Jennifer and David McNutt have
hearing from our great cloud of I
women throughout the ages throu
and edify us. This book is writter

and theological acuity, making it a ....
academy alike. Take up and read, that you may sit at the feet of many
familiar faces and others you may be meeting for the first time.

> —BRANDON D. SMITH, chair of the Hobbs School of Theology and
> Ministry and associate professor of theology and early Christianity,
> Oklahoma Baptist University; cofounder, Center for Baptist Renewal

Knowing the theologians better is really for the Christian to know more
fully their own extended family in Christ, a tribe from many times and a
household from many lands. The McNutts guide the interested student
to know more than a dozen figures from around the globe and through
the centuries, but in so doing they also tell countless other stories from
our family history. If you want to know more about the family into which
you've been adopted in Christ, this book provides a great help in getting
to know that family gathered around the table.

> —MICHAEL ALLEN, John Dyer Trimble Professor of Systematic
> Theology and academic dean, Reformed Theological Seminary
> (Orlando, FL)

Jennifer and David McNutt are such experienced, faithful teachers, and
their introduction to important theologians is certain to be a valuable
resource for all who want to delve into Christian thought.

> —BETH FELKER JONES, professor of theology, Northern Seminary;
> author, *Practicing Christian Doctrine*

Some Christians are under the impression that the gospel began in the
sixteenth century with the Reformers. Luther and Calvin undoubtedly
were visionaries, but they would have been stunned by this idea. They
knew, as we should know, that (to borrow the hymn title) "there's a
wideness in God's mercy," a breadth that includes every age and every
corner of the globe. This marvelous volume by the McNutts will help

us see something of the extent of theological contributions throughout the centuries, often outside the West and beyond male voices. If you are expecting a tedious recital, a pleasant surprise awaits you. This volume is a splendid, handy, and deeply edifying profile of the major figures in the family of faith.

—WILLIAM EDGAR, professor emeritus of apologetics,
Westminster Theological Seminary

It is thrilling to consider that the great theologians who precede us in the church are part of our spiritual family. To be a Christian is to be part of a great tradition stretching back two thousand years, and we can learn from those who walked before us as our brothers and sisters, our fathers and mothers, our friends and colaborers. David and Jennifer McNutt have selected a helpfully diverse set of sixteen key theologians from the early church to the present day. Offering a clear and engaging survey of their thought, this book will serve as a guide to beginning students of church history while also spotlighting new figures for those who already love the Christian past. Highly recommended.

—GAVIN ORTLUND, senior pastor, First Baptist Church of Ojai;
author, *Why God Makes Sense in a World That Doesn't*

In this book, Jennifer and David McNutt succeed at the daunting task of introducing the most significant theologians in the history of the church. Such a book could easily default to a superficial retelling of a few good men, but this book does much more: it highlights the historical context of each figure and their contribution to the community of believers, and it points to dozens of other theologians along the way. What is brilliant about this introduction is its capacity to dive deep while remaining accessible (and fun). The authors refrain from revealing any bias for specific denominations or interpretations of Scripture over others and instead celebrate the expansiveness of God's church.

—JESSICA HOOTEN WILSON, Fletcher Jones Chair of Great Books,
Pepperdine University; author, *The Scandal of Holiness*

As followers of Jesus in the twenty-first century, we recognize that the faith did not originate with us, nor is it meant to be lived out on our own. Our faith is received from and shaped by the great family of Jesus followers around the world and throughout church history. But how do we catch up on the story? How do we know which people to give attention to? Jennifer and David McNutt—two trustworthy voices in the field of theology and church history—have scanned the horizon and mapped the terrain for us. Like skilled guides, they know when to stop and how to draw out connections for our own journeys. This is the perfect companion for every Christian eager to grow in the faith.

—Rev. Dr. Glenn Packiam, lead pastor, Rockharbor Church;
author, *The Resilient Pastor*; coauthor, *The Intentional Year*

I loved this book! It made church history come to life. I was especially grateful to see that several female theologians were featured as important contributors to our faith history. A must-read for anyone searching the past to find answers for the present.

—Kat Armstrong, Bible teacher; author,
No More Holding Back and the Storyline
Project Bible study series

It sounds implausible: a readable, practical book about such diverse luminaries as Irenaeus of Lyons and Gustavo Gutiérrez, and dozens of great men and women in between. But that's what the McNutts have given us in this book. If only I'd had this volume twenty years ago, when my focus on ancient things kept me from trying to understand the great theologians of all the centuries. I feel I have been playing catchup ever since. But here it is—better late than never—the fast-track way to knowing who's who and what's what in the vast and beautiful ocean of Christian theology.

—John Dickson, author; host, *Undeceptions*; Jean Kvamme
Distinguished Professor of Biblical Studies and
Public Christianity, Wheaton College

At its best, theology involves communal reflection and conversation with the sacred family of God across time and diverse cultures. I highly recommend this important book, which introduces readers to key theologians from locations including North Africa, Turkey, Europe, and Latin America who have shaped our timeless, sacred family over the past two thousand years.

—ROBERT CHAO ROMERO, associate professor,
UCLA Chavez Department of Chicana/o and
Central American Studies; author, *Brown Church*

If you have ever been tempted to think theology is dull or church history tedious, then this book is for you. Pastor-theologians Jennifer and David McNutt have written an accessible and engaging introduction to some of the most significant theologians of church history in a way that is remarkably concise, nuanced, and fun. They situate each theologian in their historical context, explore their crucial insights, and introduce some of their important contemporaries. I happily recommend this book for teachers in the church and the academy, as well as anyone who just wants to learn more about their theological heritage.

—REV. DR. EMILY HUNTER MCGOWIN, associate professor
of theology, Wheaton College

KNOW
THE
THEOLOGIANS

Books in the Know Series

Know the Creeds and Councils, Justin S. Holcomb

Know the Heretics, Justin S. Holcomb

Know Why You Believe, K. Scott Oliphint

Know How We Got Our Bible, Ryan M. Reeves and Charles Hill

Know the Theologians, Jennifer Powell McNutt and David W. McNutt

KNOW
THE
THEOLOGIANS

JENNIFER POWELL MCNUTT
AND DAVID W. MCNUTT

JUSTIN S. HOLCOMB, SERIES EDITOR

ZONDERVAN

Know the Theologians
Copyright © 2024 by Jennifer Powell McNutt and David W. McNutt

Published in Grand Rapids, Michigan, by Zondervan. Zondervan is a registered trademark of The Zondervan Corporation, L.L.C., a wholly owned subsidiary of HarperCollins Christian Publishing, Inc.

Requests for information should be addressed to customercare@harpercollins.com.

Zondervan titles may be purchased in bulk for educational, business, fundraising, or sales promotional use. For information, please email SpecialMarkets@Zondervan.com.

ISBN 978-0-310-11441-3 (softcover)
ISBN 978-0-310-16571-2 (audio)
ISBN 978-0-310-11442-0 (ePub)

Any internet addresses (websites, blogs, etc.) and telephone numbers in this book are offered as a resource. They are not intended in any way to be or imply an endorsement by Zondervan, nor does Zondervan vouch for the content of these sites and numbers for the life of this book.

Cover design: Studio Gearbox
Cover images: Dreamstime; Shutterstock; Getty Images
Interior typesetting: Kait Lamphere

Printed in the United States of America

23 24 25 26 27 LBC 5 4 3 2 1

To our children: Priscilla, Geneva, and Finnegan

May you know your family of faith as you find your place among its members and may God the Father bless you with the assurance of his love, God the Son with his eternal grace, and God the Holy Spirit with unending joy.

CONTENTS

List of Profiles xiii

Foreword by Alister E. McGrath xv

Acknowledgments xvii

Introduction 1

PART 1: **EARLY CHRISTIAN THEOLOGIANS**

1. Irenaeus of Lyons 9

2. Athanasius of Alexandria. 22

3. The Cappadocian Four 36

4. Augustine of Hippo. 50

PART 2: **MEDIEVAL THEOLOGIANS**

5. John of Damascus 65

6. Anselm of Canterbury 79

7. Julian of Norwich 93

8. Thomas Aquinas. 106

PART 3: **REFORMATION THEOLOGIANS**

9. Martin Luther 123

10. John Calvin 137

11. Menno Simons 151

12. Teresa of Avila 165

PART 4: **MODERN THEOLOGIANS**

13. The Wesley Brothers 181

14. Friedrich Schleiermacher 194

15. Karl Barth 207

16. Gustavo Gutiérrez 219

    Conclusion 235

Notes 239

LIST OF PROFILES

Tertullian 13
Justin Martyr. 14
Origen. 16
Helena. 23
Jerome. 32
Frumentius (Abba Salama). 34
John Chrysostom 40
Gregory the Illuminator 44
Patrick and Brigid of Kildare 54
Pope Gregory I 59
Alopen. 67
Photius 74
Timothy I 77
Hildegard of Bingen 87
Catherine of Sienna 95
Meister Eckhart 98
Bernard of Clairvaux 101
Gregory Palamas. 109
Peter Lombard 111
Duns Scotus 114
John Wycliffe 128
Argula von Grumbach 133
Marie Dentière. 142
John Knox. 146
Heinrich Bullinger 148

Andreas Karlstadt 158

Balthasar Hubmaier 160

Ignatius of Loyola 168

John of the Cross 171

Bartolomé de las Casas 172

Matteo Ricci 175

Selina Hastings 183

Jonathan Edwards 186

William Wilberforce, John Newton, and Hannah More 190

Yun Chi-ho and Kil Sun-ju 192

Catherine Booth and William Booth 197

Søren Kierkegaard 201

Abraham Kuyper 204

Reinhold Niebuhr, H. Richard Niebuhr, and Hulda

    Clara Niebuhr 210

Dietrich Bonhoeffer 214

Dorothy L. Sayers 216

Dorothy Day 225

Albert Cleage, James Cone, Jacquelyn Grant, and Kelly

    Delaine Brown Douglas 232

FOREWORD

Know the Theologians is an elegant, accessible, and reliable guide to the wisdom of leading Christian writers down the ages who have tried to make sense of Scripture and weave together its strands in a rich and satisfying theology. We don't need to reinvent the wheel or pretend that we are the first people to try to work out how best to interpret the Bible or explain what theology is all about. We can learn from the past—from a rich tradition of faithful individuals who have passed their ideas (and their methods!) down to us.

Wife-and-husband team Jennifer Powell McNutt and David W. McNutt have given us an introduction to historical theology that is ideal for both Christian-college survey courses and for church study groups. The book focuses on sixteen key figures from church history, divided into four broad periods: the early church, the medieval period, the Reformation, and the modern period.

The theologians we are invited to know better have all been chosen with care, and they will repay study. The range of figures is impressively representative, including women and Eastern Christian thinkers. The decision to include John of Damascus is especially welcome in that he is one of the first theologians to engage with Islam—a matter of increasing importance for us today. Perhaps most important of all, this book makes studying these theologians easy without being simplistic. Readers are told enough about each writer to make us want to know more about them, with suggestions for how we can go further into them.

In the period of the early church, we are introduced to Irenaeus of Lyons, Athanasius of Alexandria, the "Cappadocian Four," and Augustine of Hippo. They're great choices, and the analysis this book provides of their ideas and their significance is lucid and helpful. We find the same pattern in the remaining three sections as we explore John of Damascus, Anselm of Canterbury, Julian of Norwich, and Thomas Aquinas in the medieval period; Martin Luther, John Calvin, Menno Simons, and Teresa of Avila in the period of the Reformation; and the Wesley brothers, Friedrich Schleiermacher, Karl Barth, and Gustavo Gutiérrez in the modern period.

In every case, we are introduced to the individual theologian in their historical context so that we can understand their life and the importance of the specific ideas that they developed. Who were they engaging with? And what is the ongoing importance of their approaches to the life of the church and to deeper reflection on faith? And while the McNutts have made some great choices for each theologian, they also include a set of more than forty sidebars that tell us something about other interesting and important figures. These brief profiles helpfully extend the book's range of engagement, giving readers pointers to where they could go next in developing their own ideas on who they might adopt as theological traveling companions as they go deeper into the study of theology.

This is an ideal resource for college introductions to theology or for church courses on going deeper into the Christian faith. I hope you enjoy reading it as much as I did.

—*Alister E. McGrath, Oxford University*

ACKNOWLEDGMENTS

Just as the church is a family of faith whose members bring particular gifts to the whole body, so too there are many people to thank who helped us bring this book into print.

We are each thankful to have grown up in families that encouraged us in our faith in Christ and helped us discern how to love God and others in myriad ways. We are also each grateful for our many teachers and professors who first introduced us to these theologians (and more), challenged us to articulate our faith, and prodded us to share it with others. Our thanks as well to the many students in the theology and church-history classes that we have taught over the years at Wheaton College, who asked probing questions, encouraged careful thought, and came alongside us as fellow disciples.

In addition, we are grateful to First Presbyterian Church of Glen Ellyn, where we both serve as parish associates, for inviting us to lead adult-education classes that introduced the congregation to these theologians over a two-year period. We are thankful to be part of a church tradition that values the teaching of the faith, and we are grateful to have had the opportunity to serve in that role.

We would also like to thank the entire team at Zondervan, which entrusted us with adding this volume to the KNOW series: Justin Holcomb, who oversees the series and graciously invited us to be part of it; Madison Trammel, who contracted us to write the book; Dale Williams, who took over the project and shepherded it through the publication process; Brian Phipps, whose careful editorial eye was a blessing to us; Emily Bruff, who brought seemingly tireless energy to marketing the book; and all those who helped to make the book what it is. We are grateful to count ourselves among Zondervan's authors.

We want to extend a special word of thanks to Alister McGrath for honoring our book with his foreword and for the inspiration and teacher that he has been to us through his work. We are also grateful for each of our friends and colleagues who took time to read and support our book.

Finally, we hope and pray that our children will continue to be strengthened in their own faith, come to know their large family of faith better, and, most important, know the grace and love of the triune God. This book is dedicated to them.

—*Jennifer Powell McNutt and David W. McNutt*

INTRODUCTION

Happy Birthday, Church!

Imagine it. Jesus has just ascended with a promise of the coming of the Holy Spirit. The disciples are gazing up to the sky with mouths open in wonder. They have been witnesses to Jesus' ministry of teaching, healing, and declaring the arrival of the kingdom of God. They have struggled through his public death on the cross, marveled at the miracle of his resurrection, and witnessed his ascension. It's a lot to take in. Two angels draw their attention back to earth and bring reassurance: "Don't worry. He'll be back again."

They travel to Jerusalem and gather in an upper room. These remaining disciples from among the original twelve have proven resilient and committed, including "certain women" and Mary, Jesus' mother, as well as Jesus' brothers (Acts 1:14). Their group has been praying nonstop, and they number one hundred and twenty (Acts 1:15). They gather to celebrate a Jewish holiday known as Shavuot, or the Feast of Weeks, which marks the giving of the Ten Commandments to Moses at Mount Sinai fifty days after Passover. On that day, however, as they gather to remember Moses' descent from the mountain, the Holy Spirit descends. With the sound of a rushing wind and with tongues of fire, the faithful believers are filled with the Holy Spirit and begin speaking in a multitude of languages. Those who have traveled to gather in Jerusalem for the feast are shocked and amazed to hear their native tongues spoken. Christ's church is born.

Peter's speech at Pentecost declares that this event is the fulfillment of the prophecy in Joel 2 regarding the descent of the Spirit, and everyone is included. God's Spirit is meant for male and female, old and young, slave and free (Acts 2:17–18). The church grows rapidly as three thousand are baptized. Soon the Holy Spirit descends upon a group of devout gentiles (Acts 13). Discipleship follows as the newly baptized "devoted themselves to the apostles' teaching and fellowship, to the breaking of bread and the prayers" (Acts 2:42).

All Christians are the spiritual descendants of those who received the Holy Spirit at Pentecost. On that day, we became family.

We Are Family

The Bible uses a variety of metaphors to illustrate the way we are connected to one another and to God through the work of Jesus Christ. One of the most important images for understanding the nature of the church and what it means to be saved and given new life in Christ is that of the church as a family. But there's more to it, and this may come as a surprise.

Scripture teaches that we are God's *adopted* children, which means that we all stand in the same position of being welcomed into a new family (Eph. 1:3–6). Through adoption, we are born again (John 3:3). Through adoption, we are given a new name. Through adoption, we receive a new inheritance. Through adoption, we are given a new way of life: "But when the fullness of time had come, God sent his Son, born of a woman, born under the law, in order to redeem those who were under the law, so that we might receive adoption as children. And because you are children, God has sent the Spirit of his Son into our hearts, crying, 'Abba! Father!' So you are no longer a slave but a child, and if a child then also an heir through God" (Gal. 4:4–7).

Adoption means thriving under the care of a Father and Mother (the church has often been described as our mother in the Christian tradition) who nurture, love, discipline (Heb. 12:7), and provide graciously and abundantly all that we need for flourishing. Adoption is gaining a brother, Jesus Christ (Mark 3:34–35), who saves. As Romans 8:28–29 teaches, "We know that all things work together for good for those who love God, who are called according to his purpose. For those whom he foreknew he also predestined to be conformed to the image of his Son, in order that he might be the firstborn within a large family." Adoption means being known by and knowing a family that is loving (1 Peter 2:17), forgiving, and reconciling. Adoption means praying a family prayer together that Jesus taught us to pray: "Our Father, who art in heaven . . ." Galatians 6:10 describes us as the "family of faith." If the church is a family, then shouldn't we get to know our family?

No doubt it's easy to focus on the church in front of us. We are certainly called to invest in the local church and serve our congregation, which embraces us, shapes us, and guides us as we mature in our faith. After all, the church is contextual. It needs our presence and gifts. But the church is also more than our local congregation.

From the start, Christianity has been on the move: north, south, east, and west. It has never been tied to one language, culture, economy, race, ethnicity, political party, sex, gender, or even region. Putting faith in Christ is not limited by these things. God's Word can bring the message of the good news of

Jesus Christ to every ear in every language. Our sacraments are common so that the signs of God's provision come from water, grain, and juice in every region. Our sacred space is such that we can commune with God anywhere our hearts are. Yes, the church is contextual, but it is also so much greater than just our little neck of the woods. When we are adopted by God, we are adopted into a big, global family.

Know the Great Cloud

But the church is not just contextual and global, it is also time- less, meaning that Christ's family includes not only those who are with us now but also those who have already gone ahead of us. In Hebrews 12:1, we read about the "great cloud of witnesses" that is cheering us on in our faith. As a people who proclaim the death and bodily resurrection of Jesus Christ and look ahead to that promise of bodily communion with Christ, our family is timeless. We are awaiting reunion by God's hand, and in the meantime, we engage in the great conversation about who God is and what God has done for us in Christ. That is the task of theology, but it requires more than our heads. It requires our whole selves: heart, soul, mind, and strength (Mark 12:30). Theology is not just for knowing but for living as members of Christ's family.

Know the Theologians will introduce you to some of the most important theologians of Christian history who have contributed to the great conversation of the church across time and who continue to shape the theology of the global church today. Our selection of theologians will highlight men and women from north, south, east, and west, reaching from early Christianity to medieval, Reformation, and modern eras. This group of theologians has made undeniably important contributions to Christian orthodoxy (right thinking) and reflect particular church traditions and trajectories. Sidebars throughout the book highlight other significant theologians involved in these important conversations in their time. Our book does not claim to be an exhaustive or definitive list of theologians. Our hope is, rather, that this book can provide a foundation for understanding the story of Christian theology, the connections between and relationships among some of the church's most important theologians, and these theologians' contributions to the church within and across traditions and throughout time, place, and space. We hope that this foundation will inspire curiosity to dig deeper into discovering the complexity and diversity of voices that have shaped Christian theology and practice over Christian history. Join us on this journey of getting to know your family!

PART 1

EARLY CHRISTIAN THEOLOGIANS

CHAPTER 1

IRENAEUS OF LYONS

PRAYER

Give perfection to beginners, O Father; give intelligence to the little ones; give aid to those who are running their course. Give sorrow to the negligent; give fervor to the spirit of the lukewarm. Give to the perfect a good consummation; for the sake of Christ Jesus our Lord.

—Irenaeus of Lyons[1]

Send Me on My Way

The dramatic growth of the early church throughout the Mediterranean basin recorded in the book of Acts did not take place in a vacuum. The most significant factor in its growth was, of course, the gospel of Jesus Christ: the good news that humans, separated from God by sin, could be reconciled to God through the life, death, and resurrection of Jesus. In synagogues, hillsides, and city squares, people heard the shocking news that the creator of the universe offered them life eternal through the actions of a crucified preacher and miracle worker from Nazareth.

But since the outpouring of the Holy Spirit on the day of Pentecost, the followers of Jesus Christ have also had to confront a dual threat to their faith: external persecution and internal heresy.

Both of these challenges are present in the New Testament. Within Scripture, we read story after story of the disciples being harassed, ridiculed, and persecuted for their faith, including the martyrdom of Stephen (Acts 7:54–60), the imprisonment of Peter (Acts 12:1–4), and the arrest and trial of Paul (Acts 21–28). In addition, it also records internal challenges to the faith: from the earliest days of Jesus' ministry, people were confused about who he was; there was infighting among the disciples (Mark 10:35–45); Peter denied Jesus three times (Matt. 26:69–75); and Judas, one of Jesus' original disciples, even betrayed him (Matt. 26:14–16).

So while the early church grew by the power and presence of the Holy Spirit, it also experienced challenges both from within and without, and this pattern continued for several hundred years. The church was able to preserve the faith throughout a tumultuous era, but it required the work of people like Irenaeus, the Greek-speaking bishop of Lyons, a city in what is today southern France.

Several factors contributed to the spread of the Christian message. The *Pax Romana*, or "Roman Peace," which lasted for more than two hundred years (from 27 BC to AD 180), meant that the early church was growing during a time of relative peace in the Roman Empire. The extensive system of Roman roads enabled easier travel, so the same roads that brought Roman soldiers to occupy Israel also allowed the early disciples to spread the gospel more quickly. Christian evangelists not only were able to appeal to Jewish Scripture and history with some audiences but also could employ the shared Greek language and Hellenistic culture and philosophy with others. The early Christians believed that they were experiencing the fulfillment of God's promise to Abram to bless all the people of the earth through his line (Gen. 12:3) and the realization of Joel's prophecy that the Spirit would be poured out on all people (Joel 2:28). But not everyone thought so.

While the early church grew, it was also subjected to intense persecution. Initially, Christianity was perceived by the Roman authorities as a religious sect within first-century Judaism, which boasted many different groups, including the Pharisees, the Sadducees, Zealots, and more. That had certain benefits because the Jewish faith was regarded as a *religio licita* ("a permitted religion"), which meant that adherents were exempt from emperor worship. Over time, however, Christianity was increasingly acknowledged as a separate faith from Judaism. This came about through both internal discussions, such as the Judaizer controversy about whether Christians had to follow Jewish law (Acts 15; Galatians 2), and external events, including the Jewish Revolt of AD 66 and the resulting destruction of the Jewish temple by Emperor Titus in AD 70. With its separation from Judaism, Christianity became a persecuted religion.

Under these new circumstances, several false charges were brought against early Christians. They were said to be cannibals. It wasn't true, but the misperception is perhaps understandable. After all, hadn't Jesus told his disciples that "unless you eat the flesh of the Son of Man and drink his blood, you have no life in you" (John 6:53)? And when he was gathered with his disciples at the Last Supper, hadn't he said to them, "Take, eat; this is my body," when he handed them the bread, and then, "This is my blood of the covenant," when he handed them the cup (Matt. 26:26–28)? These were "hard teachings" even for Jesus' followers, let alone those outside the faith. The Christians were also said to be committing incest. Again, it wasn't true, but didn't the church include "brothers and sisters" in the faith, some of whom were married (1 Cor. 1:10) and who greeted each other with a "holy kiss" (Rom. 16:16)?

Early Christians were also accused of being atheists, even though they worshiped the same God revealed in the Hebrew Bible. For Christians, the same God who created the world, entered into a covenantal relationship with Israel, and rescued the Israelites from Egyptian slavery had now taken on flesh and come into the world in Jesus Christ. They were accused of being seditious and treasonous because they did not worship the Roman emperor, who since the time of Julius Caesar had been regarded as a god. Christians worshiped God alone, but they also had been taught by Jesus to respect earthly authorities (Matt. 22:21) and by Paul to do the same (Rom. 13:1–7), even to pray for the emperor (1 Tim. 2:1–2). They were said to be the supporters of an irrational faith that preyed on the gullible because they believed that a man who was born in Bethlehem was also the eternal Son of God and that he had died but then risen back to life three days later. Such good news, it seems, has always been a "stumbling block" to some (1 Cor. 1:23).

The charges were false, but the persecution was real. And though the *Pax Romana* may have been largely a time of peace for the empire, it was not peaceful for Christians. Tertullian captured the widespread blame under which Christians often suffered: "If the Tiber rises as high as the city walls, if the Nile does not send its waters up over the fields, if the heavens give no rain, if there is an earthquake, if there is famine or pestilence, straightway the cry is, 'Away with the Christians to the lion!'"[2]

Tertullian (ca. 160–225), who was from Carthage in North Africa (modern-day Tunisia), was educated in literature and rhetoric before his conversion to Christianity as an adult. Known as "the father of Western theology" because he was the church's first significant Latin theologian, he asked rhetorically, "What has Athens to do with Jerusalem?" Unlike Justin Martyr, who believed that affinities between philosophy and Christianity could be beneficial, Tertullian viewed philosophy as intrusive to the faith—an indication that even in the church's earliest years, there were different approaches to defending the faith. Tertullian is also known for writing *Against Praxeas* and his contributions to the doctrine of the Trinity, which included coining the term "Trinity" (in Latin, *trinitas*) and developing several Trinitarian analogies.

The particular form of persecution often varied depending on the geographic region and the views of the emperor or local authority. And it ranged from being excluded from public buildings, baths, and markets to the loss of one's property, from imprisonment to public execution and martyrdom. A long line of infamous emperors persecuted Christians, including Nero (54–68), who is said to have lit his gardens by the burning of Christians and who ruled during the deaths of both Peter and Paul; Domitian (81–96) and Trajan (98–117), whose persecutions were the context for the book of Revelation; Decius (249–51), who undertook the first empire-wide persecution; and Diocletian (284–305), under whose rule Christians suffered "the Great

Persecution," with the burning of Scripture, imprisonments, and executions.

How did Christians respond to this persecution? Unfortunately, some followers lapsed under the pressure and committed apostasy by abandoning the faith. These included so-called *traditores* (the same root for the word "traitor"), who handed over their sacred Christian texts. Others, however, persevered in their faith but were martyred for remaining true, sometimes in cruel fashion. Ignatius of Antioch (ca. 50–ca. 110), a bishop of the church in Syria and one of the three Apostolic Fathers along with Clement of Rome and Polycarp, was thrown to the lions. Polycarp (ca. 69–ca. 155), the bishop of Smyrna, was bound to the stake but reportedly had to be stabbed when the fire could not touch him.[3] Perpetua, a noblewoman and nursing mother, and Felicitas, her pregnant slave, were killed together in Carthage. In response to such persecution, Tertullian said, "The oftener we are mown down by you, the more in number we grow; the blood of Christians is seed [of the church]."[4] The testimony of all those who have died for following Christ has inspired others to remain faithful under duress. But other Christians were called to defend the faith.

Justin Martyr (ca. 100–65) was a pagan native of Flavia Neapolis in Palestine. After exploring various philosophies, he converted to Christianity and wrote several defenses of the faith, including *First Apology*, *Second Apology*, *Against Heresies*, and *Against Marcion*. He is especially known for his appeal to Greek philosophical categories in developing a "Logos" (the Greek word for "word") Christology.

Defense against the Dark Arts

Today, the city of Izmir, located on the Aegean Sea, is the third most populous city in Turkey. In the early second century, it was known as Smyrna, and it was the site of the birth of Irenaeus (ca. 130–200), who traveled far and wide in support of the faith. Growing up, Irenaeus listened to Polycarp, the bishop of Smyrna, who had himself studied under John—yes, *that* John: John the Beloved Disciple, John the Apostle. Unfortunately, Polycarp was martyred, but his influence on Irenaeus was lasting. When the Christian communities in Gaul (today, France) suffered intense persecution and the first bishop of the city of Lyons, Pothinus, was killed, Irenaeus became their bishop.[5] He was certainly not the only early Christian apologist; Justin Martyr, Clement of Alexandria, Tertullian, Origen, and others were called upon to defend the faith. But Irenaeus is particularly known for his defense against one of Christianity's greatest challenges: Gnosticism.

The early church was confronted by several heresies (from the root word for "choose"; thus, heresy is, quite literally, a bad choice): for example, Marcionism, which rejected the Old Testament as authoritative for Christians; Arianism, which denied the divinity of Christ; and modalism, which denied the doctrine of the Trinity. Yet perhaps the most pervasive and persistent heresy facing the early church was Gnosticism. This second-century movement may have begun within Christianity; some regarded Simon Magus, the Samaritan magician in Acts 8, as the founder of the Gnostic sect. It was a diverse movement without a clear hierarchical organization and with different teachers, including the Syrian Saturninus and the Egyptians Basilides and Valentinus, all of whom Irenaeus opposed in his work.

Born in Alexandria, Egypt, one of the early centers of the church, **Origen** (ca. 185–254) is often regarded as the church's first systematic theologian because of his work *On First Principles*. Having studied under Clement of Alexandria, he articulated early understandings of the doctrine of the Trinity. But Origen left behind a complicated legacy, which includes, on the one hand, his biblical and theological reflections as well as his refusal to recant his faith despite being tortured, but on the other, his alleged self-castration and having his works ultimately deemed heretical by the Second Council of Constantinople (553) for their views regarding the preexistence of souls, an affirmation of universalism, and a subordinationist doctrine of the Trinity.

Despite its varieties, there were common themes to Gnosticism, most prominently its strongly dualistic worldview—good and evil, light and dark—that emphasized the spiritual over the material to such an extent that the material world was considered to be evil.

What are the implications of such a view? First, Gnosticism argued that God could not have created the world because a good and perfect God could not have been involved in the making of an evil, material world, so it theorized that a lesser deity (a "demiurge") created the world. Because of this view, it also denied fundamental aspects of Christ's life and ministry: his genuine incarnation, his physical suffering, and his bodily resurrection. It further argued that salvation could be attained only through a secret knowledge (it takes its name from *gnosis*, the Greek word for "knowledge") and that salvation entailed escaping the material and fleeing to the spiritual world. Moreover, it was antisemitic and misogynistic. For example, *The Gospel of Thomas* is one of the key Gnostic texts from the early second century (just because it's called a gospel doesn't mean it's true!), which was discovered in a jar along with other texts in Nag Hammadi, Egypt, in 1945. It states that "women are not worthy of Life" and must become men first to be saved by rejecting the physical and pursuing the spiritual.[6] If Gnosticism and other early heresies had claimed to be different faiths that required a Christian response, then that would have been challenging enough. But the greater difficulty was that they claimed to represent Christianity.

Perceiving the dramatic implications of these beliefs, Irenaeus wrote *Against Heresies* near the end of the second century. As opposed to the Gnostics, he wanted to proclaim the goodness of God's creation, which is affirmed repeatedly in the opening chapter of Genesis (Gen. 1:31), the truth of Christ's incarnation and resurrection, and the belief that salvation comes through Christ alone, not through a secret knowledge available only to some. But how was he supposed to argue that he had the correct understanding of the Christian faith, especially when the canon of Scripture had not yet been formalized?

In making his case, Irenaeus appealed to the importance of apostolic tradition, which he defined as "that tradition which originates from the apostles, [and] which is preserved by means of the successions of presbyters in the Churches."[7] Christianity has always had some version of tradition—whether oral or written— which has sought to preserve and articulate the faith in various forms. In later centuries, it developed creeds, confessions, and catechisms. But long before then, within Scripture itself, Paul pointed to the importance of "handing down" the faith, which Irenaeus appealed to:[8] "For I handed on to you as of first importance what I in turn had received: that Christ died for our sins in accordance with the scriptures and that he was buried and that he was raised on the third day in accordance with the scriptures and that he appeared to Cephas, then to the twelve" (1 Cor. 15:3–5).

While most Christians have regarded the church's various forms of tradition to be secondary to Scripture, Irenaeus showed its importance. In opposing Gnosticism, Irenaeus was able to appeal to the fact that he had studied with Polycarp, who had studied with John, who of course had been taught by Christ himself. Irenaeus was assured that his views regarding the goodness of God's creation, the reality of Christ's incarnation and resurrection, and the offer of salvation were correct because he could trace his beliefs directly to the teaching of the apostles.

In particular, that enabled him to reject the idea of salvation through secret knowledge: "It is within the power of all, therefore, in every Church, who may wish to see the truth, to contemplate clearly the tradition of the apostles manifested through the whole world."[9] Moreover, he rejected any understanding of Jesus that denied his true incarnation, suffering, and resurrection. Instead, he affirmed that Christ alone brings salvation by taking on flesh: "He who was the Son of God became the Son of man, that man, having been taking into the Word, and receiving the adoption, might become the son of God. For by no other means could we have attained to incorruptibility and immortality, unless we had been united to incorruptibility and immortality."[10]

Against Heresies was a critical text for the early church. Sadly, it was forgotten for nearly one thousand years, only to be rediscovered and published by Erasmus in 1526.[11] Despite opposition from Irenaeus and others, Gnosticism has persisted in various forms over the centuries—a good reminder that just because the church determined that a particular view was not consistent with its orthodoxy does not mean that the heresy immediately disappeared or that all Christians immediately abandoned that view. The Christian faith requires articulation and defense in every age.

Laying a Good Foundation

Irenaeus's influence was not limited to a defense of the faith. More constructively, he helped the church begin to articulate its understanding of several other key aspects of the faith, including the doctrines of the Trinity, Scripture, and the church.

As we will see, the early church painstakingly articulated a doctrine of the Trinity as the uniquely Christian understanding of the one God who is Father, Son, and Holy Spirit. It took the church centuries to declare this doctrine with clarity (even as it still presents a mystery), but early theologians had already begun to clear the church's collective throat in an attempt to express who Christians believe God to be. For his part, Irenaeus referred to the Son and the Holy Spirit as the "two hands" of the Father in reference to their work in the economy of salvation. This suggests that he affirmed the distinctions among the three persons as well as the unity of their action, seen here with regard to the divine work of creation: "For with [God] were always present the Word and Wisdom, the Son and the Spirit, by whom and in whom, freely and spontaneously, He made all things, to whom also He speaks, saying, 'Let Us make man after Our image and likeness.'"[12]

In addition, Irenaeus helped the church as it sought to determine what texts should be considered part of the church's authoritative canon of Scripture, as demonstrated in his appeal throughout *Against Heresies* to each of the four gospels and nearly every text from what is now the canonical New Testament. But as a reminder that he lived before the canon was officially closed, he regarded the Shepherd of Hermas, a Christian text from the second century, as "Scripture."[13] Finally, with regard to ecclesiology (the doctrine of the church, or the church's understanding of itself), Irenaeus ascribed a place of prominence to the Church of Rome. Perhaps that is unsurprising for one who ministered in modern-day France, but he also articulated a kind of "first among equals" view of Rome and an early version of Petrine succession that came to define Roman Catholic ecclesiology, often to the chagrin of other churches: "that tradition derived from the apostles, of the very great, the very ancient, and universally known Church founded and organized at Rome by the two most glorious apostles, Peter and Paul. . . . For it is a matter of necessity that every Church should agree with this Church, on account of its preeminent authority."[14]

It took several centuries and many controversies for the church to clarify these doctrines, but Irenaeus was among those early theologians who set the church on its course toward orthodoxy. Living under the realities of external persecution and internal threats, the first generations of Christians preserved the faith under difficult circumstances. For these early followers of Christ, there was no expectation that the persecution of their faith would ever end.

Discussion Questions

1. How does tradition function in your family, and what is its value for the church today?

2. First John 1 declares that what is known about Jesus Christ has been passed down by those who directly heard, saw, and touched him. How does this inform the way we think about Scripture?

3. Irenaeus taught that the church needs all four gospels. How does having four versions of the life of Christ enrich your understanding of the gospel?

Further Reading

John Behr, *Irenaeus of Lyons: Identifying Christianity* (Oxford Univ. Press, 2015).

Justin S. Holcomb, *Know the Heretics* (Zondervan Academic, 2014).

Irenaeus of Lyons, *Against Heresies*, in *Ante-Nicene Fathers*, vol. 1 (Hendrickson, 2004), 309–567.

Ken Parry, ed. *The Wiley Blackwell Companion to Patristics* (Wiley Blackwell, 2019).

CHAPTER 2

ATHANASIUS OF ALEXANDRIA

PRAYER

Prepare us, O Lord, to open our mouth that we may praise Thee with a pure heart, and, with a tongue that is never silent may say, "Glory to God on high, and on earth peace," . . . We praise Thee, we bless Thee. Have mercy upon us, O God, according to the greatness of Thy mercy . . . Lord, forgive us by the blood of the new covenant whereby Thou has vouchsafed us remission and mercy and salvation for ever and ever. Amen.

—Athanasius of Alexandria[1]

The Changing of the Guard

Shortly before the Battle of the Milvian Bridge north of Rome on October 28, 312, Constantine, then the deputy emperor in the Western part of the Roman Empire, had a vision. According to early-church historian Eusebius, Constantine received a vision of the "chi-rho" symbol (composed of the first two Greek letters of the word *Christ*) and was told, "By this [sign you shall] conquer."[2] With the symbol inscribed on his soldiers' shields, Constantine won the battle and subsequently rode triumphantly into Rome, eventually becoming emperor.

Attributing his victory to the Christian God, Constantine (ca. 272–337) legalized the faith with the Edict of Milan in 313, which declared that "Christians and all others should have freedom to follow the kind of religion they favoured."[3] He thus dramatically changed the state of Christianity from being a persecuted religion to being a state-supported faith. Later, under Emperor Theodosius, Christianity became the official religion of the Roman Empire in 380. In the span of less than one hundred years, Christianity went from being a persecuted faith to the sole religion of the empire.

> **Helena** (ca. 255–330) was a Greek woman of low rank who became the wife of Constantius I, a Roman emperor, and later the mother of Constantine. Raised to a prominent position when her son became emperor, Helena advocated for Christianity. She traveled to the Holy Lands late in life and was instrumental in founding churches, including the Church of the Nativity in Bethlehem and the Church of the Holy Sepulchre in Jerusalem. According to tradition, Helena discovered pieces of the true cross of Christ during her visit, which she brought back to Rome. By the medieval period, such relics became integral to the penitential life as vessels of holiness and forgiveness.

The benefits for the church brought by Constantine's conversion were significant: Christians were no longer persecuted for practicing their faith; they could worship publicly; and they could build spaces for Christian worship and create Christian art. In addition, they could take time to reflect on things that had been discussed before, but not formally determined: Exactly who is Jesus? What did that mean about God? What books should be part of the church's authoritative, canonical Scripture? Constantine's conversion meant that Christianity could now consider such questions carefully even as it grew in prestige and power, but it was also now aligned with the state—an uneasy alliance that proved challenging for the church in the years ahead.

From the Mouths of Deacons

Among the most important developments in the church following Constantine's conversion was the task of clarifying the church's orthodoxy, or "right belief." But determining the official beliefs of the church often came about only through discussion, debate, and even controversy, as seen in the christological and Trinitarian debates of the fourth and fifth centuries. One of the fundamental questions that the church took up was the same question that Jesus asked Peter and the other disciples: "Who do you say that I am?" Peter's response was simple, but profound: "You are the Messiah, the Son of the living God" (Matt. 16:15–16). Of course, the church had offered an answer to this question before Constantine's conversion, but it was thrust upon the fourth-century church in a new, and now public, way.

Heretics typically didn't set out to be heretics. And they typically were not opponents of Christianity seeking to discredit the faith. Rather, they were often Christians who attempted to articulate their understanding of the faith but came up short—radically short and with serious consequences, which is why the church needed to correct them. Arius (ca. 270–336), a priest from Alexandria, Egypt—one of the five centers of early Christianity along with Jerusalem, Antioch, Constantinople, and Rome—was one such Christian.

Is Jesus God? The answer to that question might seem obvious in light of Scripture. After all, Jesus did things that are attributed to God alone: healing the sick, calming the storm, and raising the dead. Jesus himself claimed to exist before Abraham (John 8:58), and the text affirms that he is the one through whom all things were created (John 1:10; Col. 1:16; Heb. 1:2), who is worthy of worship (Matt. 28:9, 17), and who is equal to the eternal God (John 1:1). But Arius didn't think so. Rather, he thought that Jesus was a creature: "And before he was begotten or created or ordained or founded, he was not. For he was not unbegotten."[4] For Arius, Jesus was the highest of creatures, but he was still a creature. Suggesting otherwise seemed opposed to the monotheism affirmed by both Judaism and Christianity. For Arius and Arianism, as it came to be known, Jesus was not God.

Prior to the Arian controversy, another Christian in the city of Alexandria had written about his understanding of the person of Christ. Athanasius (ca. 296–373) was a deacon under Alexander of Alexandria. In his work *On the Incarnation of the Word*, Athanasius reflected on why God, who had created the world, sent the Son into the world and how it was that Jesus achieved salvation for humanity. In addition to responding to Gnostics, who denied a genuine incarnation, Athanasius affirmed that Jesus is truly, fully divine. In making this argument, his driving concern was a question about salvation: Can Jesus actually save people? If only God—and not fellow creatures—can redeem humans and save them from their sinful state, then what does that mean about Jesus? His conclusion was that Jesus must be God to accomplish the things that Scripture claims about him: "[B]eing by nature bodiless and existing as the Word, by the love for humankind and goodness of his own Father he appeared to us in a human body for our salvation."[5] Jesus, the one through whom the universe was created, now recreates the image of God in humanity.

To resolve the controversy caused by Arius, Constantine called the first ecumenical council, which met in Nicaea in 325. Aided by Athanasius's work, the council concluded that it was not sufficient to claim that Jesus is *homoiousios*, "of similar substance," with God the Father, as some had suggested. Instead, the council affirmed Athanasius's views regarding the full divinity of Christ. To make this clear, it employed a term that was not found within Scripture but faithfully expressed the testimony that *is* found within Scripture: *homoousios*, a Greek term meaning "of the same substance." With this word, the church affirmed that Jesus shares in the same substance as God the Father: "We believe . . . in one Lord Jesus Christ, the Son of God; begotten from the Father; only-begotten, that is, of the substance of the Father; God of God, light of light, true God of true God; begotten not made; *of one substance* [*homoousios*] with the Father."[6] In short, Jesus is God.

True Human

With Athanasius's help, the Council of Nicaea clarified a fundamental affirmation of the faith: Jesus is really, truly God. But that didn't end the debate about Christology. The church spent more than a century until it came to a consensus on the person of Christ, and along the way, there were multiple controversies and councils. Briefly:

If Jesus is fully divine, then is he really human? As before, the answer may seem obvious in light of Scripture: Jesus knew hunger, thirst, and temptation, just like the rest of us (Matt. 4:2). And the facts that he took on real human flesh in the incarnation (John 1:14) and that he rose again in the flesh would seem to provide an answer. But, as before, not everyone thought so.

One feature of Gnosticism was a tendency toward docetism (from the Greek word *dokein*, meaning "to appear or to seem"). Those who held this view maintained that Jesus was indeed God, but he only appeared or seemed to be human. It denied his full humanity. Ignatius of Antioch (ca. 50–110), Irenaeus, and other early-church theologians had sought to stamp out this view. In *On the Incarnation*, Athanasius anticipated the importance of affirming Jesus' true humanity in response to Gnosticism. In Christ, he affirmed, "the incorporeal and incorruptible and immaterial Word of God comes to our realm . . . he takes for himself a body and that not foreign to our own. For he did not wish simply to be in a body, nor did he wish merely to appear [in a body]. . . . But he takes that which is ours."[7]

But a new form of docetism had emerged by this point. Apollinaris (ca. 310–90), the bishop of Laodicea in Syria, had been a staunch opponent of Arianism. Yet when it came to Jesus' humanity, he believed that while Jesus had a human body and a human soul, he could not have had a human mind. For Apollinaris, the mind was the source of sin. (Where else do we get our sinful thoughts from?) But in his desire to protect Jesus' sinlessness (Heb. 4:15), he denied Jesus' full humanity: "He is not a human being but is like a human being, since he is not coessential with humanity in his highest part."[8] Sound familiar? Unwittingly, Apollinaris had fallen into the same error regarding Jesus' humanity that Arius had fallen prey to regarding his divinity.

Gregory of Nazianzus (ca. 329–90) perceived the dangers of the docetic Christology of Apollinarianism. As with Athanasius before, his primary motivation in responding to it was about soteriology. If Jesus is not fully human, if he assumed only part of humanity's nature, then could he save people, which Scripture affirms he did? Gregory's response was simple and clear: "For that which he has not assumed he has not healed; but that which is united to his Godhead is also saved."[9] Not only did Jesus have a human body, but he was really, fully human—made like us "in every respect" (Heb. 2:17) with a human mind, a human will, and human emotions. Yes, his hunger, his thirst, and his tears were real. Yes, his temptations were real. Yes, his struggle in the garden of Gethsemane was genuine. The Council of Constantinople (381), the second ecumenical council, which was called by Emperor Theodosius I, agreed. Their condemnation of Apollinarianism and their affirmation of Gregory are enshrined in what we now call the Nicene Creed.

Surely that had resolved the matter, right?

Never Tear Us Apart (or Mix Us Up)

Long before scientists confirmed that light is both a particle and a wave, the early church struggled with how to hold these two affirmations at the same time: Jesus is truly divine, and he is also truly human. But how can we make sense of someone having two natures?

Nestorius, the bishop of Constantinople and an Antiochene theologian (a rival school to the Alexandrians), pushed this controversy to the fore. His initial concern was a desire to protect the full humanity of Jesus, a primary feature of Antiochene theology, which the church had just affirmed in the controversy with Apollinaris. For Nestorius, this entailed a rejection of the term *Theotokos*, a Greek term meaning the "God-bearer." This word was often used by Alexandrian theologians, who wanted to maintain Jesus' divinity, in reference to the Virgin Mary. They reasoned that if Jesus is God, and Mary gave birth to Jesus, then Mary is, in a sense, the "God-bearer." But according to Nestorius, this threatened Jesus' humanity. "Mary . . . did not produce the Creator, rather she gave birth to the human being, the instrument of the Godhead."[10]

While his concerns might be understandable, Nestorius overemphasized the distinction between Jesus' two natures. Rather than affirming that Christ's two natures are genuinely united in his one person, Nestorius and his fellow Antiochene theologians, like Theodore of Mopsuestia, argued for a union "by good pleasure" rather than an actual, ontological union.[11] The Nestorians thus tended to separate or divide the two natures of Christ, in effect denying that the one Jesus could be both divine and human.

In response, Cyril of Alexandria (ca. 376–444) affirmed that Jesus' two natures are really united in his one person. This union, he argued, was not simply a "union according to good pleasure," as the Antiochenes had maintained. Rather, he affirmed a "hypostatic union"—that there is a genuine union of the divine and the human in the one *hypostasis* (the Greek word for "person") of Jesus: "The natures which were brought together to form a true unity were different; but out of both is one Christ and one Son. . . . [T]he divinity and humanity, by their inexpressible and inexplicable concurrence into unity, have produced for us the one Lord and Son Jesus Christ."[12]

As has so often been the case throughout church history, theological questions were complicated by political matters. In this case, Nestorius's opposition to the term *Theotokos* rankled Pulcheria (399–453), a woman who had devoted her life to living like the Virgin Mary. She also happened to be the older sister of Emperor Theodosius II (408–50). When the emperor called the third ecumenical council, which met in Ephesus in 431, Nestorius's fate was sealed. The council affirmed Cyril's position and rejected the views of Nestorius, who was exiled into the Egyptian desert.

But that still didn't resolve the matter. Perhaps, some thought, when the divine and the human natures are united in the one person of Jesus, they are combined or mixed in such a way that there is only one nature left. Eutyches (ca. 378–454), a monastic superior from Constantinople, argued for this view, known as monophysitism (meaning "one nature"). This view was upheld by the Council of Ephesus in 449, but its implications are significant: if Jesus' human and divine natures are mixed in their union, is he still both human and divine, or has he become some third thing that is neither fully human nor fully divine?

Pope Leo I, also known as Leo the Great (ca. 400–61), perceived these dangers, and in his Tome of Leo, he affirmed that the two distinct natures of Christ are preserved even in their union: "For each of the natures retains its proper character without defect; and as the form of God does not take away the form of a servant, so the form of a servant does not impair the form of God."[13] The resulting council, which was called by Pulcheria, who by this point had assumed control of the empire following the death of her brother, Theodosius II, met in Chalcedon. The result became known as the Chalcedonian Definition, which set the boundaries for an orthodox understanding of the person of Christ: Jesus possesses two natures; he is both fully human and fully divine, and these two natures are united in his one person but remain distinct, "without confusion, without change, without division, and without separation."[14] Chalcedon's formula leaves a lot unanswered: for example, how exactly are the two natures united while remaining distinct? And it wasn't embraced by all Christians; the Coptic Church in Egypt and the Church of the East in Syria rejected it, maintaining their monophysite views. But for the rest of Christianity, and drawing upon the contributions of Athanasius, Gregory, Cyril, and Leo, it set the standard for answering the question, "Who is Jesus?"

Shaping the Practice of the Faith

Athanasius shaped not only what Christians believe (orthodoxy) but also what they do (orthopraxy). This is particularly evident with regard to the growth of monasticism and determining the canon of Scripture. After Constantine's conversion, and in the absence of martyrdom, some Christians expressed their faith by embracing asceticism, a practice that involved turning away from earthly pleasures and separating oneself from the rest of society to focus on one's spiritual life. Among the most significant figures in this new movement was Antony of Thebes (ca. 251–356), an Egyptian Christian who lived as a hermit and was the first of a group that would come to be known as the Desert Fathers and Mothers. Ironically, though he had given up everything and removed himself from society, people sought out Antony to learn from him. One of those was Athanasius, who met Antony when the monk was quite old and who wrote *The Life of Antony*, which contributed to the rise of monasticism. Later, under Pachomius (ca. 290–346), monasticism changed from the solitary hermetic life to the cenobitic (communal) monastic life that became popular across Christianity.

Jerome (ca. 345–420) is known primarily for the Vulgate, his translation of the Bible into Latin, for which he used the original Hebrew text of the Old Testament rather than the Septuagint, the Greek translation of the Old Testament. Although later translators, such as Erasmus of Rotterdam, discovered errors in the Vulgate text, the Roman Catholic Church declared it to be the official translation of the Bible at the Council of Trent. Jerome also translated Pachomius's monastic rule into Latin and wrote many commentaries on Scripture. Along with Ambrose, Augustine, and Gregory the Great, he is considered one of the four Latin doctors of the church.

What should Christians regard as authoritative texts for the faith? Once again, Athanasius came to the church's help. One part of the answer to that question concerned whether Christians should embrace the Old Testament as part of Scripture. In the second century, Marcion (ca. 85–160) had argued that the Old Testament presented a God different from the God who was revealed in Christ: the former, he thought, was a God of law, and the latter was a God of love. Irenaeus, Tertullian, and others opposed Marcionism by affirming that the God who created the world and entered into a covenantal relationship with the people of Israel is the same God who came into the world in the person of Christ. Though not uncomplicated in its interpretation and application to the Christian life, the Old Testament has been part of the church's canon ever since.

But what about the New Testament? The books and letters that became the rest of Christian Scripture were written in the decades following the resurrection of Christ until roughly the late first century. Those texts were copied, circulated, and read by Christians. Of course, other books and letters had also been written by Christians (for example, the Shepherd of Hermas, the Didache, and 1–2 Clement), so the church had to determine which texts should be authoritative for the faith and regarded as Scripture. That process, known as the "fixing of the canon," was a lengthy discussion, but Athanasius anticipated the church's eventual decision. In his Easter letter of 367, he was the first person to list the twenty-seven books and letters that ultimately were deemed the canonical New Testament. To be clear, the canon was not determined solely by Athanasius's letter; the process included councils (Hippo, 393; Carthage, 397) and a long list of criteria for each text, including its authorship, date, agreement with orthodoxy, and use among Christians. But Athanasius played a large part in helping the church to "close" the canon by the beginning of the fifth century.

When Alexander died, Athanasius became the bishop of Alexandria. He helped the church to fend off one of its greatest challenges and confirm the faith of those before him, like Peter, and shape the faith and practice of Christians for centuries to come.

The Ethiopian Orthodox Tewahedo Church is part of the Oriental Orthodox branch of the church known as the monophysite (or miaphysites, meaning "one nature" in reference to the union of Christ's two natures). Its Christian heritage is linked to Athanasius, Bishop of Alexandria, who is documented as ordaining the Phoenician missionary (from Tyre or modern-day Lebanon) **Frumentius** as bishop in 347 CE. Frumentius came to be known as **Abba Salama** and converted King Ezana of the Axum Kingdom (Ethiopia) to Christianity. This branch of the church was never subject to Rome or European colonization and survived the rise of Islam. A Judaized form of Christianity, it claims to possess and preserve the ark of the covenant.

But the fact that the church had affirmed that Jesus is truly divine did not mean that Arianism disappeared. Instead, as was often the case with other views declared heretical, Arianism persisted and lives on in some circles even today. Under Constantius II, one of Constantine's sons, who became emperor in 337, Arianism thrived, and Athanasius—the defender of the faith—spent much of the remainder of his life in exile.[15] Ultimately, though, his views prevailed and set the standard for the church's understanding of the person of Jesus Christ.

Discussion Questions

1. Why is Athanasius's teaching that Jesus Christ was fully divine so important to the Christian faith?
2. Antony of Thebes impressed Athanasius with the sacrifice

that he made based on his commitment to Christ. Who from the history of the church most inspires you to follow Jesus?

3. Athanasius was committed to the orthodox faith and to the church despite experiencing exile on numerous occasions. How do we stay committed to the church even during periods of conflict and controversy?

Further Reading

Saint Athanasius, *On the Incarnation*, trans. John Behr (St. Vladimir's Seminary Press, 2011).

Edward R. Hardy, ed., *Christology of the Later Fathers*, Library of Christian Classics (Westminster John Knox, 1954).

Justin S. Holcomb, *Know the Creeds and Councils* (Zondervan Academic, 2014).

Robert Louis Wilken, *The Spirit of Early Christian Thought: Seeking the Face of God* (Yale Univ. Press, 2005).

CHAPTER 3

THE CAPPADOCIAN FOUR

PRAYER

O Lord our God, teach us, we ask you, to ask you aright for the right blessings. Steer the vessel of our life toward yourself, you tranquil haven of all storm-tossed souls. Show us the course wherein we should go. Renew a willing spirit within us. Let your Spirit curb our wayward senses, and guide and enable us unto that which is our true good, to keep your laws, and in all our works evermore to rejoice in your glorious and gladdening presence. For yours is the glory and praise from all your saints, for ever and ever. Amen.

—Basil the Great[1]

This Is Our God

After the people of Israel, impatient with what they perceived as Moses' delay while on Mount Sinai, had given Aaron their gold to fashion into an idol in the form of a calf, they declared, "These are your gods, O Israel, who brought you up out of the land of Egypt!" (Ex. 32:4). This blasphemous announcement incited God's wrath and led Moses to shatter the first copy of the Ten Commandments. How could the people of God have forgotten that God had chosen them, rescued them from slavery, and provided for them? How could they speak about this idol as their god? A similar question faced the fourth-century church: Who is our God? How do we talk about God? How do we make sense of the one God in light of the incarnation of Jesus Christ and the outpouring of the Holy Spirit? The church needed to articulate its understanding of who God is without falling into heresy or blasphemy.

The doctrine of the Trinity, which is how the church ultimately expressed its distinctive understanding of the one God, is a bit of a high-wire act; it's easy to fall off and into the heresy waiting on either side. But with the help of several theologians, especially a group known as the Cappadocians—which included two brothers, Basil the Great and Gregory of Nyssa; their older sister, Macrina the Younger; and their friend, Gregory of Nazianzus—the church articulated its unique view of God. This fundamental tenet is not intentionally difficult, but there is an element of mystery and faith to it. Most important, it is not based on any single Scripture verse but rather seeks to make sense of Jesus' words and the whole testimony of Scripture, which rings with the affirmation—sometimes faintly, sometimes loudly—that God is both one and triune.

The belief in one God set Israel apart from its polytheistic ancient Near Eastern neighbors (Deut. 6:4–5). By the time of the New Testament, that belief was firmly in place and assumed by its authors, including Paul, who affirms that there is "one God and Father of all, who is above all and through all and in all" (Eph. 4:6). But the suggestion that God is also triune—and what exactly that means—was much more controversial.

When reading the Old Testament, early Christians did not find—nor should they have expected to find—a fully developed, explicit doctrine of the Trinity. However, when these Christians read Scripture through the lens of faith, they pointed to affirmations that God is not simply one. For example, they asked whether the first-person plural of "let us make humans in our image" (Gen. 1:26) or the threefold "Holy, holy, holy" of Isaiah's vision (Isa. 6:3) imply a plurality within God. Or might references to the wisdom, word, and Spirit of God suggest a threeness to God's being? What was implicit in the Old Testament became more explicit in the New Testament. For here, the church found clear references to the Father, the Son, and the Holy Spirit in a range of texts, including the narrative of Jesus' baptism (Matt. 3:13–17), Jesus' words in the Farewell Discourses of John's Gospel, the baptismal formula of the Great Commission (Matt. 28:19), and Paul's benediction (2 Cor. 13:13).

How might one make sense of all these passages? Or how might two brothers, their older sister, and their friend?

The Family That Theologizes Together

Throughout the church's history, there have been many families of pastors and theologians. But perhaps no family has made as great a contribution to the history of the church's thought as a fourth-century family from the region of Cappadocia in modern-day Turkey.

Macrina the Elder, a Christian woman (d. ca. 340), had fled to Cappadocia with her husband because of persecution under Roman emperors Diocletian and Galerius. Her son, Basil the Elder, married Emmelia of Caesarea, and together they raised a family of ten children with an uncommon Christian legacy. One of their sons, Basil of Caesarea (ca. 330–79), known as Basil the Great, gave up a career in law to pursue a life dedicated to

God. He established a monastic community, where he was joined by members of his family, and his writings about monastic life ended up shaping Eastern monasticism. Known for his care of the poor, Basil eventually succeeded Eusebius to become the bishop of Caesarea.[2] One of Basil's younger brothers, Gregory of Nyssa (ca. 330–95), followed in his brother's footsteps by forgoing a career as a rhetorician to seek a life in the church, eventually becoming the bishop of Nyssa.[3]

Both brothers were deeply influenced in their faith by their older sister, Macrina the Younger (ca. 327–80). More and more, Macrina is included among this group of theologians in recognition of the significant ways that she shaped and informed her brothers' thinking. She was betrothed to marry, but her fiancé died; she never married but instead devoted her life to Christ and service to her family and the church. Her brother Gregory's *Life of Macrina* chronicles her devotion to Christ through her virginity, her transformation of the family estate in Pontus into a monastic community, and her teaching on the soul and the resurrection.[4] Gregory even describes her as "the Teacher" in matters of theology and philosophy.[5] In all, five children from this remarkable family are venerated as saints: Macrina the Younger, Basil of Caesarea, Naucratius (who lived as a hermit), Gregory of Nyssa, and Peter of Sebaste (a bishop who attended the Council of Constantinople).

Meanwhile, Gregory of Nazianzus (329–90), who had met Basil as a student, joined their monastic community. Reluctantly, he was ordained as a bishop, first in Sasima and then later in Constantinople (where he was bishop during the Council of Constantinople) and, nearer the end of his life, in Nazianzus. Gregory's theological acumen, demonstrated in his *Theological*

Orations, earned him the moniker Gregory the Theologian or, sometimes, simply "the Theologian."[6] These church fathers and mothers were called on to defend the faith from distortions and to clarify the doctrine of the Trinity.

> **John Chrysostom** (ca. 347–407) was a noted Antiochene theologian and preacher. Born in Antioch, an early center of Christianity in northern Syria, John studied rhetoric and for a time lived an ascetic life as a hermit. Later, he became the patriarch of Constantinople and was particularly known for his preaching—*Chrysostom* means "golden mouthed"—which included both literal and allegorical readings of the text. As evidenced by his work *On the Priesthood*, he was also aware of the practical responsibilities of ministers. Unfortunately, his criticism of Empress Aelia Eudoxia resulted in his forced exile. Along with Basil of Caesarea and Gregory of Nazianzus, he is remembered as one of the "Three Holy Hierarchs" in the Eastern Orthodox Church.

Of course, there had been efforts to articulate the Christian understanding of God prior to the fourth century. For example, the apostolic fathers—including Clement of Rome, Ignatius of Antioch, and Polycarp of Smyrna—all employed Trinitarian language. And early apologists such as Irenaeus and Origen contributed to the church's reflection on the triune nature of God. Most notable in this earlier period was the work of Tertullian. In his *Against Praxeas*, he affirmed both God's oneness and the distinctions among the three divine persons, who he argued are "*distinct*, but not *separate*."[7] To make his argument, he developed new terms or employed terms in new ways. For instance, he coined the term "Trinity" (*trinitas*), and he applied "substance" (*substantia*) and "persons" (*personae*) to the Trinity to express God's oneness and the distinctions among Father, Son, and Holy Spirit. As helpful as these early articulations were, on the whole, they lacked clarity and specificity, and they often fell into some version of subordinationism, the view that one of the persons is somehow less than the others and thus not fully divine. Additional clarity was still needed.

Like other core tenets of the faith, the doctrine of the Trinity developed in a more intentional way in the church's post-Constantinian era. In this fourth-century discussion, the Cappadocians' influence became crucial. The divinity of God the Father, the creator and Lord of all (Ps. 47:2), is affirmed within Scripture and was assumed within the church's theology. The church's articulation of the full divinity of Jesus Christ developed in response to Arianism, with Athanasius and the Council of Nicaea (325) affirming that Christ is "of the same substance" (*homoousios*) as God the Father, and thus fully divine. This affirmation brought clarity to the church's Christology, but it also seemed to suggest the existence of two gods, even as the church maintained its monotheism.

What about the Holy Spirit?

The Ascent of the Spirit

The Spirit sometimes has been overlooked in the history of theology, but the early church found it essential to clarify the question of the nature of the Spirit. If the Holy Spirit is divine, then how is Christianity not polytheism? But if the Holy Spirit is *not* divine, then what implications might that have about Jesus? The presence and power of God's Spirit is affirmed throughout the Old Testament—for example, in creation (Gen. 1:2), in giving life to Adam (Gen. 2:7), and in bringing justice to the nations (Isa. 42:1). Likewise, the New Testament testifies to the unique work of the Spirit, who conceives Jesus in Mary's womb (Luke 1:35), empowers Jesus' ministry (Luke 4:18–19), is poured out on the disciples at Pentecost (Acts 2:1–12), inspires the authors of Scripture (2 Tim. 3:16), illumines our understanding of the truth (John 16:13; 1 Cor. 2:10), unites believers to Christ (Rom. 8:9) and each other (Eph. 4:3), and guides Christians in the process of sanctification (2 Thess. 2:13). All of this biblical testimony was crucial to the church, including the Cappadocians, in its understanding of the Holy Spirit.

Some early Christians took a particular interest in the Holy Spirit. An early sect known as Montanism, named after Montanus (ca. 135–75), emerged in Phrygia in Asia Minor. This "New Prophecy," as it was known, emphasized the presence and role of the Spirit, especially through dreams, visions, and charismatic worship. It called for its adherents to lead an ascetic lifestyle, and it affirmed a chiliastic theology (from the Greek word *chilias*, meaning "one thousand") that anticipated the imminent start of the millennium (Rev. 20:1–10). It was also known for affirming the role of women in the church—notably Priscilla (not the same Priscilla as Paul's coworker), Maximilla, and Quintilla, all of whom served as female priests or bishops. However, this proto-Pentecostal movement ran afoul of the wider church when Montanus seemed to declare himself to be a prophet, and ultimately it was deemed heretical.

Almost predictably, others denied the full divinity of the Holy Spirit. Founded by Macedonius, who at one point was the bishop of Constantinople, Macedonianism rejected the idea that the Holy Spirit is divine. These *pneumatomachoi* (meaning "opponents of the spirit" or "spirit fighters") employed arguments similar to those that Arius had used with regard to Jesus: in their view, the Holy Spirit was a creature, not divine. Who, like Athanasius before, would step up to help the church respond to these arguments?

In their works, the Cappadocians employed various arguments to demonstrate that the Holy Spirit is fully divine. In *On the Holy Spirit*, Basil affirms that, although God alone is holy (Lev. 11:45; 19:2), the adjective *holy* is rightly applied to the Spirit: "He is rightfully and properly called 'Holy Spirit,' which is above all the name for everything incorporeal, purely immaterial, and indivisible. . . . He is the source of holiness."[8] The Spirit is called holy, then, because of who the Spirit *is* and what the Spirit *does*. The Spirit does things that only God can do: the Spirit sanctifies people, making them holy (2 Thess. 2:13), which is something that no creature can do for another creature. In addition, Basil points out the significance of the fact that the Holy Spirit is included in the baptismal formula of the Great Commission (Matt. 28:19).[9] Basil died in 379, two years before the church clarified the doctrine of the Holy Spirit at the Council of Constantinople. Thankfully, the council—and his sister and brother—carried on his legacy.

What might have been Macrina the Younger's most formative teaching came at a crucial time in her family's life. Basil had just died, Macrina was on her deathbed, and the Council of Constantinople was soon to be called. In a visit between brother and sister, she spoke to her brother Gregory on the importance of believing in the immortality of the soul. This idea not only pertained to the human soul but also had important implications for how we understand God's divinity and his role as creator. She stressed that the "intelligible and immaterial Unseen" is not dependent on the material. Rather, it's the opposite. In her words, "[A]ll things depend on God and are encompassed by Him."[10]

The second ecumenical council, which met in Constantinople in 381, was an incredibly significant moment in the life of the patristic church and its determination of the orthodox faith. Not only did the council affirm the full humanity of Jesus, which Gregory of Nazianzus had argued for in opposition to the docetic Christology of Apollinarianism, but it also affirmed the full divinity of the Holy Spirit. In the words of the council, which are enshrined in the Nicene Creed, the Spirit is "the Lord and the Life-giver, that proceedeth from the Father, who with Father and Son is worshipped together and glorified together."[11]

Gregory the Illuminator (ca. 257–328) was born in Armenia and was converted to Christianity in Cappadocia during the late third century. At his return to Armenia around 300, he faced persecution for refusing to worship the Armenian goddess. Tradition remembers that when King Tiridates III became sick, it was Gregory's prayers that brought healing. Tiridates's subsequent conversion to Christianity and baptism by Gregory led to the latter's ordination as bishop, the establishment of Christianity in Armenia, and the translation of Scripture into Armenian.

The Spirit, then, possesses the same dignity, rank, and status as both the Father and the Son. In short, the Holy Spirit is God. By the end of the council, the church had articulated its belief in the full divinity of God the Father, Jesus Christ, and the Holy Spirit. But that didn't quite resolve the matter. Because now it sounded like Christians affirmed a belief in three gods. Once again, the Cappadocians were called on to provide insight.

Three Divine Persons, but Only One God

There are many ways that the doctrine of the Trinity might go wrong. Two of the most significant dangers to avoid, though, entail a denial of its basic affirmations: there are three distinct, divine persons, and yet there is one God.

In the first case, the Cappadocians found it important to affirm that the distinctions among the Father, the Son, and the Holy Spirit are genuine distinctions—that these are three distinct (but not separate) divine persons or *hypostases*. They are not one in the same. In one of his letters, Basil explains that "in the case of the Godhead, we confess one essence or substance so as not to give a variant definition of existence." At the same time, he writes, "we confess a particular *hypostasis* [person], in order that our conception of Father, Son, and Holy Spirit may be without confusion and clear."[12] To make those distinctions among the three persons evident, the Cappadocians employed terms that were particular to each within their eternal relations: God the Father is unbegotten, God the Son is eternally begotten or eternally generated, and the Holy Spirit eternally proceeds. As Gregory of Nazianzus states in his *Theological Orations*, "The personal name of the unoriginate is 'Father'; of the eternally begotten,

'Son'; of what has issued, or proceeds, without generation, 'the Holy Spirit.'"[13] These distinctions are also reflected in the work of God within the economy of salvation: for example, only the Son became incarnate, and only the Holy Spirit was poured out on the disciples at Pentecost. This notion, according to which one can "assign" or appropriate certain actions primarily to one of the divine persons (but not exclusively because there is also a unity to God's action), became known as the doctrine of appropriations. In both being and action, then, the genuine distinctions among the Father, Son, and Holy Spirit must be preserved.

Unfortunately, some did in fact deny these distinctions. Sabellius, a third-century Christian, wanted to protect the oneness of God. In this desire, however, he affirmed that the three persons are not genuinely distinct but rather only three modes or manifestations of the one God—akin to a single actor who wears a mask in one scene, then a different mask in another scene. His view became known as Sabellianism, though it is more generally known as modalism. In response, the Cappadocians affirmed that the three persons are genuinely distinct. Basil notes, "There is one God and Father and one Only-begotten [Son] and one Holy Spirit. We proclaim each of the persons singly."[14]

But that leads to a predictable question: Does that mean that Christians affirm three gods? This is the second danger to avoid: tritheism. For Christianity, a monotheistic faith whose roots are found in Judaism, the affirmation that God is one is essential. But the belief in the full divinity of three distinct persons seemed to call that into question.

Writing to one Ablabius in his work On "Not Three Gods," Gregory of Nyssa explains that the distinctions among the three divine persons do not entail three separate beings. There is, first, a unity to God's essence: "we must confess one God, according to the testimony of Scripture . . . even though the name of Godhead extends through the Holy Trinity."[15] In addition, even though each of the persons might have a particular role within the economy of salvation, there is a unity to God's action: "every operation which extends from God to the Creation . . . has its origin from the Father, and proceeds through the Son, and is perfected in the Holy Spirit."[16] When God is acting, all three persons are acting. In sum, Gregory rejects tritheism and affirms the unity of God's being and action.

To express its unique understanding of God, and after initial confusion between the East and the West because of differences in language, the church finally affirmed—with the help of the Cappadocian Four—that God is one substance (Greek: *ousia*; Latin: *substantia*), three persons (*hypostases*; *personae*). This affirmation was summarized in the Athanasian Creed, one of the most important statements of the faith along with the Nicene Creed and the Apostles' Creed: "The Father is God, the Son is God, and the Holy Spirit is God, and yet there are not three Gods but one God."[17] Here, as elsewhere, the Christian faith asks those who affirm it to hold together two notions that seem opposed to each other: God is one, and God is also triune. Yet this is who God has revealed himself to be.

Ray of Light

The entire approach of Eastern Orthodox theology, in which the Cappadocians are revered for their articulation and defense of the faith, is characterized by humility. Time and again, Orthodox theologians note the limitations of human language in describing the mysterious nature of the eternal, triune God. This approach is known as apophatic theology, or the *via negativa* (the negative way), in which one describes God primarily by saying what God is *not*. Gregory of Nazianzus, for instance, asks, "What competence have we here? We cannot understand what lies under our feet, cannot count the sand in the sea, 'the drops of rain or the days of this world' [Sir 1:2], much less enter into the 'depths of God' [1 Cor. 2:10] and render a verbal account of a nature so mysterious, so much beyond words."[18] And yet words must be spoken. However difficult the doctrine or faulty the human words employed to express it, the church has found it necessary to say, "This is our God."

It is, then, perhaps a theological irony that the Cappadocians, who emphasized the mystery of the hidden God, brought such clarity and light to the doctrine of the Trinity for the entire church in both the East and the West.

Discussion Questions

1. The Cappadocians argued in support of the divinity of the Holy Spirit. Where do you see the Holy Spirit at work in your life and at your church?

2. As Christians, we proclaim a God who is triune. What does the Trinity mean to you and your faith?

3. The Cappadocians were not only dedicated to the pursuit of robust and faithful theology, they also sought to live out their faith through ascetic and monastic ministry. What should be the relationship between Christian theology and the practice of the faith?

Further Reading

Saint Basil the Great, *On the Holy Spirit*, trans. Stephen Hildebrand (St. Vladimir's Seminary Press, 2011).

Lynn H. Cohick and Amy Brown Hughes, *Christian Women in the Patristic World: Their Influence, Authority, and Legacy in the Second through Fifth Centuries* (Baker Academic, 2017).

Saint Gregory of Nazianzus, *On God and Christ: The Five Theological Orations and Two Letters to Cledonius* (St. Vladimir's Seminary Press, 2002).

Gregory of Nyssa, *The Life of Moses*, Classics of Western Spirituality (Paulist, 1978).

CHAPTER 4

AUGUSTINE OF HIPPO

PRAYER

> *O you who are everywhere present, filling yet transcending all things; ever acting, ever at rest; you who teach the hearts of the faithful without noise of words; teach us, we pray you, through Jesus Christ our Lord. Amen.*

—Augustine[1]

Everybody's Got a Restless Heart

By all accounts, Ambrose, who served as the bishop of Milan in the fourth century, was a persuasive preacher, an expert exegete, and a gifted theologian. Yet he is perhaps best remembered for performing a single sacramental act: the baptism of Augustine. It is difficult to overstate Augustine's significance to the history of Christian theology, at least in the Western church. Over the course of his life and ministry, Augustine helped to shape the church's beliefs on matters as essential as sin, salvation, the doctrine of the Trinity, and the reality of evil, often in the midst of great controversy.

Augustine's story, like so many before and since, is one of a restless soul who meandered intellectually and spiritually until—through the work of the Holy Spirit, the prayers of those who loved him, and a dramatic encounter with the Word of God—he committed his life to Christ. But how did someone whose life, by his own admission, showed no signs of faith end up becoming perhaps the greatest theologian in the church's history?

The details of Augustine's early life up to his conversion are known to us because he took the unusual step of writing them down. His *Confessions* is regarded as the first spiritual autobiography ever to be written. Augustine was forty-three years old when he began writing the text. He had been a Christian for ten years and a bishop for two. Despite his prominent position at the time, he writes candidly about his willfully immoral life before becoming a Christian. The text is part spiritual *bildungsroman* (a coming-of-age story), part prayer, part theology. Augustine lived for another thirty-three years after he wrote *Confessions*. It is curious, and perhaps telling, that he revised all of his earlier works later in life, but when it came to the story of his conversion, he changed nothing.

Augustine (354–430) was born to a pagan father, Patricius, and a Christian mother, Monica, in Thagaste, a city in a North African province of the Roman Empire. He showed great intellectual abilities at a young age, and he applied them in rhetoric, which he studied and then taught, initially at Carthage.[2] During his early years, however, his life also revealed a reckless sinfulness. He recounts, for example, a time when he stole pears with some friends: "There was a pear tree in the neighborhood of our vineyard, but the fruit weighing it down offered no draw either in its look or its taste. . . . We filched immense loads, not for our own feasting but for slinging away to swine, if you can believe it . . .

our only proviso was the potential for liking what was illicit."[3] While in Carthage, he also had a relationship with a concubine with whom he had a son, Adeodatus. Summarizing this stage of his life in a prayer to God, he writes, "I made my way farther and farther from you, and you let me [go]."[4]

But Augustine's pursuit of knowledge and wisdom continued. Early on, his philosophical curiosity led him to embrace Manichaeism, a later form of Gnosticism, which was based on the teachings of Mani, a third-century Persian philosopher. Like its predecessor, Manichaeism was strongly dualistic, and it denied the goodness of the material world. But after a disappointing encounter with Faustus, a Manichean bishop, Augustine found that it couldn't answer his questions, so he abandoned it.[5]

He also encountered Neoplatonism, which had been advocated by Plotinus (ca. 205–70). It emphasized the unity of the divine essence and, harkening back to Plato, maintained that one could come to know full realities—truth, goodness, and beauty—by ascending through one's knowledge of lesser realities. Unlike the Manichaeism that he shed, some core tenets of Neoplatonism stayed with Augustine throughout his life. Of course, Augustine is hardly alone in appealing to philosophy in the development of his theology. This is a good reminder that philosophy has often been regarded as the "handmaid of theology" (see Justin Martyr's earlier appeal to Greek philosophy or Thomas Aquinas's later use of Aristotelian categories) and that theologians are shaped not only by Scripture and the church's tradition but also by forces beyond their control that have formed the intellectual waters in which they swim.

The path that led Augustine to embrace the Christian faith was forged by many people, but particularly by two: his mother, Monica, who continued to pray for him throughout his turbulent youth and whose faithfulness was an example for him; and Ambrose, the bishop of Milan (337–97). Augustine's skills in rhetoric took him to Rome and then the imperial court in Milan, where he met Ambrose, who was known for his intellect, his preaching, and his figurative interpretation of Scripture. In Ambrose, Augustine found an intellectual credibility that Faustus had lacked: "I now reckoned that a person could claim universal faith without embarrassment, though previously I'd thought no discourse could be launched against the Manichaeans' assaults."[6]

In a garden in Milan in 386, after years of wandering spiritually, Augustine gave his life to God: "Hardly knowing where I was or what I was doing, I sprawled under a fig tree and gave my tears free reign. . . . I was . . . weeping, with agonizing anguish in my heart, and then I heard a voice from the household next door, the voice of someone—a little boy or girl, I don't know which—incessantly and insistently chanting, 'Pick it up! Read it! Pick it up! Read it!'"[7]

In his record of this event, Augustine recalls that Antony of Thebes (ca. 251–356), the father of early monasticism, had left everything upon hearing Matthew 19:21. Taking the child's voice as a divine command, Augustine immediately picked up Paul's epistle to the Romans and read: "Let us walk decently as in the day, not in reveling and drunkenness, not in illicit sex and licentiousness, not in quarreling and jealousy. Instead, put on the Lord Jesus Christ, and make no provision for the flesh, to gratify its desires" (Rom. 13:13–14). There was no need for him to read any further: "The instant I finished this sentence, my heart was virtually flooded with a light of relief and certitude, and all the darkness of my hesitation scattered away."[8]

On the following Easter, Augustine was baptized by Ambrose. Later that year, he returned to Africa. He was ordained in 391, and reluctantly, he became the bishop of Hippo in 395. *Confessions*, then, is both Augustine's confessions of the sins of his youth and his confessions of faith in the God who continued to pursue him, took hold of him, helped him to order his loves properly, and gifted him to serve the church.

Patrick (ca. 389–461), known as the "Apostle of Ireland," was British. Born near the end of the Roman rule, he was kidnapped from his home and taken to Ireland, where, according to *The Confession of St. Patrick*, he was enslaved for six years. He managed to escape and return home, but after receiving a vision, he later returned to Ireland as a missionary. Legends abound regarding Patrick (and his collaborator, **Brigid of Kildare**), but his undoubted influence includes his conversion of the Celts and his founding of churches and monasteries.

"The Doctor of Grace" Opposes Pelagianism

Augustine's rhetorical abilities, which had been a source of status and pride for him in his early life, were called on time and time again throughout the rest of his life to help the church, which found itself in several crises. His entire ordained ministry took place between the Council of Constantinople (381) and the Council of Ephesus (431), so he didn't play a significant role in christological discussions. However, the church became embroiled in several other controversies that required careful responses, and Augustine often found himself in the middle of them. Foremost among those was a debate regarding the doctrine of salvation.

How are we saved? It's not as if the question hadn't been posed before. The early church had discussed it, and it affirmed that people are saved through Christ, not because of or through their actions. Echoing Paul, who affirmed that we are saved "by grace . . . not the result of works" (Eph. 2:8–9), first-century theologian Clement of Rome (ca. 35–99) expressed well humanity's fundamental dependence on God: "And we, too, being called by His will in Christ Jesus, are not justified by ourselves, nor by our own wisdom, or understanding, or godliness, or works which we have wrought in holiness of heart; but by that faith through which, from the beginning, Almighty God has justified all men."[9]

Pelagius (ca. 354–415), a British monk, had a quite different view. In his writings, which have been preserved by his opponents, he advocated the importance of moral living. His *Letter to Demetrias* encouraged the daughter of a wealthy widow who was about to take vows of chastity to lead a pious life. So far, so good. But in his articulation of his theology of salvation and grace, Pelagius emphasized humanity's natural strengths and abilities to do good to such an extent that the result was that humans could earn salvation. To begin, he rejected the doctrine of original sin, affirming instead that we possess an uncorrupted, free will: "Our souls possess what might be called a sort of natural integrity which presides in the depths of the soul and passes judgments of good and evil."[10] While he affirmed that our capacity for doing good is given by God, in his view, humanity is the agent responsible for achieving that good, even to the point that "the soul will climb to the very pinnacle of perfection."[11] Pelagius acknowledged the reality of sin, but he believed that it was possible to live without sin. He then spelled out the implications for our salvation: "Those who use free choice well merit the Lord's grace; they keep his commandments and deserve to be rewarded."[12] Pelagianism advocates a works righteousness according to which humanity is saved through its own efforts.

How would Augustine, who had witnessed not only his own sinfulness but also the grace of God in his life, respond to Pelagius? He began by acknowledging that God created humans with free will, with the ability either to sin (*posse peccare*) or not to sin (*posse non peccare*). However, because of Adam's fall, that free will was corrupted: "Because [Adam] abandoned God through free choice, however, he experienced God's just judgment. He was condemned along with his whole race."[13] Our corruption was so great after the fall that humans cannot *not* sin (*non posse non peccare*). What we need, then, is something we cannot achieve on our own. We need healing. We need a physician. We need someone who can liberate our wills, which are captive to sin. We need divine grace: "When God promises something, we do not achieve it by choice or by nature. He accomplishes it himself through grace."[14] Salvation is a gift from God, not a reward for our good works. While we are still called to do good works—Augustine affirmed cooperative grace, whereby humans cooperate with God in their salvation—salvation is not a reward for the good we have done. God's promise for humanity's heavenly state is far greater than humanity's original state because in heaven, humans will be unable to sin (*non posse peccare*).[15]

For his continual emphasis on humanity's need for God's

grace, Augustine is sometimes referred to as the "doctor of grace." He had helped the church navigate the Pelagian controversy, but this was not the only theological minefield that would require his wisdom.

An Imperfect Body

What should the church do when believers who have lapsed in the faith repent and want to come back? That was the practical question the early church faced during persecution, when some Christians who had abandoned the faith wanted to return. And the answer, of course, is obvious: welcome them back! In practice, it's more complicated.

After persecution under Emperor Decius began in the middle of the third century, which was the first empire-wide persecution, some Christians who had left the faith wanted to return. At first, they were opposed by Novatian (ca. 200–58), a priest from Rome. However, Cyprian of Carthage (ca. 200–58), who had studied under Tertullian, argued that preserving the unity of the body was more important: "This unity we ought to hold and preserve, especially we who preside in the Church as bishops, that we may prove the episcopate itself to be one and undivided. Let no one deceive the brotherhood with falsehood; no one corrupt our faith in the truth."[16] This set a pattern for the church's response, but what should it do when the lapsed believer is a leader, a bishop?

Just this scenario played out later during the persecution under Emperor Diocletian, which is often considered to have been the worst for Christians. Among those who lapsed in the faith during this time was Felix, the bishop of Aptunga. When he repented and returned to the church, Felix began to do all the things that bishops do: baptize infants, celebrate the Mass, hear confession, and consecrate other bishops. (In this case, he consecrated Caecilian as Bishop of Carthage.) But like Novatian before him, Donatus (ca. 311–55) opposed this reinstatement. He believed that Felix's lapsing invalidated his actions as a bishop after his return, including his consecration of Caecilian. What Donatus and his followers wanted was a pure church, free from the failings of those who were entrusted with its care, so he set himself up as a rival bishop of Carthage.

Once again, Augustine was called upon, this time to respond to the Donatists. The church, he argued, is a mixed bag, full of both wheat and tares. Returning to a theme he knew all too well from his own life, he pointed to the sinfulness of all Christians, including the Donatists. All sin, including lapses in faith, is serious, but who would be left in the church if all the sinners were kept out? The schismatic Donatists were, in Augustine's view, guilty of greater sins: forgetting the grace of God and splitting the church. In addition, their view suggested that the sacraments depended on the holiness of the person who administered them.[17] Instead, Augustine argued that the sacraments are effective not because of the minister or the recipient but because they are given by Christ: "however great be the perverseness of understanding on the part either of him through whom, or of him to whom, it is given, the sacrament itself is holy in itself on account of Him whose sacrament it is."[18] At a time when the church was still trying to define itself, Augustine reminded this imperfect body of believers that it depends not on its own holiness but on the holy and gracious God.

Pope Gregory I, or Gregory the Great (ca. 540–604), lived in a monastic order before becoming Bishop of Rome (the first pope to have been a monk). He is known for his writings, including *Dialogues*, his support of clerical celibacy and missionary efforts, and his advocacy of the arts and music, which included the use of images in the church's worship. Along with Ambrose, Jerome, and Augustine, he is considered one of the four Latin doctors of the church.

It's Kind of Like This

Analogies have a long history in theological discourse. This is especially true when it comes to analogies for the Trinity. Tertullian, for example, appealed to several analogies in an effort to explain God's triune nature: a root, a tree, and its fruit; a spring, a river, and a stream; the sun, its rays, and the apex of the ray.[19] At their best, theological analogies are helpful ways for people to express imprecisely something that is true about the nature of God, who is ultimately beyond all human language. But they are inadequate because they are, after all, only analogies.

In his work *On the Trinity*, written over roughly twenty years at the start of the fifth century, Augustine offered a thorough discussion of God's triune nature as Father, Son, and Holy Spirit. After a lengthy discussion of how the doctrine of the Trinity is founded on Scripture, Augustine considers how we can come to understand God's triune nature by looking within creation for *vestigia trinitatis*, vestiges of the Trinity. In particular, he argued that we should look at ourselves because humans alone are created in God's image (Gen. 1:26–27): "Where then is a trinity? Let us look into the matter as closely as we can, and call upon the everlasting light to enlighten our darkness . . . and let us see in ourselves as far as we are permitted the image of God."[20] Through his so-called psychological analogies, he examines both our internal constitution and our external experience.

Internally, he identifies several trinitarian patterns, including our memory, understanding, and will, as evidence of the triune God: "These three, then, memory, understanding, and will, are not three lives but one life, nor three minds, but one mind. So it follows of course that they are not three substances but one substance."[21] Externally, he again identifies Trinitarian patterns in our subjective experiences, most notably our experience of love: "When I who am engaged on this search love something, there are three: I myself, what I love, and love itself."[22] These three, Augustine suggests, correspond to the Father, the one who loves; the Son, the beloved; and the Holy Spirit, the "bond of love" between them. Like all analogies, Augustine's fall short of the full reality of God, but they have been highly influential in the church's understanding of God as triune.

A Heartfelt Response to Suffering

The fall of the Roman Empire, which had existed since before the time of Christ, was a reality-altering event. Militarily, it can be traced to a series of conquests, including the sack of Rome by the Visigoths (who were actually Arian Christians) in 410, the siege of Rome by Attila the Hun in the mid-fifth century, and eventually the surrender of Emperor Romulus Augustulus to Germanic Vandals in 476. The collapse of the empire created huge shock waves with political, economic, and social consequences that swept through the ancient world. But it also raised theological questions. After all, if the Roman Empire had embraced Christianity as its official religion (as it did with the Edict of Thessalonica in 380), did its fall imply that the Christian faith was false?

Of course, Augustine was no stranger to the realities of suffering, which he had witnessed in his life and in the lives of those he served as a bishop. In attempting to explain the reality of evil, in an earlier work, *On Free Will*, he had argued that evil does not have a positive existence on its own. Rather, evil is the absence of the good (in Latin, *privatio boni*), a turning away from God: "The movement of turning away, which we admit is sin, is a defective movement, and all defect comes from nothing."[23] But the sack of Rome raised the stakes significantly. It demanded a response. In *The City of God*, Augustine contrasted two cities, which "were created by two kinds of love: the earthly city was created by self-love reaching the point of contempt for God, the Heavenly City by the love of God."[24] The former was plagued by the reality of original sin, but in the latter, those predestined by God, who are strangers in the earthly city, become "by grace . . . citizen[s] above."[25] It is God's grace and not the power of Rome that is lasting.

Augustine died as the Vandals were besieging the city of Hippo in 430, but his life was a testimony to the grace of God. It could be argued that the history of the Western church since his death is as much a history of interpreting Augustine as it is interpreting Scripture. In the coming centuries, both Roman Catholic and Protestant theologians claimed Augustine as their own, though for different reasons. His insights into the doctrine of salvation, God's triune nature, and the reality of evil are significant aspects of his theological legacy. But perhaps his greatest contribution is showing the church what it looks like for a restless heart to finally find peace in God.

Discussion Questions

1. If you were to write a spiritual autobiography as Augustine did, what turning points would you highlight from your faith journey?
2. Augustine's mother, Monica, was an important influence in his life and theology. What should our commitment be to theological mentoring in the Christian family?
3. Augustine navigated a range of disagreements and controversies confusing and dividing the church. How should Christians navigate theological disagreement well?

Further Reading

Augustine, *The City of God* (Penguin, 2003).

Augustine, *Confessions*, trans. Sarah Ruden (Modern Library, 2017).

Peter Brown, *Augustine of Hippo: A Biography* (Univ. of California Press, 2013).

Justo L. González, *The Mestizo Augustine: A Theologian between Two Cultures* (IVP Academic, 2016).

PART 2

MEDIEVAL THEOLOGIANS

CHAPTER 5

JOHN OF DAMASCUS

PRAYER

O Lord, you have nourished me with spiritual milk, with the milk of your sacred Word. You have sustained me with the solid food of the body of our Lord Jesus Christ, your only-begotten and most holy Son, and you have blessed me with the sacred life-giving chalice which is his blood that he shed for the salvation of the world. O Lord, we praise you, for you have loved us and given your only-begotten Son for our redemption. Amen.

—Adapted from John of Damascus[1]

The Fall of Rome, the Rise of Islam

With the political power vacuum created by the fall of Rome, the bishop of Rome (the pope) became an increasingly important figure in the West. The church had been tied to the state ever since the conversion of Constantine, but during the medieval period, the relationship between the two became even more complex. This is perhaps best seen in the crowning of Charlemagne (ca. 742–814). On Christmas Day in 800, he was crowned the first emperor of what became the Holy Roman Empire by Pope Leo III at Old Saint Peter's Basilica in Rome, thus symbolizing both the pope's capacity to crown the emperor and the emperor's role as protector of the church. The first Western emperor since the fall of Rome, Charlemagne united Europe and initiated a "Carolingian Renaissance," which included cultural, intellectual, and religious developments.[2]

While the Western church was dealing with the far-reaching implications of the fall of Rome, the Eastern church was confronting a new challenge: the rise of Islam. Based on the teachings of Muhammad (ca. 570–632), a military leader who was considered by his followers to be a prophet and the last messenger of God, Islam was founded in the seventh century. With its staunch monotheism, rejection of the divinity of Christ, dismissal of the doctrine of the Trinity as blasphemous, and refusal of the use of images in worship, Islam (which means "submission") introduced religious, political, and cultural tensions with Byzantine Christians. During the seventh century, Eastern Christianity lost two-thirds of its land to Arab conquests, including Syria, Palestine, and Egypt, which had been centers of Christianity for generations. The rapid spread of Islam meant that some Christians—including John of Damascus—were forced to live under Islamic rule. Later, Western Christians began efforts to reconquer these territories, including the Holy Lands, under the banner of the Crusades from the eleventh to the thirteenth centuries. The tensions between Islam and Christianity were on full display later still, when Islamic Turks conquered Constantinople in 1453, thus ending more than one thousand years of the reign of Byzantine Christianity.[3]

The Hagia Sophia, the Church of the Holy Wisdom, was completed in 537 in Constantinople under Justinian I. For nearly a millennium, it had stood as the largest cathedral in the world and the center of Eastern Orthodoxy. Worship at Hagia

Sophia was so moving that it reportedly impressed emissaries of Vladimir I of Kiev (ca. 958–1015) to the point that he converted to the faith, which later resulted in the mass baptism of the Rus' people.[4] But after the Islamic conquest of Constantinople, the Hagia Sophia was converted into a mosque. A more dramatic example of the sweeping changes taking place in the East over the centuries could hardly be imagined.

Syrian bishop **Alopen** traveled to Chang'an (modern-day Xi'an in China) from East Persia along the Silk Road in 635. He wore a white tunic and carried Scripture and crosses. The second emperor of the Tang Dynasty, Taizong (considered the Constantine of China), welcomed him to the capital city. The emperor commissioned Alopen to translate Christian texts into Chinese. The Xi'an Stele, which was engraved in 781 (discovered in 1624), recounts this history of the earliest arrival of Christianity to China through the Church of the East.

Constantinople, We Have a Problem

At the heart of the Christian life is not just an affirmation of theological beliefs, such as the two natures of Christ or the doctrine of the Trinity, but also the practice of the faith. Christian orthodoxy (right belief) should be expressed in and align with Christian orthopraxy (right practice). And central to the practice of the faith is worship of the triune God. But worship has also been at the center of some of the church's greatest controversies. One persistent question for Christian worship over the centuries has been whether the church may use images or icons within the context of worship. Are these helpful aids to the true worship of God? Or are they distractions? Or worse still, do they create opportunities for, or perhaps inevitably lead to, idolatry?

Images have been part of Christian worship since no later than the second or third century. Under Pope Gregory the Great (ca. 540–604), the Western church distinguished the educational benefits of images in worship—people who could not read could still learn the story of Scripture—from the adoration of images, which infringed on the worship of the triune God. This distinction between proper and improper use of images in worship has, in one form or another, characterized much of Western worship ever since (though some Protestants later rejected them).

In the East, however, the role of icons became a divisive issue that plagued the church during the "iconoclast controversies" of the eighth and ninth centuries. On one side, iconophiles or iconodules like John of Damascus argued that icons (representations of Jesus, Mary, or the saints in a stylized pose, often with both eyes looking directly at the viewer) were beneficial aids in worship that served as "windows to the divine." On the other side, iconoclasts were concerned that such images violated the second commandment (Ex. 20:4–6; Deut. 5:8–10) and would lead to idolatry, so they called for their removal.

The controversy began in 726, when Byzantine emperor Leo III (ca. 685–741) prohibited the use of icons in worship and ordered their destruction throughout the empire. They were already being used in worship, so why did he make this change? Scholars are divided on this question. Perhaps Leo recognized the theological challenge that images could not reflect the fullness of the person of Christ, who is both fully divine and fully human. Perhaps the use of icons in worship was inhibiting conversions from or increasing tensions with Judaism and Islam, both of which are strongly iconoclastic faiths. Perhaps it was a combination of theological, political, and liturgical motivations. Whatever his reasons, Leo removed something that had been a regular feature of the doxological life of Eastern Christians and threw the Byzantine church into a turmoil that lasted nearly one hundred and fifty years. His decision was upheld by the Council of Hieria in 754, which prohibited the veneration of icons and called for their destruction. In its view, images of Christ fail to depict the reality of his two natures, either mixing them or separating them, thus falling into classic christological heresies.[5] With the stakes this high, it's no wonder that the issue of icons in worship was so divisive.

The two pressing matters for the Eastern church during this time—the rise of Islam and the question of icons in the church's worship—deeply shaped the life of a Syrian theologian who has been called "the last of the church fathers," but who also signals the shift to medieval Christianity: John of Damascus.

On the Road from Damascus

Today, with a Christian population of less than 10 percent, Syria is not regularly thought of as a center of Christianity.[6] However, it played a major role in the life of the early church and the spread of the gospel. Some of the Christians who fled Jerusalem settled in Syria, which at the time was a Roman province, and in its cities, such as Antioch, Edessa, and Damascus. It even has been said that "Christianity was born in Syria."[7] It was in Antioch, after all, that the followers of Jesus were first called "Christians" (Acts 11:26). And Saul's dramatic encounter with the risen Christ, which led to his conversion to faith, took place on the road to Damascus because he was seeking out the followers of "the Way" (Acts 9:1–2).

John of Damascus (ca. 660–750), also known as John Damascene, was born into this rich Christian history and into a prominent Christian Arab family. But he was also born at a time when Muslims ruled Syria, having conquered Damascus in the mid-630s. Like his grandfather and his father before him, John initially served in the court of a Muslim caliph. But when the caliph wanted to "purify" his court and make it more thoroughly Muslim, John left his courtly life to become a monk. In a sense, John took the same road as Paul, but in the opposite direction, moving from Damascus to the Mar Saba monastery near Jerusalem, where he lived the rest of his life.[8]

John's theological interests were wide ranging. His *Fount of Wisdom* includes reflections on creation, the incarnation, angels, Mariology, the sacraments, and the doctrine of the Trinity. Carrying on the tradition of the Cappadocians, John developed the Greek notion of *perichoresis* (in Latin, *circumincession*) to describe the harmony of the internal and eternal relations among the Father, Son, and Holy Spirit. He also wrote poems and hymns that became part of the Greek liturgy. Yet John is known particularly for supporting the iconophiles during the iconoclast controversies and for writing three treatises in support of the use of icons in worship.

Flesh and Blood

After Leo III banned the use of icons, some Eastern theologians rose to their defense, including Germanus, the patriarch of Constantinople (ca. 634–733), and Theodore of Studios (759–826), both of whom were exiled for their views. But the best-known response came from John of Damascus.

It is important to note that John was not unaware of the dangers of idolatry, and he clearly affirmed that Christians are called to worship God alone: "I believe in one God . . . in three persons, Father and Son and Holy Spirit, and I worship this one alone, and to this one alone I offer the veneration of my worship."[9] Moreover, John acknowledged that it is impossible to depict God, whom he describes as "incommensurable and uncircumscribable and invisible,"[10] employing typical Eastern apophatic terms. What, then, would legitimate the making of icons?

For John, Christ's incarnation changed everything. Prior to the incarnation, "God the incorporeal and formless was never depicted, but now that God has been seen in the flesh and has associated with human kind, I depict what I have seen of God."[11] In response to the iconoclasts, John draws a distinction between the material icons and the one who created the material world and came into the material world in Christ: "I do not venerate matter, I venerate the fashioner of matter, who became matter for my sake and accepted to dwell in matter and through matter worked my salvation."[12] In the view of John and the iconophiles, rather than leading to idolatry, icons enhance Christian worship.

John's defense of icons did not immediately change the Eastern church's liturgical practice. Under Leo and a succession of emperors, the doxology of the church remained staunchly iconoclastic. Eventually, Constantine V (771–805), the great-grandson of Leo III, came to the throne. But because he was only nine years old at the time, his mother, Empress Irene (ca. 752–803), ruled as regent. During her reign, she called the

Second Council of Nicaea in 787, which reinstated icons on the basis of Christ's incarnation and the belief that when icons are used in worship, one venerates the person who is depicted, not the icon itself: "For the honor which is paid to the image passes on to that which the image represents, and he who reveres the image reveres in it the subject represented."[13]

However, that didn't resolve the matter. Instead, the pattern was repeated. Two years after Leo V (775–820) came to the Byzantine throne in 813, he reintroduced the proscription against icons. But eventually, Empress Theodora (ca. 815–67), who was ruling as regent for her son, Michael III (840–67), restored icons in worship. Her decision was confirmed by the Fourth Council of Constantinople (869), which affirmed the use of icons and, in the process, elevated their status as equal to that of Scripture: "We decree that the sacred image of our Lord Jesus Christ, the liberator and Savior of all people, must be venerated with the same honor as is given to the book of the holy Gospels."[14]

In all, there were two periods when iconoclasm was the official policy of the Byzantine Empire, and each time, icons were restored under the leadership of female regents. Ever since this contentious era, icons have held an essential place in Eastern Orthodox worship. To this day, the Orthodox church continues to carry on the legacy of John of Damascus by celebrating the Triumph over the Iconoclasts on the first Sunday of Lent each year.

It's All Eastern to Me

While he is best known for his defense of icons, John of Damascus also reflects other emphases of Eastern Orthodox thought, including its apophatic approach to theology, its understanding of salvation as deification, and its appeal to the tradition of the Eastern church fathers.

Throughout their reflections, Eastern theologians tend to employ the *via negativa* (the negative way), or apophatic theology. Such an approach acknowledges that God is ultimately mysterious and beyond human comprehension, so it often describes God in terms of what God is *not*: for example, God is not finite (infinite), does not change (immutable), does not suffer (impassible), and does not die (immortal). As seen in Gregory of Nyssa's *The Life of Moses*, apophatic theology finds something of a theological exemplar in Moses: one who acknowledged his creaturely shortcomings and was completely dependent on God for divine revelation (in a burning bush, no less), yet learned even the very name of God (Ex. 3:14) and encountered God on Mount Sinai (Ex. 20:21).

John of Damascus exhibited a similar caution. In his preface to *The Fount of Knowledge*, after pointing out that Moses regarded himself unfit to the task of speaking for God, John asks, "[H]ow am I, who have not sufficient power of speech to express such concepts, to utter those divine and ineffable things which surpass the comprehension of every rational creature? With these considerations in mind I have hesitated to undertake this book."[15] Yet the task of theology is to express what God has revealed and to articulate the faith that has been handed down. Words must be spoken. John did write the book.

What is salvation? The answer to this seemingly simple question reveals another distinctive element of Orthodox theology and a difference between the East and West. Whereas Western theology, broadly speaking, tends to focus on legal categories such as justification and atonement, the East has preferred to view salvation primarily as sharing in God's divine nature or being made divine, known theologically as deification or *theosis*. Perhaps the best-known articulation of this view is found in Athanasius's *On the Incarnation of the Word*, when, speaking of the benefits of Christ assuming flesh, he writes, "For he was [made] incarnate that we might be made god."[16] That may sound strange or rather stark to Western ears, but for Eastern Christians, deification is precisely what Scripture means when it affirms that through God's promises, we "may participate in the divine nature" (2 Peter 1:4 NIV). In his work, John of Damascus similarly affirms, "[T]he Son of God for our sake became as we are and made us sharers of the divine nature, that 'we might be like him'" (1 John 3:2).[17] As with so many issues in theology, this one comes down to a matter of how one reads the text.

Photius (ca. 810–93), the patriarch of Constantinople, played the central role in what became known as the Photian Schism between the East and the West, which lasted from 863 to 867. After his initial appointment from layman to patriarch was challenged by Pope Nicholas I, Photius was deposed for a time, so that he was patriarch on two separate occasions (858–67; 877–86). He is known for arguing against the Western church's doctrine of the procession of the Holy Spirit from the Father and the Son (*filioque*) in works such as *Mystagogy of the Holy Spirit*. Though resolved, the Photian Schism anticipated the later Great Schism between the East and the West in 1054.

According to Eastern Orthodox theology, while God alone is divine by nature, humanity's salvation entails sharing in the divine nature. By grace, we become partakers in the very life of God.

Throughout his work, John of Damascus regularly interacts with and appeals to both Scripture and the work of Eastern church fathers. You'll find references not only to texts across the canon but also to Dionysius the Areopagite, Basil of Caesarea, Gregory of Nyssa, Gregory of Nazianzus, and John Chrysostom. That inclination reflects the importance of tradition within the Eastern Orthodox Church, which is sometimes called "the Church of the Seven Councils." We have explored the first four ecumenical councils and their contributions to the church's orthodoxy, especially its Christology and the doctrine of the Trinity: the First Council of Nicaea (325); the First Council of Constantinople (381); the Council of Ephesus (431); and the Council of Chalcedon (451). And we have discussed the seventh ecumenical council, the Second Council of Nicaea (787), which confirmed the use of icons in worship.

But what about the other two? The Second Council of Constantinople (553), the fifth ecumenical council, was convened by Emperor Justinian I (482–565), whose reign of nearly four decades was marked by the recapturing of some Muslim-controlled territories, the construction of the Hagia Sophia, and a strong defense of Chalcedonian orthodoxy in opposition to monophysitism. This council is known primarily for condemning the works of Origen and those associated with him, including Didymus the Blind (ca. 313–98).

Finally, the sixth ecumenical council, which was the Third Council of Constantinople (680–81), took up the question of

Christ's wills. If Jesus is both truly divine and truly human, then did he have one will or two wills, human and divine? This question largely was ignored in the West, which had embraced the Chalcedonian formula regarding Christ's two natures. But in the East, where both Chalcedonian and non-Chalcedonian churches—including the Oriental Orthodox Church and the Church of the East (also known as the Nestorian Church)—persisted, it became a matter of dispute. The debate largely followed the previous controversy about Christ's natures. Some—including Pope Honorius I and Sergius I, the patriarch of Constantinople—argued in favor of monothelitism, the belief that Jesus had only one will. Maximus the Confessor (ca. 580–662) rejected this view and instead followed the implications of Chalcedonian Christology, arguing that just as Jesus had two distinct natures, so too he had two distinct wills. Taking the example of Christ's prayer in Gethsemane (Matt. 26:39), Maximus argued that Jesus had both a divine will and a human will, but there was "no opposition between them."[18] For his efforts, Maximus was put on trial, his tongue was cut out, his right hand was mutilated (so he could neither speak nor write about his beliefs), and he was sent into exile. But his views ultimately were vindicated in the late seventh century at Constantinople.

These seven councils—bookended by two councils in Nicaea, and three of which took place in Constantinople—reflect the importance of the church's tradition, which often was clarified only in the crucible of controversy, to the Orthodox church. John of Damascus's contribution to that tradition included his defense of icons, which helped the Byzantine church to clarify its worship practices. Unfortunately, the tensions between the East and the West did not abate. In fact, things were just starting to heat up.

Timothy I was the patriarch of the Church of the East from 780–823, and during that time, he brought reform, promoted missions beyond the borders of Persia, and wrote numerous pieces (pastoral letters, polity, theology). Like John of Damascus, Timothy navigated the Christian faith under Islamic rule. In 781, he dialogued with the third Abbasid caliph, Mahdi. His account of that conversation via letter was written in Syriac and translated into Arabic, and is regarded today as a theological defense for East Syrian Christianity. In this account, Timothy shows respect for the caliph's faith and demonstrates his basic familiarity with the Qur'an as he addresses questions regarding the virgin birth, the Trinity, Jesus' death on the cross, Scripture, and more. He is considered one of the greatest East Syrian patriarchs in Christian history, with a reach that included Tibet, Turkey, Yemen, India, and China.

Discussion Questions

1. Consider the place of images in the worship of your church. Do they have a place in your tradition? Should they have a place? Why or why not?

2. John of Damascus claims that Christ's incarnation justifies the use of images or icons in worship. What is persuasive about that view? What might be concerning?

3. The Eastern tradition celebrates God's transcendence beyond human understanding. How can recognition of that transcendence enhance the Christian faith? How do we balance that with an affirmation of God's revelation to us?

Further Reading

Sidney H. Griffith, *The Church in the Shadow of the Mosque: Christians and Muslims in the World of Islam* (Princeton Univ. Press, 2010).

John of Damascus, *Three Treatises on the Divine Images*, trans. Andrew Louth (St. Vladimir's Seminary Press, 2003).

Maximus the Confessor, *On the Cosmic Mystery of Jesus Christ*, trans. Paul M. Blowers and Robert Louis Wilken (St. Vladimir's Seminary Press, 2003).

Richard Viladesau, *The Beauty of the Cross: The Passion of Christ in Theology and the Arts, from the Catacombs to the Eve of the Renaissance* (Oxford Univ. Press, 2006).

CHAPTER 6

ANSELM OF CANTERBURY

PRAYER

Come then, Lord my God, teach my heart where and how to seek You, where and how to find You. . . . Teach me to seek You, and reveal Yourself to me as I seek, because I can neither seek You if You do not teach me how, nor find You unless You reveal Yourself. . . . I do not seek to understand so that I may believe; but I believe so that I may understand.

—Anselm of Canterbury[1]

The Not-So-Dark Ages

References to the Middle Ages continue to conjure up notions of the "Dark Ages," when European society was supposedly full of nothing but ignorance. The phrase was apparently coined by the father of Renaissance humanism, Italian Francis Petrarch (1304–74), who used it to connect the rebirth of his time to classical Greco-Roman culture and also to conveniently demarcate both of them from the medieval period. But as we will see, the time from the early Middle Ages (ca. 700–1000) to the High Middle Ages (ca. 1000–1300) was hardly a dark age. Rather, it was a season of great intellectual progress, cultural vitality, and religious devotion. While the Eastern church was struggling with the rise of Islam and navigating the iconoclast controversies, Western Christianity was experiencing a time of flourishing, especially beginning with the Carolingian Renaissance under Charlemagne (ca. 742–814). This vibrant season in the Western church both enriched the existing institution of monasticism and led to the rise of scholasticism. Both of these developments are reflected in the life of Anselm, an Italian monk who spent his most formative and productive years in France and later became the archbishop of Canterbury in England.

Monasticism had been a feature of the church's life since the conversion of Constantine, so it was well-established by the medieval period. Following the fall of Rome, monasticism helped Christianity to survive and expand geographically during many tumultuous years until the crowning of Charlemagne. Foremost among those who shaped its Western expression were Benedict of Nursia (ca. 480–547), who established a community in Monte Cassino, Italy, and whose *Rule of St. Benedict* was adopted by the Western church, and Pope Gregory I (ca. 540–604), the first pope who had previously been a monk. Monasteries served a vital role in medieval society. They were not just the sphere of silent religious reflection; they provided education, medical care, respite for travelers, and social welfare. In many ways, monasteries were the hub of medieval society.

But they were not without their problems. The land owned by the church provided extensive wealth, and problems arose within the clergy, including moral decadence, nepotism, simony (the selling and buying of church offices), and concubinage (when priests did not remain celibate). Some recognized the need for reform, resulting in the Cluniac Reforms of the tenth century and, later, the Cistercians of Citeaux in the eleventh century, whose members included Bernard of Clairvaux (1090–1153) and who called for a return to the principles of Benedict's *Rule*. The Fourth Lateran Council (1215) also sought to fix practical matters by addressing the abuses of the clergy (in addition to other noted decisions, such as affirming transubstantiation and requiring confession of all Christians at least once per year). The Protestants of the sixteenth century were not the first to notice the need to reform the church!

Another change within the monasticism of the medieval church was the establishment of several new religious orders during this time: the Dominicans (the "Order of Preachers," or the "Black Friars"), founded by Saint Dominic (1170–1221); the Franciscans (the "Brown Friars"), founded by Saint Francis of Assisi (1181–1226); the Carmelites (the "White Friars"), founded in the twelfth century and later reformed under Teresa of Avila; and the Augustinians, whose members came to include a young Martin Luther. Both the monastic reforms and the creation of new orders highlight the religious vitality of the era. However, by the end of the medieval period, many of the same issues of corruption and excessive wealth that had plagued the monasteries persisted.

But it wasn't just the monasteries that were undergoing change during the Middle Ages. Another major development was the rise of a movement known as scholasticism. Engaging in theological reflection was, of course, nothing new in the church. It had been, in an informal way, part of the Christian life since the earliest disciples attempted to understand who Jesus was. And theological study had long been connected to monasteries, which often emphasized study as part of their daily routine. But a change that signaled the start of something new was the establishment of universities throughout Europe, which grew out of the cathedral schools. Among the earliest universities were the University of Bologna in Italy, the University of Salamanca in Spain, the University of Oxford and the University of Cambridge, both in England, and the University of Paris, known as the Sorbonne, which became a center of Roman Catholic theology. In these institutions, the seven liberal arts were taught (grammar, logic, rhetoric, arithmetic, geometry, astronomy, and music), but theology was regarded as "the queen of the sciences," the foundation for all other intellectual pursuits.

The developments that were taking place in both monasticism and scholasticism were reflected in the life of Anselm of Canterbury (ca. 1033–1109), who is often regarded as "the father of medieval scholasticism." Born into a noble family in Aosta, Italy, Anselm entered the Benedictine Abbey in Bec (located in modern-day Normandy, France) in 1059.[2] His theological reflections came to shape Western theology on matters as significant as the existence of God and how Christ's death on the cross benefited believers. But five years before he set foot in the monastery in northern France, a titanic shift in the bedrock of Christianity shook the church.

As Far as East Is from West

An issue that separated East from West in their respective theologies and that contributed to a long-lasting schism concerned the eternal relations among the Father, Son, and Holy Spirit in the Godhead. In its explanation of the doctrine of the Trinity, the church employed specific terms to describe the distinctions among the three divine persons. The Father is affirmed as the "unbegotten," the Son is eternally begotten or generated, and the Spirit eternally proceeds or is eternally spirated. That view was confirmed in the Nicene Creed, which states that the Spirit is "the Lord and the Life-giver, that proceedeth from the Father, who with Father and Son is worshipped together and glorified together."[3] Notice, in its original version, the creed states that the Spirit proceeds *from the Father* alone. But later, when the Western church was facing a resurgence of Arianism, which rejected Jesus' full divinity, in the Iberian Peninsula, it decided to tweak the creed. To reassert the fact that the Son is equally divine, it added the phrase "and (from) the Son" (that's *filioque* in Latin) to the creed so that it now affirmed that the Spirit proceeds from the Father *and the Son*.

For the West, such an affirmation helpfully showed that the Son is on par with the Father, doing what the Father does, even in the eternal Godhead. Moreover, it could be supported biblically by Jesus' words that he will send the Spirit (John 15:26), the fact that he breathes the Spirit on the disciples (John 20:22), and references to the Spirit as "the Spirit of Christ" (Rom. 8:9; Phil. 1:19). Western theologians have regularly affirmed the "double procession" of the Spirit (from both the Father and the Son). Among them was Anselm, who later defended the *filioque* clause at the Council of Bari (1098).[4]

Predictably, the East did not respond well to this change. Not only was the West altering an agreed-on ecumenical creed, but in so doing, it was asserting its authority over other churches. Moreover, while the addition of the phrase might be interpreted as elevating the status of the Son, it could also be seen as demoting that of the Spirit. Whether this change was biblically warranted might be questioned by the testimony that Jesus is conceived by the Holy Spirit (Matt. 1:20; Luke 1:35), the Spirit descends on Jesus at his baptism (Mark 1:9–11), and the Spirit empowers Jesus' entire ministry (Luke 4:18). For their part, Eastern theologians down the line rejected the *filioque* clause.

Centuries later, during Anselm's lifetime, the *filioque* controversy was one of several factors that contributed to the Great Schism in 1054. Other matters included Rome's assertion of authority over other churches, differences in language (Greek in the East, Latin in the West), differences in practices, such as the use of icons and whether priests were allowed to marry, and differences in theology, including the *filioque* clause. But matters sharply intensified in 1054 when Pope Leo IX sent Cardinal Humbert as a papal representative to Constantinople. According to accounts, Humbert delivered a papal bull to the patriarch of Constantinople, Michael Cerularius, on the eucharistic altar in Hagia Sophia, that excommunicated all of Eastern Christianity. The East responded in kind with excommunications of their own, officially breaking fellowship between the East and the West. Later, in 1204, during the Fourth Crusade, as Western armies were supposedly attempting to recapture the Holy Lands, they stormed Constantinople and ransacked the Hagia Sophia. The mutual excommunications between East and West remained in place until 1965.[5]

Over the next several centuries, the East continued to struggle against encroaching Islamic forces, which eventually conquered Constantinople in 1453. Meanwhile, the West was experiencing a theological renaissance, and Anselm played a key role.

Lord, Help My Belief

After he entered the abbey in Bec, Anselm showed great promise, and he quickly rose through the ranks, becoming a prior and later an abbot. During this season of his life, he wrote both *Monologion* and *Proslogion* (1078–79), works of such personal devotion and intellectual insight that they earned him a reputation as a noted theologian. He might have remained there, but church politics intervened. After the Norman invasion of England in 1066 under William the Conqueror, Lanfranc of Pavia, who had previously served as a prior at Bec, became the archbishop of Canterbury. Following Lanfranc's death, King William II needed to appoint a new archbishop. He chose Anselm, who took on the role in 1093. Yet Anselm's longest-lasting contributions to the church turned out to be theological.[6]

Like Augustine before him, Anselm viewed theology as an act of faith—something that required God's help even as one pursues greater knowledge of God. Anselm found support in his reading of Isaiah 7:9: "Unless I believe, I shall not understand."[7] Hence, Anselm's theological methodology is often characterized by the phrase *fides quaerens intellectum*, or "faith seeking understanding."

This approach to theology is on full display in one of Anselm's most important contributions: the ontological argument, which he articulated in his *Proslogion*. Though it is often characterized as a "proof" for God's existence, it is perhaps better thought of as an outworking of Anselm's faith through the use of his reason. Allow us to quote part of the argument at length:

> Now we believe that You are something than which noth-
> ing greater can be thought. . . . And certainly this being

so truly exists that it cannot be even thought not to exist. For something can be thought to exist that cannot be thought not to exist, and this is greater than that which can be thought not to exist. Hence, if that-than-which-a-greater-cannot-be-thought can be thought not to exist, then that-than-which-a-greater-cannot-be-thought is not the same as that-than-which-a-greater-cannot-be-thought, which is absurd. Something-than-which-a-greater-cannot-be-thought exists so truly, then, that it cannot be even thought not to exist. And You, Lord our God, are this being.[8]

Let's see if we can follow Anselm's logic and, in the process, not get lost in all the "that-than-which" statements. First, notice how Anselm defines God. He does not refer to Scripture, the Trinity, Jesus Christ, or the Holy Spirit. Rather, he defines God as "something than which nothing greater can be thought." (Important: that is decidedly *not* the same thing as "the greatest thing that you can think of.") For Anselm, God is perfect, the greatest possible being, so nothing and no one is greater than God. This definition of God, he argues, necessarily entails God's existence. How so?

We each have an idea of God in our mind, he suggests. But wouldn't existing in reality be greater than existing only in someone's mind? If God exists only in our minds and not in reality, then God would no longer be the perfect, greatest possible being that Anselm affirms God to be. If God does not exist, then we would have only the idea of God, not the reality. Therefore, for God to be "that-than-which-a-greater-cannot-be-thought," God must exist in reality. To put it another way, if God is perfect, then God must exist because it is more perfect to exist than not to exist.

Not everyone was convinced. Gaunilo of Marmoutier, a contemporary of Anselm's and a Benedictine monk, attempted to refute Anselm's ontological argument by offering a "reply on behalf of the fool" (a reference to the fool of Ps. 14:1). The crux of Gaunilo's response was this: just because you have an idea of something in your mind doesn't mean that the something exists in reality. Take the example of a perfect island, he said. Just because I have an idea of a perfect island in my mind doesn't mean that that island exists. Likewise, the mere idea of God does not entail God's existence. Anselm countered by saying that Gaunilo's response applies to perfect islands or any other created thing. But God is in a different ontological category, so the argument holds, at least for Anselm.

Whether the ontological argument might rightly be considered a proof for God's existence has been much disputed.

Hildegard of Bingen (1098–1179) was a preacher, abbess (meaning monastic leader), poet, theologian, and mystic. She entered the convent at eight years old and was educated in Latin. At nearly forty years old, she was elected to lead her order and began to experience visions, which she wrote down in her work *Scivias*. After concerns of heterodoxy were raised, her work received the direct approval and encouragement of the pope. Her wisdom was sought after from the lowest to the highest levels of society, including emperors and popes. She is remarkable for being formally confirmed as a theologian by the pope in her lifetime even though she received no formal theological training.

The argument has been replayed over the centuries in theological and philosophical discourse (for example, with Rene Descartes playing the role of Anselm and Immanuel Kant playing Gaunilo). What is evident is that Anselm is not actually beginning with a blank slate. Although he does not use biblical language to define who God is, he certainly has some preconceived ideas about who God is. It is thus perhaps best to view his argument as an example of "faith seeking understanding," in which Anselm employed his reason to seek further knowledge of God.

Rescue Me

The early christological councils spent a great deal of time and energy answering the question, "Who is Jesus?"—which is about the *person* of Christ. They were less focused on articulating an answer to the question, "What did Jesus do?"—which is about the *work* of Christ. Of course, the person and work of Christ are intimately related because his identity is revealed in what he does, and what he does is possible only on the basis of who he is. The early church certainly affirmed that Christ had taken on real human flesh, really died on the cross, and really risen to redeem lost humanity. But exactly how does Jesus' death save us and bring about reconciliation between God and humanity? The mechanics of the atonement became a matter of dispute in the Middle Ages.

Understanding Christian theories of the atonement (which derives from the Latin word for reconciliation) requires acknowledging the broader context of the sacrificial system in the Old Testament. As described in Leviticus 16, the covenantal relationship between God and Israel required sacrifices to atone for the sins of the people. In the New Testament, atonement between

God and humanity is achieved not by a series of ongoing sacrifices but rather in light of the one-time sacrificial death of Jesus Christ (Heb. 9:12; 10:10).

Since the time of the early church, the dominant theory of the atonement had been what is known as the ransom theory. This idea interpreted Christ's work on the cross as part of a larger cosmic drama in which the forces of good and evil were in conflict. According to this theory, Satan held humanity captive because of the reality of sin. Humanity was helpless, subject to the one whom Scripture calls "the prince of this world" (John 14:30 NIV), "the god of this age" (2 Cor. 4:4 NIV), "the ruler of the kingdom of the air" (Eph. 2:2 NIV), and "the evil one" (1 John 5:19). Christ's death on the cross, then, is seen as a ransom (Matt. 20:28; Mark 10:45) that buys back sinners from Satan. Through his resurrection, Jesus is victorious over Satan, delivering humanity from captivity and destroying "the one who has the power of death, that is, the devil" (Heb. 2:14).

For roughly the first thousand years of the church's life, this dominant understanding of Christ's work was popularized by figures such as Gregory of Nyssa, Gregory the Great, and Maximus the Confessor. Anselm developed a different theory of the atonement, one that was clearly rooted in his time but sought to point to the universal need for and accomplishment of Christ's work.

In *Cur Deus Homo* (*Why God Became Man*), Anselm describes how humanity's sin dishonors God by failing to render all of the honor that is due to God. This honor must be repaid, so someone must make satisfaction to pay for this debt. Anselm explains that humanity *should* pay the debt, but we are unable to do so. And because only God *could* pay the debt, what is required is someone who is both human and divine, the God-man, Jesus:

"If God only *can*, and man only *ought* to make this satisfaction, then necessarily One must make it who is both God and man."[9] It is helpful to remember that Anselm was writing in the eleventh-century context of feudalism. For him, God is akin to a feudal lord, and humans are like serfs, whose disobedience dishonors their lord, but who could never repay their debt. In this way, Anselm's satisfaction theory is a great reminder that all theology is done within a particular context.

Among Anselm's critics was Peter Abelard (1079–1142), a French theologian and philosopher who taught at the University of Paris. If you've heard of Abelard, then it might be because of his romantic relationship with Heloise, a nun with whom he fell in love. In keeping with his experience, Abelard's atonement theory appealed to love. For Abelard, Anselm's theory was far too transactional. You might say that he was—wait for it—dissatisfied with the satisfaction theory. For Abelard, rather than providing satisfaction for the damage done to God's honor, Christ's death on the cross was primarily a demonstration of God's love (Rom. 5:8). Christ's sacrifice is therefore an example of love for us, such that "our hearts should be enkindled by such a gift of divine grace, and true charity should not now shrink from enduring anything for him."[10] His theory of the atonement thus came to be known as the moral influence theory.

In subsequent centuries, the church developed more atonement theories that sought to describe Christ's work on the cross. For example, the penal substitution theory, often associated with John Calvin, argues that Christ took our place, substituting himself for us and suffering the penalty that we should have suffered: "Death held us captive under its yoke; Christ, in our stead, gave himself over to its power to deliver us from it."[11] The moral government theory, which was developed by Hugo Grotius (1583–1645), an Arminian theologian, argues that Christ's death demonstrates his obedience. Rather than encouraging people to love (as in the case of Abelard's theory), here the cross reveals God's wrath against sin, which should deter people from sinning and thereby preserve the moral governance of the world. Finally, the *Christus Victor* (meaning "Christ is the victor!") theory, articulated by Gustaf Aulén (1879–1977), a Swedish theologian, bears some similarities to the ransom theory from the early church. Developed shortly after World War I, this theory emphasizes God's liberating victory over evil and the powers that keep humanity in bondage (1 Cor. 15:57).

Though some Christian traditions or denominations have preferred one of these atonement theories over the others, there is no single, orthodox theory of how Christ's death on the cross redeems humanity. Scripture itself uses different images to try to capture the breadth and depth of Christ's saving work, and new theories developing today might enhance our understanding of Christ's work. Since the time of the early Christian apologists, theologians like Anselm of Canterbury have sought to show how faith can be supported by the use of reason. Meanwhile, other theologians, like Julian of Norwich, explained their faith by appealing to their personal, mystical experiences.

Discussion Questions

1. What role do you think reason should play in the Christian faith? Is understanding a prerequisite for salvation?
2. What do you find to be convincing arguments for the existence of God today?

3. How would you describe what happens in Christ's death on the cross? How does it save us?

Further Reading

Anselm of Canterbury, *The Major Works*, ed. Brian Davies and G. R. Evans (Oxford Univ. Press, 1998).

G. R. Evans, *The Medieval Theologians* (Wiley-Blackwell, 2001).

Hildegard of Bingen, *Hildegard of Bingen: Scivias*, trans. Mother Columba Hart and Jane Bishop, Classics of Western Spirituality (Paulist, 1990).

Joshua M. McNall, *The Mosaic of Atonement: An Integrated Approach to Christ's Work* (Zondervan Academic, 2019).

CHAPTER 7

JULIAN OF NORWICH

PRAYER

God, of your goodness give me yourself, for you are enough for me, and I can ask for nothing which is less which can pay you full worship. And if I ask anything which is less, always I am in want; but only in you do I have everything.

—Julian of Norwich[1]

Women Behaving Ascetically

Beginning with Mary's response at the annunciation of Jesus' birth (Luke 1:26–38) and highlighted by Mary Magdalene's witness to the resurrected Christ (John 20:11–18), the church has been profoundly shaped by women committed to following Christ and contributing to the ministry and theology of the church even in the face of numerous barriers and formidable challenges because of sex and gender. Christian history is filled with women behaving "ascetically," and not only as hermits and monastics.[2] We saw how from the earliest days of Christianity women such as Perpetua were courageous martyrs for Christ at the hands of the Roman Empire. These acts of faithful valor and self-denial were offered from positions not only of persecution but also of power.

Women of political importance have used their influence to shape Christian theology, practice, and policy, as we saw with Empress Pulcheria's presiding over the Council of Chalcedon. In the structure of the church, we know that women ministered as deacons (see Abbess Radegunde, ca. 520–87) and served as bishops (see the Montanists). If early Christian frescos from the Catacomb of Priscilla are interpreted correctly, women administered communion in the early church (later in the medieval practice of "masses without priests"[3]). Numerous accounts of women preaching, authorized or not (celebrated or not), are remembered throughout the record of Christian history.

No other space in the church, however, has provided more opportunities for women to engage in formal ecclesiastical leadership than monasticism. From the start, even as the paradigm of the pious shifted from martyrdom to the hermit's life to the communal religious order, both men and women have always participated. (See Pachomius's houses for men and women.) If we recognize Jerome's role in the establishment of Western monasticism, we should also remember his collaboration with Marcella and Paula and the joint monastic community they established in Bethlehem in 386. To celebrate Patrick's evangelistic and monastic ministry in Ireland, we should not overlook his collaboration with Brigid of Kildaire. When it adopted the *Rule of St. Benedict* in the sixth century, the Western church began to formalize the transition from the abba/amma hermit life of the Syrian desert to the nuns/monks/friars (abbots/abbesses, etc.) of Europe. Among them was Julian of Norwich, an anchoress who gained prominence and significance by the fourteenth century.

Catherine of Sienna (1347–80) was a mystical theologian who experienced visions and the stigmata. She was a member of the Dominican Order and worked on behalf of the poor. She dictated numerous letters, including her *Treatise on Divine Providence*. Out of her zeal for reform and her abilities in diplomacy, she visited Pope Gregory XI to urge him to move the papacy back to Rome after many years in Avignon, France. In 1377, the papacy returned to Rome. She was canonized in 1461 and, in the twentieth century, became the second woman after Teresa of Avila to be named a doctor of the church.

An Anchored Life

What do Geoffrey Chaucer, John Wycliffe, and Julian of Norwich all have in common? They were English contemporaries who advanced the common language and religious culture through literature, Scripture, theology, and ministry. Julian's book *A Vision Showed to a Devout Woman* (a.k.a. *Showings*, plus a later and longer version called *A Revelation of Love*) is regarded as the first English book authored by a woman. There is little we can confirm about her life, including her true name, but she is believed to have been born in Norwich, England, around 1342/3. Her name may derive from the church that she was attached to: the Church of Saint Julian. It is evident from her writings that she was educated and knowledgeable of the Latin Vulgate. By her own account, her writings began after a rapid sickness that left her on her deathbed and receiving last rites when she was around thirty years old.[4] In May 1373, she experienced sixteen "showings" or revelations from God, which she recorded in short and long forms. The short text version (*Showings*) was likely written around the 1370s and 1380s, and she later wrote several versions of the long text version, likely in the 1390s, while she was an anchoress.

Before Julian was fifty years old, she dedicated her life to the church as an anchoress. Given her emphasis on mothering and pregnancy, some scholarship claims that she was married around age sixteen and then perhaps lost her husband and child during the black plague.[5] Various wills from the region and period bequeathed money to her ministry, which corroborates her remembered name and position at the church.[6] Clearly, she was recognized and valued in her time and within her community.

To describe Julian as an "anchoress" (meaning to withdraw) indicates that she served the church as an ascetic recluse in an isolated cell literally anchored to the church. Her anchorage was a small room outfitted with an altar, and she lived there on modest provisions. The focus of her life as an anchoress was one of solitary prayer on behalf of the community, but she was also a resource for spiritual guidance to those in need. A visit to the church today, which is both a tourist and pilgrimage site, reveals a cell with a small window accessible to those outside the church. Fully withdrawing was rarely possible for ascetic recluses, who, by virtue of their extreme commitment, became beacons of spiritual wisdom. Julian lived in one of the busiest neighborhoods in one of England's largest cities, which meant that she was paradoxically also a "public figure."[7] She stood at the border between two communities, an intermediary of the spiritual.[8] Julian's writing further extended that legacy and inspired a new wave of anchorites in the life of the church.

Extreme Ways

Julian's theology has an important place within the corpus of medieval Western mystical theology. This approach to theology is described as rooted in a heightened awareness of God's direct presence with special emphasis on the bond between knowing and loving God.[9] Knowing God, and therefore God's love, frequently derives from visions and mystical experiences that serve as metaphors for theological truth. The approach is accessible to women because education is not a condition for hearing directly from God, and the medieval church recognizes that ultimately God can speak through anyone. Experiences of visions, divine locutions or meetings with God, and even raptures or ecstasies communicate God's presence and activity uniting the believer to Christ. In that regard, both male and female mystics often emphasize marriage and courtly love to describe the bond that is formed between God and the individual.

In the recounting of these events, mystics describe an overwhelming experience of body, mind, and emotion that can generate "ecstatic" feelings. Female mystics tend to focus on matters of food, disease, and the body.[10] They also stress the physical toll exacted by their divine encounters, particularly when meditating on Christ's suffering on the cross. Some practiced severe acts of penance such as fasting or injuring the body in observance of the "mortification of the flesh."[11] These dynamics are present but also tempered in Julian's writings. From the start of the Short Text, she prays for three gifts of God's grace: visions of Christ's passion, bodily sickness, and a gift of three wounds. (In her case, these "wounds" are contrition, compassion, and desire for the will of God.)[12] God answers her prayer, but always in a way that leads to a greater reliance on and understanding of his love. In this way, "wounds" become avenues for grace in Julian's writings.

Self-effacing tendencies are also present among female mystics, who are known to stress their lowliness as "mere women" (not just sinful humans) as a means of emphasizing God's power at work within them like filled vessels. Julian writes with pronounced humility to the benefit of "every" Christian,[13] but scholars have also noted a shift between the two texts in this regard. In the first version, the Short Text, she describes herself as devout, but also as an uneducated, feeble, and frail woman who has no intention of teaching. By the Long Text, she is simply an "unlettered creature,"[14] which may be an indication of how entering the office of anchorite transformed her sense of calling and enabled her to embrace the authority that came with her official entrance into the church. While the two texts—in their similarities and differences—have complicated her legacy and the readings of her theology, at the same time, they have provided a rare opportunity to see how the theology of a female mystic developed as she moved into her mature years as she lived well beyond the average lifespan of the time. As she came to better understand the visions that God revealed to her, the overarching message of God's love was magnified.

Meister Eckhart (1260–1327) was a German Dominican teacher and preacher. He emphasized the value of an inward spiritual experience of God in pursuit of union with God. But the idea of discovering the divine within was judged heretical by the church. Mystics were frequently evaluated by the church with some level of suspicion until proven orthodox.

JULIAN OF NORWICH | 99

Love in the Time of the Black Death

Several shared traits across mysticism are evident in Julian's writings, but the central message of her work is that the gracious love of God sustains all things. God's love is manifest even in the smallest of created things, she taught as she gazed at a tiny hazelnut in her hand: "And in this he showed me something small, no bigger than a hazelnut, lying in the palm of my hand. . . . What can this be? . . . I was amazed that it could last, for I thought that it was so little that it could suddenly fall into nothing. And I was answered in my understanding: It lasts and always will, because God loves it; and thus everything has being through the love of God."[15] For Julian, the hazelnut came to reveal God as creator, who both loves and preserves even the smallest thing, and that only in union with God is there love, rest, and true happiness waiting for her. Like Augustine, her restlessness was a beckoning to find true rest in God and to know God, who desires to be known.

In reflection of Christ's passion, the foundation for her confidence in God's love, Julian famously writes that Jesus declares "readily and sweetly with his words, and says: But all will be well, and every kind of thing will be well."[16] This is a good word for all who will be saved by the Holy Spirit (she is not a universalist), and she stresses that Jesus offers it tenderly and without blame or judgment. But this too is the work of the Trinity and not only of Jesus, Julian makes clear. The Trinity created all things out of nothing and promises to make all things well in God's perfect timing.[17] The day of judgment, in Julian's teachings, is delayed out of compassion and love for creation. Any compassion, then, that believers offer to others is the evidence of Christ within.

The message is remarkable perhaps because it was far from obvious during her lifetime. In the first place, Julian was living through the bubonic plague. After a series of droughts and poor harvests in Europe, a malnourished population was prone to infectious disease. The black death began to spread around the world during Julian's childhood through Constantinople (1347) until finally reaching England in June 1348. Italian ships had never been better designed to sail faster and farther, and consequently, ports had never been deadlier. Urban centers became breeding grounds for rats carrying disease-ridden fleas. As it turned out, the disease spread not only through flea bites but via airborne transmission. It was a perfect storm.

To emphasize God's love in the time of the black death is no small matter.[18] The infected and their families were forced into terrible moral dilemmas of either abandoning loved ones or facing almost certain death. Many clergy were criticized by survivors for abandoning their flocks at the breaking point and neglecting obligations of administering the sacrament of last rites on the deathbed. Disillusionment with the clergy over failed pastoral care of the sick proved a lasting resentment into the Reformation. In the end, the disease is estimated to have killed approximately 30 percent of the population. Christians blamed events on their own sins and some practiced extreme public flagellation of their bodies, overt veneration of the saints, and severe scapegoating of the Jews as a way to pacify divine retribution. If only that were the only challenge at the time.

Julian also wrote during the Hundred Years' War (1337–1453), which dragged on between the French and the English. During this mess, Joan of Arc (1412–31), a peasant girl turned mystic and military leader, was captured by the English, tried, and burned at the stake at age nineteen for heresy and for wearing trousers. Being a woman of visions was not a straightforward calling. From where did Julian's confidence come?

Witnessing Christ's suffering and bleeding as evidence of God's love is a prominent theme in Julian's writings. Noting the copious amounts of his spilled blood, Julian communicates the sufficiency of Christ's sacrifice to cover sin.[19] The dying face of Christ serves as the assurance of God's love for every Christian.[20] She describes putting on Christ as wearing love like clothes that wrap and enfold you.[21] This is not to say that the sinful life has no role in the believer's life. Julian speaks of a "gentle fear" paired with consolation for believers when faced with the reality of sin while wrapped in the love of Christ.[22] She emphasizes the role of prayer and penance (contrition, confession, and satisfaction) as medicine that heals wounds but not scars. Nevertheless, she revels in God's gracious plan: "[A]ll shame will be turned into honour and into greater joy." [23] This is the gentle and kind love that God has in store for those who will be saved.

Bernard of Clairvaux (1091–1154) was a French abbot of Clairvaux who led reform in the Benedictine Order and founded the Cistercians at Citeaux in 1112. In 1174, Bernard was canonized, and he was later named a doctor of the church in 1830. He wrote extensively on God's love and the mystical union between the bridegroom Jesus and his bride in the Song of Songs. Bernard taught about the right ordering of love and employed an "affective mysticism" that emphasized the experiences of the senses in the meeting of God.

Mama and the Trinity

Although the act of addressing God or Jesus as "mother" is often attributed to modern feminism, the practice began well before then. Many early church fathers (Clement, Origen, Irenaeus, John Chrysostom, Ambrose, and Augustine) were known to address Jesus as mother, and medieval monasticism followed suit. Comfort with maternal imagery when addressing God and Jesus stemmed not only from appreciation for a good metaphor in theology but also especially because Scripture connected those dots (Isa. 49:1, 23; 66:11–13; Ps. 21:10–11).

The father of scholasticism, Anselm of Canterbury, developed his teaching on Jesus as Mother in his *Monologion* based on Matthew 23:37. He identified Jesus with the actions of motherly love insofar as a mother gives birth, even giving up her life for her child, provides refuge and comfort from hurt, and revives her child by the milk of her breast.[24] This manner of referring to Jesus gained prominence among twelfth-century monks, mystics, and scholastics and particularly among the Cistercians in the writings of Bernard of Clairvaux.[25] Julian stands within this tradition and also extends it in her Long Text.

Julian's theology is especially attentive to the Trinitarian dynamics of the faith. She describes deep joy in reveling over the Trinity's role as our maker, protector, and eternal spouse.[26] She pairs this with sound, orthodox Christology: affirming the codivinity and coequality of the Father and the Son, the fullness of Christ's two natures, and the atonement that he can offer as a result.[27] Chapters 58–63 are rich with reflection on God as Father, Mother, and Spouse (and Jesus as Savior and Brother);[28] she is the first theologian to comprehensively discuss

God as Mother within a Trinitarian framework. She writes, "God almighty is our loving Father, and God all wisdom is our loving Mother, and with the love and the goodness of the Holy Spirit, which is all one God, one Lord."[29] Julian identifies Jesus as the true Mother who is reforming, restoring, and perfecting us. Mother Jesus is gracious and patient, protecting us by his love. Themes of bearing, birthing, and nursing are attributed to Jesus as a loving mother who is attentive to her child's every need. (Julian has a high view of mothers!) Mother Jesus teaches wisdom and illumines understanding with tenderness; he may allow us to fall but is always there to pick us up. By this motherly bond of love, we are attached to him, and in that attachment, we are united to God so that we will never perish.

Even with vibrant metaphors, visions, and physical experiences of God, Julian's teachings affirm the mystery of God (a theme of apophatic theology). God is hidden still and not all is revealed. The fullness of knowledge that awaits us comes only in uniting with him eternally.[30] In the end, Julian's message is powerfully pastoral and points to a God who "loves us and delights in us, and so he wishes us to love him and delight in him and trust greatly in him, and all will be well."[31]

A Meeting of Two Mystics

Around 1413, the English mystic Margery Kempe (b. ca. 1373) visited Julian in her seventieth year. Their meeting is recounted in *The Book of Margery Kempe*, which is considered the first autobiography in the English language. Kempe was in Norwich visiting a Carmelite friar, who encouraged her to trust that the Holy Spirit was at work in her life through the experiences and visions she was having and assured her of God's love. She then followed God's prodding to visit the anchoress in Norwich called "Dame Julian."[32] Their conversation about meditation, divine encounters, and contemplation lasted several days. Though strangers before meeting, they found connection "in the love of our Lord Jesus Christ."[33] Julian counseled Kempe powerfully against fear of the devil by identifying the evidence of the Holy Spirit at work through Kempe's experiences. She reflected on the teachings of Paul and Jerome, weighing her situation with pastoral care. After all, in Kempe's words, "the anchoress was expert in such things and good counsel could give."[34]

The account of the meeting of these two women mystics is a remarkable gift to the church, marking their faith in Christ and confirming their presence and contributions in ways that often don't happen for women. Their writings also reveal the growth of texts that were written in common languages from the thirteenth century on and how that development provided women with a special opportunity for direct self-expression of their theology and spiritual lives (rather than through a male chronicler[35]). Less than forty years later, the introduction of the moveable-type printing press by Johannes Gutenberg further extended the reach of female theological writings, offering direct access to their spiritual experiences. Strasbourg Protestant printer Margarethe Prüss (yes, a female printer) took risks to publish Katharina Shütz Zell (the self-described "Church Mother" of Strasbourg and wife of Reformer Matthew Zell), on the one hand, and the visions of radical reformer and illiterate female prophet Ursala Jost on the other.[36] The potential for visibility as women in theology and in the church had never been greater. Even so, theology as the "queen of the sciences" at the medieval university was still a man's privilege in a man's clerical world with one man (Aristotle) especially dominating the conversation.

Discussion Questions

1. Julian of Norwich taught that "all will be well." How might we respond as Christians to the evil that we encounter in the world?
2. Withdrawal from the world is something that Jesus practiced during his ministry. What can be the spiritual value of disentangling ourselves from everyday life?
3. What could it mean to think about God as Mother in light of Scripture's metaphors?

Further Reading

Samuel Fanous and Vincent Gillespie, eds., *The Cambridge Companion to Medieval English Mysticism*, Cambridge Companions to Literature (Cambridge Univ. Press, 2011).

Julian of Norwich, *Showings*, trans. Edmund Colledge and James Walsh (Paulist, 1978).

Alister E. McGrath, *Christian Spirituality* (Oxford: Blackwell, 1999).

Veronica Mary Rolf, *An Explorer's Guide to Julian of Norwich* (IVP Academic, 2018).

CHAPTER 8

THOMAS AQUINAS

PRAYER

> O merciful God, grant that I may desire ardently, search pru-
> dently, recognize truly, and bring to perfect completion whatever
> is pleasing to You for the praise and glory of Your name. . . . Give
> to me, O Lord my God, understanding of You, diligence in seeking
> You, wisdom in finding You, discourse ever pleasing to You, and
> confidence in finally embracing You. . . . You Who live and reign,
> God, world without end. Amen.

—Thomas Aquinas[1]

I'm Bringing Aristotle Back

Western Christian theology during the Middle Ages is characterized by the influence of the pre-Christian Greek philosopher
Aristotle (384–322 BC). Initially, encounters with Aristotle's
writings were limited until the tug-of-war between Christendom
and Islam began over control of the Iberian Peninsula. In the
thirteenth century, Spanish and Portuguese Christian rulers
recaptured Muslim-controlled land in Iberia, which had been
lost or compromised since the eighth century. In the clash and
exchange of civilizations, the Western world gained exposure to

certain works of Aristotle and commentaries on his writings that previously had not been accessible in Latin.

Only Aristotle's *Categories* and *On Interpretation* had been known in Latin education from the sixth century because of Boethius. But by the midtwelfth century, with a renewed awareness of Aristotle's works, Christian theology began to embrace Aristotle's concept of substances in the *Categories*, his "four causes" in *Physics*, and his notion of the "unmoved mover" in *Metaphysics*. Meanwhile, influential commentaries became essential reading at the university in Córdoba, including works by Jewish philosopher Moses Maimonides (1135–1204) and the Muslim philosopher Ibn Rushd (1126–98), who is known as Averroës or "the Commentator." Both Aristotle's physics and metaphysics were viewed with suspicion to the point that the University of Paris forbade professors in the faculty of Arts to lecture on those writings (1215), and so did certain papal bulls in the coming decades. The controversy grew even more heated when in 1255 the faculty of Arts adopted a new syllabus that removed the ban on Aristotle's natural philosophy through reading and lectures. The following year, Thomas Aquinas became a master in theology at Paris. The timing could not have been more auspicious for the kind of work that he was about to contribute. The only complication was that he was a Dominican.

Walk like a Mendicant

For families of nobility in Thomas's time, the Benedictine Order was a comfortable place to send a son or daughter. Wealth and family status often determined access to and inclusion in the order, and the order's vows of poverty leaned toward being more of a formality. No one was going hungry in a Benedictine Order, it seemed. The son of minor nobility, Thomas was born in the family castle of Roccasecca, located between Rome and Naples. He began his studies at the premier Benedictine Abbey of Monte Cassino (the first house of the Benedictine Order that had been established by Benedict of Nursia) from age five. After receiving a foundation in Bible and exposure to Augustine (both key sources in his theological writing), Thomas pursued a liberal arts education at the University of Naples, where he was likely trained in Aristotelian natural philosophy and metaphysics.[2] In 1244, Thomas joined the Dominican Order against his family's wishes. They were so opposed to his involvement with the mendicant (begging) order that they held him captive in a castle for fifteen months to force him to change his mind. He refused, and with that, the direction of his life became increasingly tied to higher education in Paris.

Thomas was sent to Paris in 1245 to the convent of Saint James, where he studied under Albert the Great. Through Albert's teaching, he was exposed to Pseudo-Dionysius and Aristotle's *Ethics*, though Aristotle's place in the Christian corpus was an open and contentious question. After teaching in Cologne as an assistant, Thomas returned to Paris to serve on the faculty, though he faced opposition from those who barred mendicants from the university, which proved taxing. Even so, over the course of his life, Thomas wrote a variety of works alongside his biblical commentaries and *Summa Contra Gentiles*, an apologetic handbook to assist Spanish friars in the conversion of Muslims. He had become an important teacher and leader in the order, which was tasked to prepare others for the ministry of teaching and confession. But the greatest theological accomplishment of his life—and perhaps in Christian theological history—was writing the *Summa Theologiae* (1265–73).[3]

As mendicants moved into the university, Eastern monastics were drawn into controversy over hesychasm, a silent prayer practice that regulates breathing and invokes the name of Jesus (1 Thess. 5:17). Disagreement emerged over the idea that such prayer provided direct access to God and enabled one to see the divine light. **Gregory Palamas** (ca. 1296–1359), archbishop of Thessalonica, defended the practice against accusations of violating the apophatic approach to theology. The hesychasts were affirmed at the Fifth Council of Constantinople (1341–51).

Head over Heals

For Thomas, the goal was clear: he was writing a theology textbook, or what he called *sacra doctrina*, to be used for training in the Latin university. He intended it to replace *Four Books of Sentences*, the work of his predecessor, Peter Lombard. To that end, the *Summa* explores a range of complex and intricate theological and philosophical topics related to God as creator, the fall and restoration of humanity, and how the person and work of Christ bring about salvation. Theological topics and themes mirrored those set by Anselm, Abelard, and Lombard before him. Along the way, Thomas "baptized" (so to speak) Aristotle with an impact that continues today. How did it all fit together?

Here's the deal. Scholastics favored dialectical reasoning. They practiced an approach that posed a question (saying,

"Whether it is the case that . . ."), affirmed that question, offered three contentious answers, contended with those answers ("I answer"), and then arrived at a summative and responsive answer. To be sure, tracking the conversation is not for the faint of heart. The result of that effort was that Christian theology was bound to Greek philosophy at a molecular level. Even the form and method of theology helped to shape its meaning (which is why the Protestant Reformers took issue with Aristotle and prioritized Scripture so that the form of their theology was also transformed).

That does not mean Scripture is lacking in the formation of Thomas's theology. There are twenty-five thousand biblical citations in the *Summa* alone, which indicates Scripture's prominence.[4] Nevertheless, Thomas wrote commentaries or expositions on Aristotle and even cited him next to Scripture as "the Philosopher" when it supported his theological teachings (along with engaging with church fathers and even Muslim sources). And though Thomas did on occasion disagree with Aristotle, nonetheless Aristotle held a crucial place for Thomas in both the form and the content of his theology, whether he was explicitly cited or not.

Even Plato's fingerprints are found in his work, though Thomas had hardly any access to Plato's writings, and there were few historical details known about the relationship between Plato and Aristotle.[5] As it happened, to follow in the theological footsteps of Augustine and Pseudo-Dionysious (as Thomas sought to do) was to absorb the teaching of Plato,[6] so that any way you look at it, Greek philosophy has had a truly immense impact on Christian theology from the start. How does that come through in Thomas's theological teaching?[7]

Scholastic theologian **Peter Lombard** (ca. 1100–60) was a student of Peter Abelard's and was supported by Bernard of Clairvaux. His *Four Books of Sentences* became the standard textbook among theology students in his time. The method of his text was to highlight quotations from early Christian sources and group them into doctrinal themes. He is attributed with confirming and developing the sacramental life of the medieval church, including formalizing the seven sacraments.

Get Real

Thomas is identified as being from the first school of scholasticism called the *via antiqua* (literally, "old school"). Two schools eventually emerged at the medieval university that became differentiated over philosophical assumptions about how we know what we know (epistemology), and Thomas was a "realist." Realism trusted that a person could use reason to determine the truth about specific/individual and universal/common concepts from their sense of things. That meant that you could encounter, for example, a white rock, and even though you held only the one white rock in your hand (as opposed to every white rock in the world), you could still understand from the one instance the common traits of them all. The accidents (size, weight, color) and essence/substance (being a rock) of the thing are not merely constructs of our minds but true manifestations of reality. There's continuity between what the human mind can understand about the world and what the world is really like. This is the case not because of the abilities of the human mind to understand but because all things exist in the mind of God so that coherence and correlation are possible.

For Thomas, this continuity did not demote God's revelation or the role of Scripture but nonetheless affirmed that there is a lot that human minds can know about the world as rational creatures created in God's image, and that anything we can know can help us to know God better. This expectation was on full display at the start of the *Summa* in his discussion of the existence of God, a question that Anselm of Canterbury, before Thomas, had famously explored and answered with the ontological argument. Applying Aristotelian concepts to the question, Thomas identified five ways for proving the existence of God apart from revelation.[8]

Consider motion, the first way. Based on sense experience, Thomas reasoned that because the world is not static but dynamic, nothing can move without a mover. He observed that every motion has a mover, which has another mover, and so on, until you arrive at what must have been the original mover. Thomas then identifies the Christian God with Aristotle's "unmovable mover" (with the important caveat that God is an active creator, according to Scripture). Similarly, the second way was causation. Thomas applied the dynamics of cause and effect to the question of God's existence. He noted that effects require a cause, and there must be a first cause, or an uncaused cause, to explain the ultimate cause.

According to Thomas, the third way to prove God's existence is contingency. It's easy to observe that all things in the world are contingent, but apart from an infinite sequence of contingent beings, there must be a first being whose existence is not contingent but necessary. Thomas points us to degrees as the fourth way to affirm God's existence. The fact that humans can imagine ideals and principals like truth, goodness, and nobility at levels of gradation (because some things are better than others) indicates that there must exist the ultimate embodiment of those ideals. Something has brought those ideas into being. For Thomas, God is both the exemplar (the ultimate source of goodness) and the formal cause of all perfections. This teaching also resonates with Plato's notion of the forms and God's perfections. Likewise, for the fifth way, Thomas invites Christians to look around and notice how the world indicates traces of design. God is the designer who orders all things. Everything moves toward a *telos* or goal, another idea from Aristotle, thereby possessing potency (the potential for change that is inherent to all living things on earth) with the goal of actualization or perfection.

Thomas's reliance on Aristotle was immense. Can you see it? Thomas employed Aristotle not only in his argument for God's existence but also regarding the nature of God as omniscient (all knowing), omnipotent (all powerful), and omnipresent (everywhere). Thomas leaned heavily on Aristotle in defining God as pure form or being, who is fully actualized and without change. God's essence and God's actions show no differentiation, which provided Thomas with the groundwork for affirming divine simplicity.[9] This framework for understanding God also confirmed an Aristotelian worldview for how the earth related to the cosmos, which in turn informed social/political/gender structures that were not overturned until well after the Scientific Revolution began in the midsixteenth century.

Nevertheless, the idea of the Trinity—God as Father, Son, and Holy Spirit—for Thomas remained firmly and securely in the category of faith and revelation. The Christian God is triune, and for Thomas, there is no explaining the mystery of the incarnation of the Son apart from believing in the Trinity.[10]

An important scholastic of the next generation, **Duns Scotus** (ca. 1265–1308), was a critic of Thomas. Scotus was a Franciscan who also taught at the premier universities of Oxford, Cambridge, Paris, and Cologne. His writings challenged Thomas on God's relationship to natural law, arguing that these laws were examples of God's will rather than his limitations. While Thomas stressed reason's transformation in salvation, Scotus emphasized the will's transformation. Thomas understood knowledge as the path to salvation, but Scotus emphasized love. For Scotus, ethics should be based on God's revelation rather than on natural-law ethics.

This Is My What?

One of the ways that scholasticism shaped the worship life of the church through Thomas was in clarifying the theology of the Mass. Once again, Aristotle was key. The Feast of Corpus Christi was instituted by Pope Urban IV in 1264 based on the advocacy of Belgian mystic Juliana of Cornillon (1192–1258).[11] For that service, the "Lauda Sion," which became part of the Roman Catholic Mass, was written by Thomas at the pope's request. The hymn is still popular today and reflects how theology and liturgy meet in the life of the church.

Scripture records that at the Last Supper, when Jesus gave bread to his disciples, he said, "This is my body" (Matt.

26:26). But what did he mean exactly? What happens when we receive the communion elements, bread and wine? Questions over the mechanics and meaning of the Mass were not new to the church. During the ninth century, two monks at the same monastery disagreed over what happened to the bread and wine during the Mass. Abbot Paschasius Radbertus and monk Ratramnus of Corbie argued over whether the elements literally became Christ's body and blood or Jesus' words were intended to be metaphorical. After controversy erupted in the eleventh century, the Synod of Rome (1079) declared that the transformation of the substance into the true body and blood of Christ was accomplished through the consecration or the words of institution, even though the change of substance was still deemed mysterious. In 1215, the Fourth Lateran Council used the term *transubstantiation* for the first time while still preserving the mystery of that change. Thomas invited Aristotle to the table, and his understanding of the Mass endures within Roman Catholicism to this day.

To explain the doctrine of transubstantiation, Thomas applies Aristotle's distinction between a substance (the essence of a thing) and its accidents (what is perceived by the senses).[12] The question is, If the bread converts to the body of Christ in its substance, then why does it still look like bread, taste like bread, and smell like bread? Employing Aristotelian categories, Thomas argued that the substance of the bread was changed entirely into the substance of Christ's body (and the wine into his blood), but the accidents remained the same. He declared the transformation of the substance to be an act of the power of God so that believers are—in a material way—consuming the grace of Christ's flesh under the form of bread. For Thomas, this provides an infusion of grace necessary for the justification of the believer, akin to taking medicine for healing.

These teachings of Thomas were confirmed at the Second Council of Lyons (1274). By the end of the century, elevating the host and ringing bells at the end of the consecration signaled transubstantiation. In the fourteenth and fifteenth centuries, the theology and praxis that developed around the Mass (such as prohibiting the laity from the cup) came to concern the forerunners of the Reformation (both John Wycliffe and Jan Hus) and the Protestant Reformers, starting with Martin Luther.

Saved by Grace (but Do Your Part)

While Thomas sought to replace Peter Lombard's theological textbook with his *Summa* on the one hand, he also worked to emulate Augustine on the other hand, even citing him some ten thousand times throughout his work (more than any other church father, and he was familiar with both Greek and Latin fathers).[13] Augustine's influence is apparent even when Thomas does not mention him, and there's no better way to see that dynamic at work than in his teachings on the doctrine of grace.

Over and over, Thomas teaches that grace or divine help is necessary for humanity to will and do good since God is the first mover.[14] That means that it is not possible, by one's natural powers, to achieve salvation full stop because it would require one to initiate and "produce meritorious works commensurate with eternal life."[15] Thomas was no Pelagian. For him, we can neither start the process of salvation nor meet the requirements. We need grace to heal our nature (which is fallen because of Adam and Eve's sin) and also to help us follow God's will.[16] To Thomas, even the disposition for receiving grace is a gift of God rather than something that a person can prepare themselves to receive.[17] This ensures that human justification—being made acceptable before God—relies on God's free grace or divine assistance each step of the way.[18] Walking in Augustine's footsteps, Thomas affirms the grace that goes before us (prevenient grace) and turns our hearts to God (operative grace), which in turn enables our wills to cooperate with God's will (cooperative grace).[19] The process is initiated by God, but the person is enabled then to participate in his or her justification.

Where Thomas seems to diverge from Augustine is in how he understands the impact of sin. At several points, he notes that sin does not entirely corrupt human nature, so that it can still do some good.[20] He teaches that the impact of corrupt nature is seen in our natural inclination toward virtue, which he claims is "diminished" rather than lost.[21] A person is unable then to fulfill the *entire* good that is required, which differs from a will that is so depraved by sin that no good is possible. In his estimation, Thomas is protecting human reason and ensuring that humans are always responsible for their sin. In effect, though, he is opening the door for the second school of scholasticism (the *via moderna* or "new school") to reject prevenient grace and to conclude that people are able to prepare themselves for the reception of grace that leads to justification.

Theologian Meets World

In the many biographies that touch on his life and thought, Thomas Aquinas has often been depicted as something of a late bloomer or a quiet student whose brilliance was first underestimated in Paris by his fellow classmates. Reportedly, after a fair amount of teasing from his peers, Albert the Great famously declared, "We call this one the Dumb Ox, but I tell you that the whole world is going to hear his bellowing."[22] Myth or not, Albert's prediction was right, but the reception was far from immediate, and Thomas was not treated as being beyond critique.

Just two years after Thomas's death, in 1277, the Synod of Paris condemned the *Summa Theologiae* for its reliance on Aristotle. The following centuries reveal a variety of responses, with the bulk of criticism stemming from identifying Thomas too closely with Muslim scholars or the Averroists. Thomas's theology, meanwhile, stepped outside of Western Christendom by reaching Eastern Orthodox theologians of Byzantium and Jewish rabbis.[23] Even with Pope John XXII's canonization of Thomas in 1323, there was still ambivalence around his legacy. Significantly, a few years after the final session of the Council of Trent and at the height of the Counter Reformation, Thomas was declared a doctor of the church by Pius V. His writings were turned into a significant source of Roman Catholic defense against Protestant theology, especially in the council's session on the doctrine of justification. In the nineteenth century, interest in Thomas's theology was again revived by the papacy. The papal encyclical *Aeterni Patris* (1879) encouraged a return to Christian philosophy and elevated Thomas as the chief teacher in the corpus of classic Roman Catholic doctrine. Subsequent popes followed with their approval of Thomas in the twentieth century, which led to his identification as the preeminent Roman Catholic theologian of Christian history.

The relationship between faith and reason or theology and philosophy is one of the enduring questions of Christianity from its inception in the Roman Empire to today's postmodern world. Thomas's theology offered rich, compelling, and biblically informed ways for navigating that dynamic. But for Protestant Reformers like Martin Luther, Thomas and the Roman Catholic theology that he came to represent were sources of contention.

Discussion Questions

1. Thomas valued the role of the university in shaping Christian thought. What should be the role of education in the Christian life?
2. What can we learn about God by looking at the world? How can that approach be helpful? How might it be problematic?
3. Consider the way your church celebrates communion. What do Jesus' words at the Last Supper about the bread and the cup mean to you and how does that align with Scripture?

Further Reading

Thomas Aquinas, *Thomas Aquinas: Selected Writings*, ed. Ralph McInerny (Penguin Classics, 1999).

Frederick Christian Bauerschmidt, *Thomas Aquinas: Faith, Reason, and Following Christ*, Christian Theology in Context (Oxford Univ. Press, 2013).

Brian Davies, ed., *The Oxford Handbook of Aquinas* (Oxford Univ. Press, 2012).

Eleonore Stump and Thomas Joseph White, eds., *The New Cambridge Companion to Aquinas* (Cambridge Univ. Press, 2022).

PART 3

REFORMATION THEOLOGIANS

CHAPTER 9

MARTIN LUTHER

PRAYER

Dear God and Father, I pray for you to so nurture me that I may be to you as a beautiful garden, so that many people may enjoy your fruit and be attracted through me to all godliness. Write into my heart, by your Holy Spirit, whatever is abundantly found in Scripture. Let me constantly keep your word in mind, and permit it to become far more precious to me than my own life and all else that I cherish on earth. . . . To you be praise and thanks in eternity. Amen.

—Martin Luther[1]

You've Come a Long Way, Friar

On July 2, 1505, in the middle of a vicious thunderstorm, Martin Luther feared that he was on the verge of losing his life. This son of a miner made a vow to Saint Anne, the mother of the Virgin Mary and the patron saint of miners, that he would become a monk if he survived. He was true to his word and entered the Augustinian monastery at Erfurt two weeks later. And so it was that Luther's unexpected journey into church leadership began with a lightning bolt and was followed by the thunder of a hammer twelve years later.

There is nothing in Martin Luther's early life that can prepare us for what happened to him and to the church through him. His father, who had descended from peasants, was resourceful and able to work his way into the successful ownership of mines. His mother's side of the family, however, tended toward the law profession, so Luther studied law at the University of Erfurt. The monastery was not in the game plan.

However, upon entering the monastery, Luther's concern for reform was inward facing. He worked out his spiritual angst through confessional practices. Luther felt his sins acutely and struggled to believe that he was good enough for God. Spiritual peace was elusive, and he was known to trouble his confessor, Johannes von Staupitz, with the smallest concern.[2] By all accounts, he was devout, but it was a devotion that offered neither peace nor assurance.

The life of the mind turned out to be the balm of Gilead for Luther as he turned his attention to the study of Scripture and the writings of Augustine. He lived during the sunset of the Renaissance era and the pinnacle of humanism, an educational reform movement born of criticism of scholasticism in its effort to recapture the learning of the classical age. *Ad fontes* or "back to the source" was its mission and vision. For theology that meant rediscovering the languages of Scripture (Hebrew and Greek) and using grammar to understand and translate those teachings. Renewed interest in the Greek and Latin church fathers as well as ancient philosophers transformed the conversation of the university and then the church.

When Luther began teaching theology at the University of Wittenberg, which had only recently been founded by Frederick, elector of Saxony, he was shaped by the scholastic theology of William of Ockham (ca. 1287–1347) and the *via moderna*'s teachings on justification. According to this view, God was so gracious that he would accept an unworthy effort on the person's part and reward it as meritorious even though it was not worthy of grace. Significantly, a person could even "do what is within them" and turn to God according to their will to merit the first grace. Consequently, God's gift of grace was determined by human choice and action rather than God's free will. Had they resurrected Augustine's age-old enemy, Pelagius? What do we have to do to be saved? It was a fair question. While lecturing on Romans from 1515 to 1516, Luther experienced a kind of theological renaissance or "rebirth" of his own, which he later identified with his reinterpretation of Romans 1:17.[3] In his lecture on that passage, he warned his class, it's not about what you can or can't do, it's about what God has done for you through Christ, for "the righteousness of God is the cause of salvation."[4] To Luther, discovering that insight was akin to being born again.[5]

Can't Buy Me Love

By the early fall of 1517, Luther, who was now an Augustinian friar and Wittenberg professor, had completed a treatise that he was eager to share in his scholarly circle. The text was daring in its critiques, and Luther expected it to cause a stir. The piece was *Disputation against Scholastic Theology.* (Not what you were expecting?)

Over the course of the treatise, Luther critiqued the *via moderna* school of scholasticism in which he had been trained. First, he challenged the grip that Aristotle maintained over the form and content of theology. In addition, rather than starting with the seeds of human potential, Luther taught—like Augustine before him—that the human will is captive to sin. Because human sin requires grace, Luther denied that we are "able to do what is within" us to earn that grace (as taught by the Ockhamist Gabriel Biel). True to an Augustinian outlook, Luther appealed to the doctrine of predestination to protect grace as a gift. God did not elect based on our choosing of him (*post praevisa merita*) but elected according to his gracious free will (*ante praevisa merita*). This theology was reflected in Luther's pastoral criticism, as district vicar since 1515, of the selling and buying of indulgences. The underlying question was the same: Are you saved by what *you* do or by what Christ does?

For the early modern Christian, from the cradle to the death-bed, grace was mediated through the sacraments. Among the seven sacraments confirmed by scholastics like Lombard and adopted by the Western church at the Fourth Lateran Council of 1215, the act of penance loomed large over Christian practice. As Christians sorted out with their priest and confessor the impact of their sin on their afterlife destination (heaven, hell, or purgatory), they were taught that the weight of their merit served as a counterbalance to the debt of their sin. Penance invited Christians to enter a cycle of contrition for sin, confession of sin, and completing satisfaction for sin. Fasting, prayers, alms, and pilgrimages were all common practices for satisfying the debt of sin, but sin could also be resolved by purchasing a certificate of indulgence, like spiritual insurance. It would seem that indulgences could buy God's love, and not only for yourself but for those who had already passed on. But is that what Scripture intended? Luther thought something had to be said.

Nailed It!

As the story goes, on All Hallows' Eve, October 31, 1517, Luther took his newly written *Ninety-Five Theses* and nailed them to the doors of the Castle Church in Wittenberg. Today, the church remembers the instigation of the Protestant Reformation with that act by way of the bronze "Theses Doors," which were installed in 1858 to commemorate Luther's 375th birthday and have inscribed on them the Latin form of the theses. Whether or not this event took place, we know that Luther mailed a letter, the theses, and an essay on indulgences that day to Albrecht of Brandenburg (1490–1545), who was the highest-ranking church authority in the Holy Roman Empire. For a hefty sum, Albrecht had acquired from the pope the archbishopric of Mainz, side-stepping more than a fair share of canon law in the process. Pope Leo X had his eyes set on the completion of Saint Peter's Basilica in Rome, started under the previous pope, Julius II. The reissuing of "Peter's Indulgence" was enough to ensure the project's completion and cover the cost of Albrecht's loan from the Fugger bank. Upon receiving Luther's letter and attachments, he knew trouble was not far off, and he sent the theses promptly to the theology faculty of Mainz and to Rome. In the coming months, the *Ninety-Five Theses* was translated and rapidly distributed.

Luther's theses hit at the heart of papal power and the penitential system. To start, Luther recast Jesus' command in Matthew 4:17 as pursuing a life of repentance rather than taking part in penance (here, he adopted the argument of Renaissance humanist Desiderius Erasmus, ca. 1466–1536). Luther rejected the idea that the pope possessed powers that could move a soul from one place to the next in the afterlife.[6] He also taught that

God prefers that believers help a neighbor in need and provide for the needs of one's family rather than give over precious coin for the building of Saint Peter's Basilica.[7] God does not need your money, Luther stressed; your neighbor in need does. Over and over Luther's theses stressed that God's Word, the cross, and acts of love and mercy were all greater than indulgences.[8] In the end, a truly contrite heart is more precious to God than any indulgences, since money can't buy God's love.[9] A coin in the coffer will ring, but that does not mean a soul from purgatory will spring![10]

After the indulgences controversy blew up in 1517, Luther continued to write, teach, preach, and develop his understanding of salvation and the Christian life according to the principle that believers are justified by faith in Christ alone rather than by their own righteousness. In 1518, Luther's *Sermon on Indulgences and Grace* opened the conversation up to Germany, and Luther became a bestselling author.[11] By 1521, he had attracted not only recognition and notoriety but also opposition from the two greatest powers of his time: the pope and the Holy Roman Emperor.

John Wycliffe (ca. 1328–84) was a precursor to Luther in his rejection of both transubstantiation and indulgences. He was the first person to translate the Latin Vulgate into the first complete English Bible (1382) and believed in the supremacy of Scripture as the highest authority. His views were increasingly regarded as dangerous and radical by the end of his life. Although he died in 1384, his bones were dug up and burned by order of the Council of Constance (1415).

First, he was excommunicated by the pope, and then he was banned by the emperor, essentially receiving the condemnation of both soul and body. Before the indulgences controversy, Luther turned to Augustine to challenge scholasticism. But now he moved beyond Augustine in ways that have profoundly and enduringly shaped the church's teachings today. What was Luther declaring?

Let Freedom (in Christ) Ring

Each of Luther's writings carries its own context and purpose in its time, but taken together, they form a coherent picture of how his theology was crystalizing in the face of opposition, need, and interest in those early years. In each case, he treated Scripture as the highest authority (above pope or council, though in conversation with church fathers), and this was no mere ideal but the true foundation of Luther's theology from start to finish.

The centering of Luther's theology around the importance of Christ's suffering on the cross (his "theology of the cross") and his elevation of Scripture's authority above all became most evident in 1518–19. At the Leipzig Disputation, Luther was pressed by Roman Catholic theologian Johann Eck (1486–1543).[12] There Luther provocatively reinterpreted Matthew 16 from its traditional reading of Jesus' words to Peter after his confession of faith as the basis for Petrine supremacy to declare that not only was the pope fallible but so were councils. Luther shocked his onlookers by openly criticizing certain church fathers and overturning common Western sentiment about the salvation of Eastern Orthodox Christians and "schismatics" like the Bohemians. Luther was increasingly walking in the footsteps of Bohemian

(Czech) protoreformer Jan Hus (ca. 1369–1415) and, to an extent, Italian Dominican friar Girolamo Savonarola (1452–98). But those similarities did not bode well for him; Hus and Savonarola had both been burned at the stake.

One of the challenges that Luther faced was that the papacy had grown resistant to reform efforts in reaction to "conciliarism," the idea that a general council has more authority than the papacy. It was no longer in the pope's best interest to call a council, given the realignment of power. Just one year before Luther's *Ninety-Five Theses*, Pope Leo X decreed by papal bull that only a pope could call a council and only a council could reform the church. Conciliarism was essentially blocked as an avenue for calling reform apart from the pope's consent just as Luther was leaning into Scripture's authority alone.

Could the church reform apart from the pope? In August 1520, Luther dedicated his *Letter to the German Nobility* to the newly elected emperor, Charles V, with that very possibility in mind. Luther identified three "walls of Jericho" that were blocking reform and needed tumbling down: that the church is over the state (as Boniface VIII in *Unam Sanctam*), that the interpretation of Scripture is limited to the pope, and that no one may call a council but the pope. To tear down these walls, Luther pointed to the doctrine of the priesthood of all believers. All Christians are part of the royal priesthood, he taught, since they have received the anointing of baptismal waters (1 Peter 2:9 and Rev. 5:10) and are part of the one body of Christ (1 Corinthians 12). With this doctrine, Luther empowered the princes to be involved in church affairs just as he also made clergy accountable to civil law and flattened the spiritual hierarchy of medieval society. Luther taught that the clerical office was necessary in terms of function, but not greater in status. In this way, Luther made room for Christ to be the true and only mediator of all and for every believer to participate in the "power of the keys" (Matt. 16:19).

In October 1520, Luther tackled the complexity of the nature, number, and role of the sacraments in the Christian life with his treatise *Babylonian Captivity of the Church*. Controversy had first arisen over sacraments when Renaissance humanist Erasmus pointed out the false equivalence between the Latin word for "sacrament" and the Greek word for "mystery" in the Vulgate. If every mystery was not a sacrament, then what was a sacrament? Luther accused the papacy of keeping the sacraments captive in three significant ways that defy the teachings of Scripture: withholding the cup from the laity, upholding transubstantiation, and teaching communion as a good work rather than God's gift.

In response, Luther argued that all Christians should receive communion in two kinds (meaning both bread and the cup) as commanded by Christ, who says, "Drink from it, all of you" (Matt. 26:27).[13] Luther then contested with the Thomists and sided with Wycliffe on transubstantiation. Using Ockham's razor (which holds that the simplest explanation is preferred), he reasoned, "It is not necessary in the sacraments that the bread and wine be transubstantiated and that Christ be contained under their accidents in order that the real body and real blood may be present."[14] Luther insisted that both the bread/wine and the body/blood are present at the same time. In his words, "The Holy Spirit is greater than Aristotle."[15] In addition, Luther exposed the financial corruption within the church system that treated the Mass as a good work and a sacrifice. The only thing necessary for participation is faith (as opposed to money). By the time Luther had finished, he had embraced only two sacraments as instituted by Christ (contrary to Lombard's seven sacraments). By that point, his excommunication was imminent.

Luther's *Freedom of a Christian* (November 1520) was written between receiving the papal bull threatening him with excommunication (*Exsurge Domine*) and his decision to publicly burn the bull and canon law in defiance. In the interim, Luther explored the true meaning of freedom in Christ. Citing Paul in 1 Corinthians 9:19, Luther argued that freedom in Christ means being subject to no one and—paradoxically—subject to all because of Christ.[16] Such freedom is not secured by good works; on the contrary, "faith alone, without works, justifies, frees and saves."[17] At the same time, faith does not free us *from* works but frees us *for* them.

Well before Luther married former nun Katherina von Bora (1525), he explained the doctrine of justification by way of a marriage metaphor (tipping his hat to medieval mystic Bernard of Clairvaux). The believer is united to Christ like a bride to a bridegroom; the two become one flesh (Eph. 5:31). In this "joyous exchange," the bride and the groom pledge to belong to each other, and wedding rings are a mark of that faith. All that is Christ's is given and shared, and vice versa, but to our benefit. Luther here repeats from his sermon *Two Kinds of Righteousness* (1519), where he declared, "Everything which Christ has is ours, graciously bestowed on us unworthy men out of God's sheer mercy, although we have rather deserved wrath and condemnation, and hell also."[18] For Luther, union with Christ through faith is the only thing that can free believers to love God and neighbor.[19]

Argula von Grumbach (1492–1563/8)[20] was a German noble-woman who became a bestselling Protestant author. Her open letter to the faculty at the University of Ingolstadt in 1523 in sup-port of Martin Luther went through fourteen editions. A woodcut image of her challenging the divinity faculty alone with just a Bible marks her significance as the first female Protestant published author.

With or Without You

On January 3, 1521, Luther was officially excommunicated from the Roman Catholic Church. By April of that year, Luther stood before Holy Roman Emperor Charles V at the Diet of Worms to answer accusations of heresy and to potentially resolve his excommunication. The authorities' concern over Luther's grow-ing popularity was palpable, and rightly so.

While Luther's bold declaration of "Here I stand!" before the papal officials and the emperor still lingers in our collective remembrance as the ultimate expression of his defiance, he made a more substantive declaration (and one more certain in the historical record) that gives us greater insight into his driving conviction. At the end of his examination, he declared, "My conscience is captive to the Word of God."[21] That captivity is reflected in Luther's prioritization of the translation of Scripture throughout his adult life, starting with initial translations found in his early lectures at Wittenberg and reaching all the way to his final years working on the 1541 and 1545 editions of the complete German Bible. Bible translation was not an afterthought for Luther but held primacy of place in his work as professor and pastor. Before his excommunication, Luther had declared that the only thing necessary for the Christian life, for righteousness and freedom, was the Word of God—the gospel of Jesus Christ.[22]

Although Luther left the diet in the worst possible state (banned and excommunicated), he immediately turned his attention to translating the New Testament into German, aided by Philip Melanchthon, who was the first professor of Greek at the University of Wittenberg. For his safety, Frederick had secretly arranged for Luther to be transported to Wartburg Castle, where he spent eleven weeks completing the German New Testament based on the second edition of Erasmus's Greek New Testament. The resulting September Testament has been described as a printing phenomenon, a sensation, and a bestseller. By 1522, within just five years of his posting the *Ninety-Five Theses*, Luther's New Testament, along with other pamphlet publications, made him the most published author in Europe ever.[23]

Global Luther

The primacy of Scripture and the reception of salvation by grace alone, through faith alone, and achieved by Christ alone were convictions that rallied others to Luther's call for reform. A Swiss German movement led by Reformer Ulrich Zwingli developed with a potential for expanding political alliances with Germany through theological alliances.[24] Similar to Luther's reform, the Swiss Reformed tradition emphasized the authority of Scripture and the freedom of a Christian. The importance of the complete Bible in the common language, church services in the common language, and communion in two kinds were points of agreement between the traditions. Nevertheless, disagreement over the theology of communion proved difficult to navigate. Luther and Zwingli developed a heated exchange via published pamphlets over the question of Christ's bodily presence before meeting for the first time at Marburg in 1529.[25] The question was not whether Christ was present but how he was present. Zwingli's metaphorical reading of Christ's words, "This is my body" (Matt. 26:26), clashed with Luther's literal reading of those same words. While Zwingli emphasized Christ's bodily ascension and therefore his spiritual presence in communion, Luther stressed the bodily presence of Christ in the sacrament because of the transformation of his human nature after the resurrection that allowed for him to be everywhere. (How else could he walk through walls in John 20:19?) Although both Luther and Zwingli signed the Marburg Articles, their dispute over the Christology and hermeneutics of communion created division among Western Christian camps as well as among future generations. Lutheran theology, including its perspective on communion, was codified in the Book of Concord (1580) by Jakob Andreae and Martin Chemnitz.

Luther did not initiate reform in the church with the intention of cultivating a newly born Western branch of the church. On the contrary, he sought to reroot the church in Christ and in the witness of Scripture. The technology of the printing press brought his call to faith in Christ alone to places with a speed and reach that had never before been possible, and many people were inspired by that call. Today, a movement that started on the European continent is centering on the African continent, but Luther's reform was not the only one to have a global reach.

Discussion Questions

1. What about Luther's life and theology resonates with your faith journey and tradition?
2. What lasting legacy has the Reformation forged for Christian belief and practice that you either appreciate or struggle with?
3. How does the doctrine of the priesthood of all believers shape how you see your place and role in the body of Christ?

Further Reading

Robert Kolb, *Martin Luther: Confessor of the Faith*, Christian Theology in Context (Oxford Univ. Press, 2009).

Martin Luther, *Martin Luther's Basic Theological Writings*, ed. William R. Russell and Timothy F. Lull, 3rd ed. (Fortress, 2012).

Alister E. McGrath, *Reformation Thought: An Introduction*, 4th ed. (Wiley-Blackwell, 2021).

Timothy Wengert, ed., *The Pastoral Luther: Essays on Martin Luther's Practical Theology* (Fortress, 2017).

CHAPTER 10

JOHN CALVIN

PRAYER

Heavenly Father, I know that beginning well means little unless one perseveres. So, I ask you to be my guide, not only today but for all my life. Increase your grace in me each day, until you have brought me into full union with your Son, Jesus Christ our Lord, who is the true Sun of our souls, shining day and night forever. Amen.

—John Calvin[1]

Wholehearted, Not Coldhearted

In 1543, an anonymous book appeared in Venice called *Beneficio di Cristo (The Benefit of Christ's Death)* that quickly became a bestseller, selling some forty thousand copies within six years. *Beneficio* has been regarded as one of the most influential books in spreading Reformation ideas, and the strength of its content was drawn from Reformer John Calvin's magnum opus, *Institutes of the Christian Religion.* Even in its day, the reach of Calvin's theological masterpiece was wide and the impact swift. The second wave of the Reformation after Luther's generation was defined by the life, theology, and pastoral ministry of John Calvin.

Today, Calvin's presence is remembered in Geneva by way of a sixteen-foot statue that stands out from the Reformation Wall, erected to mark the four hundredth anniversary of Calvin's birth. The monument is built into the old walls of the city so that the statue faces the University of Geneva, which was established by Calvin in 1559. The statue is striking. In one way, it is an apt representation of Calvin's immense legacy, global and enduring; in another way, it is a reflection of how Calvin is viewed today: cold, hard, and immovable. But wasn't this also the man who loved the Psalms so much that he read his life story through its pages and introduced them to others as the heartbeat of the Christian life? Wasn't this the man who took for himself an emblem of his hand holding out his heart to the Lord because it was all he could do when God called him to a place he did not want to go to spend his life doing a ministry he had never intended to do? Wasn't this the man who wrote and preached tirelessly for the church right into an early death? Wasn't this the man who feared that his grave would become a pilgrimage site and insisted on an unmarked grave so as not to draw attention to himself? By looking beyond the sixteen-foot statue, we can better see the sixteenth-century man, whose work and ministry became the fulcrum of the Reformed tradition.

Born to Run

John Calvin was a Frenchman, born in 1509 in a city that eventually disinherited him for his Protestant view of the faith. Unlike Martin Luther in Germany, whose name, history, and every waking step (honestly, that's not an exaggeration) were eventually marked and even recognized with the fastest-selling Playmobil toy of all time[2] (Little Luther), Calvin was maligned and exiled by his native country in his time and after his death. His theology developed on the run, born of a crisis of displacement. Where would this religious refugee, forced to leave his native France, find a home?

When Calvin was growing up, his father handled finances for Noyon Cathedral and was able to secure church benefices (stipends) that made it possible for Calvin, the second oldest of seven children, to receive a first-rate education. All roads were directing Calvin into professional training as a lawyer, but in the end, it was his self-study of theology, Scripture, and biblical languages that proved to be his passion and calling. Keep in mind that he was only eight years old when Luther's *Ninety-Five Theses* took off in 1517, but by the 1530s, Calvin had begun to embrace a Protestant view of the gospel. The "sudden conversion" that he experienced was actually a softening of his heart, as he described it later in 1557 in the preface to the Psalms commentary, that helped him to see the "abyss of mire" he had accepted for true faith and practice.[3] He marveled at becoming open to God's redirection, and ultimately, his whole life took a path he had not anticipated.

Prior to Calvin's conversion, the Reformation had entered France under the wing of Queen Marguerite of Navarre, the king of France's cherished sister and confidante.[4] A group of reform-minded clergy guided by the bishop of Meaux and blessed by Marguerite's patronage were instrumental in bearing those first reforming fruits. Nonetheless, radical acts of resistance to Catholicism within the ever-growing movement brought the king to a breaking point. The Placard Affair of 1534 (when posters maligning the Mass were placed throughout the city of Paris and just outside the king's chambers) was swiftly met with royal persecution, capital punishment, and forced exile. Calvin had been implicated among Protestant circles in Paris the year before, had fled from northern France, and was residing in the southwestern region when it became imperative for him not only to leave France briefly (heading to Basel) but also ultimately to leave France permanently.

On the run in July 1536 in Basel, Calvin published the first edition of the *Institutes of the Christian Religion*, which he returned to again and again, expanding it over his career. Meanwhile, an unexpected overnight stay in Geneva proved to be a life changer. At the urging (actually more the threatening) of Reformer Guillaume Farel, who had already brought the Reformation to the city, Calvin agreed to stay and partner with him in rebuilding the church. There was a lot of work to be done, and it helped to have a lawyer involved. Calvin began to lecture on the Bible, assist in theological disputations, and lay the groundwork for catechism and congregational singing in the city. But by the second year, Calvin and Farel fell into dispute over church discipline with civil leaders who ended up exiling them from the city. Calvin's first phase of ministry in Geneva ended in apparent defeat.

Surprised by Strasbourg

At the invitation of Reformer Martin Bucer, Calvin was invited to Strasbourg, where he served as pastor of the French refugee church and married a widow, Idelette de Bure. During this joyful season of his life, Calvin was prolific, writing his first biblical commentary (that's right, Romans) and the second Latin edition of the *Institutes*. In time, he began to translate the Latin *Institutes* into French to reach a broader audience.

A turning point came when Geneva's civil leadership realized how much they needed Calvin to set and defend a vision of reform. While under pressure to return the city to Rome, they reached out to Calvin for help. Rather than revel in their change of heart and circumstances, Calvin came to their aid, though it went against every fiber of his being, and he described the struggle to submit his will to God's and offer his heart as a sacrifice. In 1541, Calvin returned to Geneva to resume his pastoral leadership in the city. As it turned out, he would never return to France, though he always directed his ministry toward the hope of her reform and the ceasing of persecution.

Building the Theological Infrastructure

One of Calvin's most notable contributions to the Reformed tradition was to give it form according to his reading of the New Testament church. Calvin organized the Genevan church around four key offices: pastor, elder, doctor, and deacon. Institutional committees (yes, Presbyterians love their committees!) promoted shared church governance and carried the load of pastoral ministry in various ways throughout the city, whether in the parishes (both rural and urban), in the hospitals, through education, or through the disciplining body (called the consistory). A new liturgical calendar was adopted to establish a reformed rhythm of life that filled the week with worship services. A considerable amount of Calvin's time, energy, and even finances were directed toward aiding fellow Protestants within the city and beyond, such as through the restoration of the diaconate. In Calvin's mind, structure and order rooted in renewal secured the marks of a true church: the right preaching of God's Word and the right administration of the sacraments. But Calvin's shaping of the church involved more than its polity.

Marie Dentière (ca. 1495–1561) converted to Protestantism in the 1520s because of Luther's writings. Her departure from the Augustinian convent in Tournai, France, led to two marriages (she was widowed in 1533) and eventually to settling in Geneva in 1535 before Calvin's arrival. She was likely the first person to publish an eyewitness account of the Reformation in Geneva, and she was also a defender of Calvin against Geneva's civic leaders. Dentière's open letter to Queen Marguerite of Navarre encourages women to use their God-given talents to proclaim the gospel through teaching and preaching. In 2002, Marie's name was added to the wall of Reformers in Geneva.

Over the course of his ministry, as Calvin grew in knowledge of Scripture and theology while also gaining experience in pastoring, he expanded the size, content, and complexity of the *Institutes* until it became a four-volume work that was five times larger than the first edition. Calvin's initial hope for the book was that it would serve as a kind of confession for fellow French Protestants, or "Huguenots." He dedicated the book to the king of France to counter false impressions that had inspired royal persecution, including the notions that the Protestant movement sought political anarchy and that it was innovative in its theology by ignoring the church fathers. Initially, Calvin's theological content was shaped by Luther's Shorter Catechism in the topics selected and in their order. Eventually it became its own piece according to Calvin's reading of Scripture, his interaction with the church fathers (particularly Augustine), and the challenges he faced and the wisdom he gained through his pastoral ministry.

The flow of the books covered doctrines relating to God, then Jesus Christ, then the Holy Spirit, and finally the church. Calvin engaged with the Apostles' Creed, the Lord's Prayer, and the Ten Commandments extensively, which were all staples of Protestant worship and catechesis by this point. Polemics were also never far from his pen as he explained the mistakes of Roman Catholicism, the Anabaptists, the Jews, and even certain Lutherans.

Book 1 focuses on the doctrine of God as creator and Father. Calvin famously taught that the knowledge of ourselves and the knowledge of God are tied together.[5] How can we truly know ourselves if we do not know our creator?[6] Calvin starts here because knowledge gets at the heart of what it means to be human: not only created by God but set apart from every other living creature as uniquely made in God's image. Unfortunately, sin clouds our understanding of ourselves and of God and distorts our vision of the world. There is a seed of divinity within us,[7] not extinguished by the fall, but apart from Scripture, it serves only to lead us into idolatry, since we were made to worship God.[8] We walk through life with blurry vision unless we don "the spectacles of Scripture"[9] that can help us to see clearly, including the world as the theater of God's glory.[10] Scripture, then, is an expression of God's loving accommodation to humans. Calvin famously described the teachings of Scripture as akin to how a mother talks to a child.[11] In this, we are reminded that the Bible is meant to connect not only with the elite and highly educated but also with everyday people and their common experience of the world.

For Calvin, God is an attentive father who adopts fallen children mercifully out of love and goodness.

Book 2 explores the impact of the fall on the will,[12] our total depravity (as in every part of us is affected),[13] common grace,[14] the relationship between the Testaments of the Bible, and Jesus' role as our sole mediator.[15] The threefold office of Christ as prophet, priest, and king allows Calvin to read the New Testament through the Old Testament by emphasizing Christ's fulfillment of the Old. The sinless and priestly Christ enters the holy of holies and provides the only sufficient sacrifice that can ensure salvation: himself. Another major theme of Calvin's theology is our adoption into God's family. To be welcomed into God's family, not by anything that we have done but by the work of our brother Jesus Christ, is to receive all the promises of inheritance that Jesus has received. The gift of adoption comes with the assurance of bodily resurrection and eternal life. God's kingdom is inaugurated now (though only in a spiritual manner),[16] but one day it will be on earth as it is in heaven.[17]

Book 3 teaches on the role of the Holy Spirit, who acts as advocate in all things and secures the benefits that Christ promises.[18] The Holy Spirit illumines our understanding of Scripture and confirms its divine origins through an "inner testimony."[19] The primary roles of the Holy Spirit are to lift us up in mind and heart to Christ, illumine our faith, incite our repentance, bind us to him, and restore his image in us.[20] By the Holy Spirit, we are united to Christ, and through that bond, the Holy Spirit sanctifies us daily. The assurance of that union is the result of justification by faith in Christ (the "main hinge on which religion turns")[21] rather than because we live a perfect life or have full comprehension of faith.[22] Christ's gift to us is to dwell in us and become partakers of every good.[23] Calvin teaches a "double grace": one grace that justifies us apart from ourselves, and one grace that transforms us within so that we too may become righteous like Christ.[24] Perfection on this side of heaven is elusive, but we strive for obedience out of love for God.[25] For Calvin, regeneration in Christ is the crux of Christian freedom.

Of all the topics that Calvin explored in the *Institutes*, his section on prayer is the longest.[26] Here the pastoral side of his work meets the theological side as Calvin teaches on the importance of bringing faith and hope to the act of prayer. Prayer is not possible because of human worthiness but because of Christ's. In humility, we pray with assurance that God hears prayer and is at work. Though God already knows what is in the hearts and minds of his people, the act of prayer is the opportunity for the believer to grow in faith. For Calvin, prayer, which takes place through the Holy Spirit, is the primary exercise of faith. Through this spiritual practice, true piety is fostered in which love and reverence for God are joined.[27]

One of the greatest misconceptions about Calvin is that the doctrine of predestination is the center of his theology. But it is only after laying this groundwork that he comes to the doctrine of predestination, which he roots in the idea of adoption.[28] Like Augustine before him, Calvin relied on Ephesians 1, which teaches that adoption is rooted in God's good pleasure to bestow on the chosen the inheritance that is sealed in us by the Holy Spirit.[29] To ensure that salvation is completely unmerited (free for us, though costly for the Son of God), Calvin pointed to Romans 1:18–21 and concluded that humanity is otherwise inexcusable before God.[30] Predestination confirms the freedom of God's will to choose[31] and the assurance and certainty of that gift because it is dependent not on human merit but on Christ's. In this way, Calvin's view of predestination differed from Augustine, since Calvin believed that the perseverance of the saints was assured by God's election.[32] As the *Institutes* makes clear, predestination and the promise of bodily resurrection cannot be separated.[33] Though Calvin's doctrine of double predestination ("eternal life is foreordained for some, eternal damnation for others") has often been criticized, it was good news because it pointed to the assurance found in God's good will alone.[34]

Finally, in book 4, Calvin addresses the doctrine of the church, which includes his definition of the true church, an affirmation of infant baptism, his understanding of the Lord's Supper, and his discussion of the spiritual practices that shape the Christian life as well as the relationship between the church and the state. No other issue, however, generated more disagreement than communion.

Scotsman and Reformer **John Knox** (1514–72) was a graduate of the University of St. Andrews who converted to the Protestant faith in the 1540s under the preaching of George Wishart. As a Marian exile (one who fled the reign of Mary Tudor), he found refuge in Calvin's Geneva, where he pastored Geneva's English-speaking church and was involved in the translation of the Geneva Bible. In 1556, he described Geneva as "the most perfect school of Christ." Taking this teaching back to his home country, Knox was instrumental in launching the Scottish Reformation and establishing the Scots Presbyterian kirk tradition.

I'm the Problem; It's Me

As a gifted rhetorician with a brilliant legal and theological mind, Calvin was drawn into debates ranging from the doctrine of the Trinity to the meaning of the Lord's Supper. In upholding the traditional view of the Trinity, he opposed the writing of Spanish theologian Michael Servetus, known today as a father of the Unitarian tradition. Servetus wrote *On the Errors of the Trinity* (1531), which rejected the orthodox view of the Trinity and put a target on his back until his execution in 1553 for heresy. This incident is sometimes the only thing that some people know about Calvin, which has complicated his reputation.[35]

Calvin's role in the debates surrounding the Lord's Supper, or communion, meanwhile, show a willingness to moderate or accommodate for the sake of unity. He signed, after all, Philip Melanchthon's variation of the Augsburg Confession in 1540. Along with Luther and all Protestants, he rejected transubstantiation (that the substance of the bread and wine change into Christ's real body and blood through the words of institution, while the accidents remain the same). But several key questions remained: is Jesus present when we celebrate communion and what does Scripture teach us? If he is present with us at communion, then how is he present and in what way? These questions had been generating disagreement among Protestants since 1525, but Calvin was determined to find a way through.

The Reformed tradition, starting with Zurich Reformer Ulrich Zwingli, looked to Jesus' ascension to answer questions about his presence at communion. Reformed Christians taught that Christ ascended bodily to sit at the right hand of God the Father meant that Jesus could not be bodily present at communion. A Reformed critique of Luther's teachings was that it unnecessarily yanked Christ from his heavenly seat to be bodily, though invisibly, present during communion.[36] Instead, Calvin countered, Christ is spiritually (not bodily) present with us, because the Holy Spirit lifts believers to the ascended Christ during the celebration of the Lord's Supper.[37] In that moment, a "spiritual banquet" occurs where Christ is received as spiritual nourishment for the soul through faith and the power of the Holy Spirit.[38] Calvin considered this to be a special moment of union with Christ that is also a glimpse of what is to come.[39] After Calvin's death, this teaching gained prominence in Reformed circles in the Second Helvetic Confession, written by Heinrich Bullinger, Zwingli's successor in Zurich.

Heinrich Bullinger (1504–75)[40] took over the helm of pastoral leadership and reform at Zurich in 1531 with the sudden and brutal death of Ulrich Zwingli in battle. Bullinger and Calvin corresponded for nine years about the theology of the Lord's Supper before they came to agreement with the *Consensus Tigurinus* (signed in 1549). Bullinger is best known in the Reformed tradition for developing covenant theology and for writing the Second Helvetic Confession.

Calvin's Geneva in the Rearview Mirror

For centuries, Geneva served as a "Mother Church" and even the "Rome of Protestantism" as Reformed Christians in France continued to be persecuted into the eighteenth century.[41]

But the Reformed tradition's story also reaches beyond France and Geneva in large part because of population displacement from exile and persecution. As the second wave of the Reformation was developing, the Reformed tradition spread to England, Scotland, Hungary, Poland-Lithuania, Transylvania, the Netherlands, and about a dozen German principalities. Its role in forming the English and Scottish Reformations is notable.

It was through the reign of Henry VIII's son, Edward VI, that Protestant reform shaped the Church of England so indelibly, which was then confirmed by one of Henry's daughters, Queen Elizabeth I (with the staunchly Catholic Mary Tudor I ruling in between them). Under the leadership of Thomas Cranmer, the archbishop of Canterbury, the Book of Common Prayer was introduced with English liturgy, homilies on justification by faith alone were taught, the English Bible was promoted, and the (eventually) Thirty-Nine Articles were adopted as the Anglican confession of faith. The journey of these documents, as they took shape, moved decidedly from a Lutheran expression of faith to a Reformed expression through the influence of Martin Bucer of Strasbourg, Peter Martyr Vermigli of Italy, John à Lasco of Poland, and John Knox of Scotland. The next generation of Reformed Puritans added the Westminster Standards.

Today, Myung Sung Presbyterian Church in Seoul, Korea, is the largest Reformed church in the world, marking the tradition's global reach. The legacy of Reformed theology in churches today around the world is evident in the ongoing use of the Heidelberg Catechism, published in 1563 by Zacharias Ursinus and Kaspar Olevianus. The very first question and answer in the catechism captures the heart of the Reformed tradition theologically and echoes the words of Calvin:[42] Q: "What is your only comfort in life and death?" A: "That I, with body and soul, both in life and in death, am not my own, but belong to my faithful Savior Jesus Christ."[43] There is perhaps no better example of how Reformed theology was shaped by experiences of persecution and displacement. Yet their theology was not alone in being informed by the reality of suffering.

Discussion Questions

1. Have you ever thought that your life was going in one direction, only for it to suddenly change course? How did you grow in your faith because of that experience?
2. How does Scripture illuminate your understanding of God's creation and your place in the world?
3. How does the global reach of Calvin's theology today inform our understanding of the one body of Christ?

Further Reading

John Calvin, *Institutes of the Christian Religion*, ed. John McNeill, trans. Ford Lewis Battles, 2 vols. (Westminster, 1960).

Bruce Gordon, *Calvin* (Yale Univ. Press, 2009).

R. Ward Holder, ed., *John Calvin in Context* (Cambridge Univ. Press, 2020).

Elsie McKee, *John Calvin: Writings on Pastoral Piety* (Paulist, 2002).

MENNO SIMONS

PRAYER

Lord! Consider your troubled and poor servants. You examine every heart. You know me. You know that I seek and desire nothing but your will. Loving Lord, direct and teach me in your truth. For you alone are my God and Lord, my salvation. Apart from you I know no other. You alone are my hope, my comfort, my shield, fortress and protection. I place my trust in you and in my fear, tribulation and suffering I daily wait on you.

—Menno Simons[1]

Don't Forget the Radicals

When we consider the Reformation story, Martin Luther and John Calvin most likely are the first names to pop into many heads. After all, they were the most prominent leaders of their generations, and their theological writings have shaped two of the most significant Protestant traditions worldwide today. But to limit the Reformation to Luther and Calvin misses a significant piece of the puzzle, then and now. A fuller image of the Reformation includes the radicals of their time because of how they pushed limits and challenged norms to bring their own versions of reform to the church. In many ways, they lived in the wings of church and society because of their ideas and actions, and yet they were at times also center stage as Reformation disruptors. What is their story?

Reformation-era radicals are a diverse group who sit under a broad umbrella. Some outright rejected the office of clergy, the practice of sacraments, and even the gathering of the church body (think "spiritualists" like Caspar Schwenckfeld). Meanwhile, other radicals rejected the doctrine of the Trinity and rekindled every early Christian controversy, including the divinity of Christ and the personhood of the Holy Spirit (think "evangelical rationalists" such as Michael Servetus). And then there were the radicals who established a "community of goods" based on the precedent set in Acts 2:44–45 and sought to realize the community of the saints (think Jacob Hut and the Hutterites).[2] The radical side of the Reformation complicates what we mean when we say "Protestant." The radical reformers' ideas pushed mainline Reformers like Luther and Calvin (often called "magisterial" for their partnership with civil rulers) to clarify and defend their views in significant ways and vice versa. Unfortunately, reconciliation was elusive and hostility the status quo.

But some Reformation-era radicals might not seem particularly radical to the modern-day observer. Nevertheless, they too were regarded as heretical and a threat to the political, religious, and social order of Reformation Europe. Their story is particularly troubling because they were ruthlessly persecuted by church and civic leaders, including magisterial Protestants and Roman Catholics. Collectively, this group rejected infant baptism, so they were called the "Anabaptists," meaning "rebaptizers," which was intended in the most derogatory way. In nearly every case, they wrote their theology while on the run for their lives or in prison cells while awaiting capital punishment for heresy. Most often, they suffered the life of the refugee, migrating from Western to Eastern Europe in search of a place to settle. An Anabaptist martyrology, the *Martyrs Mirror*, features the story of Dirk Willems, who was fleeing from authorities after being tortured. He successfully slid across the ice away from his pursuer only to watch as the ice cracked and his pursuer plunged into the water. Rather than allow him to drown, Willems graciously pulled him from the ice, saving his life, only to be arrested and burned outside of Asperen (1569).[3] Stories of martyrdom like Willems' emboldened the tradition, which traced its legacy to the first Christian martyr, Stephen (Acts 7).

Against all odds, the Anabaptist movement proved to be profoundly influential in shaping Western Christianity and theology in ways that endure today, especially through the legacy of Menno Simons. Under the leadership of Menno, Anabaptists survived crisis and adversity as well as clarified their theological views and practices to become a thriving Protestant tradition.

I'm a Survivor

Menno Simons' humble beginnings in his birth to dairy farmers in the Netherlands belie the greatness he achieved during his life and within the living legacy of the Anabaptist tradition. Even though Charles V put a price on Menno's head in 1542, Menno successfully dodged authorities for the rest of his life and died of natural causes in 1561. One of the most unlikely parts of Menno's story was that he was buried in his cabbage garden rather than burned at the stake.[4] Even before his peaceful passing, his Anabaptist followers became known according to his name.[5]

Menno became a priest in 1524 without ever having cracked the Bible open, explaining later that he feared it would confuse him.[6] He experienced doubts over Roman Catholic teachings on transubstantiation (the view that the bread and wine become the actual body and blood of Christ during the celebration of the Mass). As his conscience grew troubled, he was driven to Martin Luther's writings and Scripture. How could this be the true body and blood of Christ? Menno's rejection of transubstantiation and the Roman Catholic Mass was just the beginning of his alignment with the reforming branches of the Western church. During the 1530s, Anabaptism grew in Friesland (a northern province of the Netherlands), where Menno lived, and he was shaken to the core by the execution of Anabaptist Sicke Freerks (1531), whom Menno admired. Menno turned to Scripture again, but this time, he was dissatisfied with disagreements he found between prominent interpreters, including Strasbourg Reformer Martin Bucer and Zurich Reformer Heinrich Bullinger. In the end, despite the consequences, he claimed that his rejection of infant baptism (or pedobaptism) was directed by the Holy Spirit: in his view, Scripture did not allow infant baptism.[7] But to go against the rest of the Western church on this matter of Scripture and theology also had civic and social implications.

Sorting Out Baptism

It may be difficult to imagine why views on baptism were so controversial that they could be treated as a capital offense. But it's important to keep in mind that in the sixteenth century, infant baptism was a mark of citizenship. The baptismal record was a kind of modern-day passport or even social-security card as well as entrance into society and church. To renounce infant baptism was akin to renouncing one's citizenship and the fellowship of the church at the same time.[8]

In 1525, the first recorded believer's baptism was carried out among the Swiss Brethren of Zurich in the private home of Felix Manz, when Conrad Grebel baptized George Blaurock, a former Catholic priest. It was fairly shocking. Even though for centuries Christians had practiced infant baptism, the Anabaptist conviction in Scripture alone (sola Scriptura) led to the conclusion that Scripture taught no precedent and offered no allowance for infant baptism. Anabaptist teaching maintained the importance of the right order of Jesus' Great Commission in the gospel of Mark (16:16): teaching and then baptizing.[9] The significance of John the Baptist and Jesus' baptism were treated as affirmations of believer's baptism. Part of the challenge was that Protestants no longer believed that baptism was necessary for washing away original sin (as Augustine had once taught), so one might ask, What was the point of infant baptism?[10]

Zurich Reformer Ulrich Zwingli developed a theology of baptism in response to the Swiss Brethren that continues to shape the practice of infant baptism in the Reformed tradition today. Zwingli responded with a typological reading of infant baptism as a New Testament replacement for Old Testament circumcision. Though considered by some to encourage a replacement (or "supersessionist") reading of sacraments that excludes Jews, Zwingli taught that infant baptism was a sign of the new covenant in Christ,[11] and this emphasis on covenantal theology developed further with Zwingli's successor, Heinrich Bullinger. For Zwingli, the foremost danger of believer's baptism was in believing that one's faith required perfection before baptism, as though your salvation depended on you. This struck Zwingli and others as a new kind of monasticism. Zwingli pointed out that even living by faith in Christ and after baptism, Christian perfection was still elusive.[12] He consistently taught regarding sacraments that their efficacy was solely dependent on the movement and will of God rather than the will of the recipient. In these ways, baptism intersected not only with politics and church membership but also with crucial theological doctrines of sin, justification, soteriology, ecclesiology, and the human will. For the magisterial Reformation, there was no better example of salvation by grace alone than the baptism of an infant. For Anabaptists, it was a false tradition that had no place in the church.

The backlash against Anabaptism was intense. Rebaptism quickly became a capital offense in Europe with rare exception, and authorities began to practice a so-called third baptism to punish Anabaptists: death by drowning as capital punishment. But the Anabaptist rejection of infant baptism for theological and biblical reasons was not the only theological controversy that Menno and his followers faced.

It's the End of the World as We Know It

Europeans of the early modern period believed they were living in the end times, and this belief had much to do with the Muslim Turks, who were threatening to burst through the door of Western Europe. The Siege of Vienna in 1529 was frightening for all of Europe. Was Christendom on the brink of destruction?

In this climate, some early Anabaptist groups regarded themselves as facilitators of God's judgment and encouraged violence against the nonelect. Their task, so they thought, was to rightly harvest the wheat from the tares using the Lord's sickle,[13] which assumed their ability to rightly discern between those who were saved and those who were not. Old Testament accounts of aggression served for biblical precedent. Thomas Müntzer, a former Roman Catholic priest, was instrumental in shaping a theological outlook of violence and apocalypticism.

Müntzer was a dynamic preacher whose teachings seemed to align with a group of radical prophets in the town of Zwickau. He eventually led a peasant army to attack anyone deemed outside the elect. In his early work *Sermon to the Princes* (1524), he identified himself as a new Daniel and declared, "For the godless have no right to live except that which the elect decide to grant them."[14] Before Müntzer's involvement, the uprising had started powerfully and peaceably with a bestselling pamphlet, *The Twelve Articles of the Upper Swabian Peasants*, that innovatively rooted peasant demands in Scripture's teachings. The pamphlet represented the concerns of some thirty thousand peasants amassed in Upper Swabia, and their questions about the implications of Christian freedom were provocative. Are we not free in Christ, not from all authority but from being treated as property? "Release us from serfdom," they demanded, "or show us from the gospel that we should be serfs."[15] But what began with a sympathetic start took a violent turn and brought the Peasants' Revolt (1525) to a bloody end.

A tension was brewing among early Anabaptists that would not be fully settled until Menno. The first wave of Anabaptism (Andreas Karlstadt and the Swiss Brethren) taught resistance through nonviolence and the willingness to be martyred. Michael Sattler's *Schleitheim Confession* (1527) responded to the Peasants' Revolt and began the process of formalizing a nonviolent theology.[16] This first confession of the Anabaptist tradition highlights the importance of preserving the purity of the church, which defines the ecclesiology of the church as the visible gathering of the elect (rather than Augustine's wheat and tares, elect and nonelect). Because they viewed the church that way, Anabaptists elevated separation from the world to preserve the holiness of the church; likewise, they emphasized the importance of voluntarism in faith and practice. It was their conviction that no one should be forced to conform in matters of faith, since the heart could not truly be compelled. These are the same touch points that spurred the replacement of infant baptism with a baptism anchored in the confession of faith. After all, to be plunged into the waters of baptism was akin to dying on the cross with Christ, just as rising out of the water signaled rebirth into Christ's righteousness (Rom. 6:3–4).

Andreas Bodenstein von Karlstadt (1486–1541) was a professor of theology and a colleague of Martin Luther's at the University of Wittenberg. Karlstadt participated in the Leipzig Disputation of 1519 and led Wittenberg into reform during Luther's absence by administering the first evangelical public mass. Karlstadt was also the first reformer to renounce his vow of celibacy and marry. His tendency to advance swift reform led to his expulsion from the city and tensions with Luther. He ended up serving in Zurich as deacon at the Grossmünster with Ulrich Zwingli and finally teaching at the University of Basel at the end of his life.

The theological perspective was compounded by the fact that separation entailed more than just believer's baptism.

The radicalism of Anabaptist actions also included their rejection of loyalty oaths to the state, refusal to participate in civic leadership, and unwillingness to use the sword under any circumstances, including self-defense. Their commitment to nonviolence was often expressed in shocking ways for the times, such as when Sattler declared at his trial that even "if the Turks should come, we ought not to resist them. For it is written [Matt. 5:21]: Thou shalt not kill. We must not defend ourselves against the Turks and others of our persecutors."[17]

Meanwhile, the Anabaptist community had a different way of dealing with the wayward within. To further preserve the purity of the church, Anabaptists banned from the community those who fell into sin until they showed proper repentance (a practice based on Matt. 18:15–20).[18] Menno and his followers, who came to be known as Mennonites in his lifetime, were known to moderate the practice when banning proved harmful to families in the community: "Mildness, politeness, respectfulness, friendliness to all mankind becomes all Christians."[19] The Good Samaritan served as an inspiration for showing mercy.[20] The church's efforts to preserve the purity of the community also included electing their own pastor.[21] Doing so, Anabaptists rejected the authority of the episcopacy or the monarchy to make such decisions, and provided a way to overcome the medieval practice of simony (the selling and purchasing of church offices, which had become common practice by the eve of the Reformation and reached all the way to the papacy).

The conviction that nonviolence was a core Christian

practice was not accepted by all Anabaptists in those early years before Menno. So much of the conversation hinged upon interpreting Jesus' command to Peter in the garden of Gethsemane to put his sword away (Matt. 26:52). Andreas Karlstadt wrote in 1524 against Müntzer's teachings by emphasizing that "Christ ordered Peter to sheath his sword."[22] The question remained: did Jesus mean that his followers should never pick up a sword again? The duration of Christ's command was contested, and the same year that Sattler declared pacifism as the true practice of Anabaptism was the year that Balthasar Hubmaier presented a third option for Anabaptist communities. Persuaded by Romans 13, Hubmaier claimed that the sword could rightly be carried by the "pious ruler" and used according to God's will.[23] It should be noted that at the time, Hubmaier was also benefiting from the protection of the Moravian princes, so his theology aligned well with his circumstances. In the midst of disagreement, Menno's response to the crisis at Munster settled the matter once and for all.

Balthasar Hubmaier (ca. 1485–1528) was a German Anabaptist. He served as preacher at Regensburg before he was appointed parish priest at Waldshut. He became embroiled in the Peasants' Revolt and fled to Zurich for refuge. There he was forced to recant his views regarding believer's baptism to preserve his life. He retracted and settled in Nikolsburg, Moravia, in 1526 where he wrote theological texts on free will, the Lord's Supper, and pacifism. After being extradited from Moravia, he was burned in Vienna in 1528.

It was not until the Munster debacle that Menno hitched his wagon to the Anabaptist cause. The Munster crisis involved the prophetic teaching of a former fur merchant by the name of Melchior Hoffman. Although Melchior was banished from city to city, he still managed to publish *The Ordinance of God* (1530), which limited the Lord's Supper to memorialism (remembrance only), baptism to believers, and justification to righteousness coachieved by human free will. Most important, Melchior's insistence that Christ's second coming would occur in Strasbourg in 1533 generated a level of apocalyptic fervor that spread beyond his control as he suffered in prison until his death. His followers (known as the Melchiorites), meanwhile, altered his prophecy, predicting that Christ's second coming would occur in 1534 in the city of Munster. There, Reformer Bernhard Rothmann welcomed Anabaptist pilgrims with open arms to the "New Jerusalem." Whether a political coup or a landslide took place, Anabaptists ascended to political leadership, which led Lutheran and Roman Catholic inhabitants to abandon the city. Protestants and Catholics then united to lay siege to the city for sixteen months. Bizarre events transpired that deeply troubled Europe. The breakdown of city leadership as well as the hardships of starvation and military fighting degenerated into forced polygamy, the implementation of Jewish law enforced by capital punishment, and the reconstitution of the twelve tribes of Israel under a new "King David." Massacre and reconquest of the city took place, and the bodies of Munster's leaders were hung in three cages from the top of Saint Lamberti Cathedral as a warning. Cages still hang there today. In this time of crisis, Menno's leadership became a lifeline for Anabaptism.

An Unlikely Legacy

In the aftermath of the debacle at Munster, Menno regarded himself as a shepherd called to guide the wayward, scattered, and lost sheep of Anabaptism. His brother, Peter Simons, may have even died in the siege. Menno's first Reformation writing came from a place of compassion for the Munsterites, whom he regarded as led astray by the false prophecy and corrupt leadership of John of Leiden, whose name grew in infamy throughout Europe alongside another Munster orchestrator, Jan Matthys. In 1536, Menno officially renounced the Roman Catholic priesthood and was rebaptized probably later that year by Obbe Philips. Even though he was never involved at Munster, the events that transpired there ruined the possibility of implementing a peaceful Anabaptist Reformation in Europe. Menno spent the rest of his life decrying any association with Munster's sword, polygamy, king, and earthly kingdom.[24] He consistently stressed the necessity of pacifism. After all, Christ refused Peter's sword for his defense,[25] and his kingdom was inaugurated not by the sword but suffering.[26]

Constructively speaking, Menno's theological contribution focused on the transformed life of the believer as a new creation (*The New Birth*, 1537) marked by believer's baptism (*Christian Baptism*, 1539).[27] Regeneration, rebirth, and the possibility of Christian perfection in imitation of Christ became prominent themes in his theology. The concern to overcome human sin led Menno to teach an unorthodox understanding of the incarnation, which claimed that Christ was without sin because he did not receive human flesh from Mary, though he was born of her (*The Incarnation of our Lord*, 1554). This teaching became a sticking point of disagreement, in addition to the controversy over baptism, when Menno met to dispute with Polish Reformer John à Lasko (or Laski) in Emden (1544). It was a view that did not long endure, even in Mennonite circles.

As the movement centered in Amsterdam, Menno began to systematize his theology in what is considered his magnum opus, *The Foundation of Christian Doctrine* (1539–40). The piece is both an apologetic and a confession, entreating magistrates to read and better understand his theological position in the hope of quelling persecution. He taught that the order of salvation began with repentance and contrition, followed by baptism as the expression of faith, which became the foundation for a life of obedience. True faith in Christ would manifest itself in obedience to God's Word alone (not church fathers or biblical scholars) and no matter the cost.[28] In an important step for the movement, Menno removed the apocalypticism that had troubled early Anabaptism by rejecting chiliasm (millennialism, or the idea that Jesus will reign on earth one thousand years) as misguided. Above all, the willingness to endure worldly suffering and persecution with patience, out of a biblical commitment to the cross of Christ and in pursuit of holy living through separation, proved to be the most notable outworking of Mennonite theology. The following helpfully summarizes Menno's theology: "Then I, without constraint . . . renounced all my worldly reputation, name, and fame, my unchristian abominations, my masses, infant baptism, and my easy life, and I willingly submitted to distress and poverty under the heavy cross of Christ."[29]

In 1632, the Mennonite tradition codified its beliefs in the Dordrecht Confession of Faith, including believer's baptism, footwashing as a mark of servanthood, church discipline, and nonresistance. The Amish later emerged as a subgroup of the Mennonite tradition, tracing their historical roots to Swiss Anabaptist/Mennonite Jakob Ammann (1656–1730). To this day, Mennonite believers emphasize the Christian life as one of regeneration. In answer to the question, "Are you a Christian?" the Mennonite responds, "Ask my neighbor."

Discussion Questions

1. What is the relationship between our justification in Christ alone and living a faithful life according to God's will? How do those two affirmations connect in Scripture?
2. What is the role of baptism in your church tradition? What does your baptism mean to you?
3. How should Christians navigate the conflation of or divide between church and state? What is the ideal situation, if there is one, for the church to thrive?

Further Reading

Michael G. Baylor, ed., *The Radical Reformation*, Cambridge Texts in the History of Political Thought (Cambridge Univ. Press, 2008).

William R. Estep, *The Anabaptist Story* (Eerdmans, 1995).

Daniel Liechty, ed., *Early Anabaptist Spirituality* (Paulist, 1994).

George Williams, *The Radical Reformation* (Westminster John Knox, 1962).

CHAPTER 12

TERESA OF AVILA

PRAYER

> *May you be blessed, my Lord, that from such filthy mud as I, You make water so clear that it can be served at Your table! May you be praised, O Joy to the angels, for having desired to raise up a worm so vile!*

—Teresa of Avila[1]

Roman Catholic Reformers?

Too often when we hear "Reformation," we equate it with "Protestant." But one of the reasons why the Reformation was so momentous for Western Christianity is because reform also took place *within* the Roman Catholic Church, even as it sorted out its response to Martin Luther and other Protestant Reformers. But who were those reform-minded leaders who maintained ties with the Roman curia (church leadership) and influenced the reforming practices of the Catholic Church? Teresa of Avila is the most remembered female theologian among them today and one of the most important Roman Catholic reformers of all time.

Before Teresa came on the scene, it was not so clear that the break that was happening between Luther and Rome was irreparable. The sides had not yet been barricaded, so to speak, even after Luther's excommunication. During the 1520s on, a group of reform-minded Roman Catholic leaders known as the Spirituali (or Italian evangelicals) gained prominence. Among them included the well-known Renaissance artist Michelangelo (yes, that one!), the poet-theologian Vittoria Colonna,[2] the English cardinal Reginald Pole, and the Italian cardinal Gasparo Contarini.

Contarini was present at the Diet of Worms as the Venetian ambassador to the imperial court. He was already sympathetic to Luther's emphasis on grace because he himself had come to the profound realization in 1511 that Christ's sacrifice was truly enough to cover his sins. But what could be complex about admitting that? If Christ was the true mediator, reliance on the sacrament of penance and the mediation of the cult of the saints came under scrutiny. Contarini's view of the doctrine of justification leaned in Luther's direction to the point that just a few years after Worms, in 1523, Contarini wrote, "I have truly arrived at the following firm conclusion; although I had formerly read it and knew how to repeat it, nevertheless only now, as a result of experience, do I fully grasp its meaning. It is this: nobody can justify himself or purge his soul of worldly affections through works. We must have recourse to divine grace which we obtain through faith in Jesus Christ. . . . [W]e must justify ourselves through the justice of another, namely Christ. Joining ourselves to him, his justice becomes ours."[3] In Contarini's mind, here was an enormous opportunity for healing the ever-widening breach.

When Contarini rose to the rank of cardinal in 1535, Pope Paul III appointed him to serve on a commission the following year that exposed systemic corruption in the church surrounding indulgences and clerical abuse. Reform was needed; everyone agreed. In 1541, the finest minds on all sides of the theological issues (sans Luther because of the imperial ban) met at Regensburg. Even a young John Calvin was there watching the proceedings with anticipation. The most astonishing development to work itself out was the agreement they managed over the doctrine of justification.

In the quest for a faithful understanding of the process of soteriology (salvation), Regensburg adopted the concept of double righteousness. This *duplex justitia* taught that a sinner received the gift of faith by the Holy Spirit, who both imputed and imparted Christ's righteousness so that a double righteousness was received.[4] In this way, Protestant concerns to maintain justification by faith alone were upheld even as Catholic concerns for the practice of good works was addressed. The believer was freed, by Christ alone, to live into righteousness starting with Christ's righteousness. It was the best of both worlds.

Reaching this was a big deal. You could say that they successfully summitted the Mount Everest of all theological issues for the time, but they could not resolve the issue of the papacy or transubstantiation. Regensburg proved to be a point of demarcation in the relationship between Luther and the pope. Afterward, the Roman Inquisition was reinstated to curb the threat of Protestantism, and the Index of Prohibited Books resumed, with Luther's works among them.

While the Spirituali diminished in influence and number, the Jesuits, or Society of Jesus, gained standing. Protestants were busy engaging with Europe as a mission field in need of re-Christianization[5] when Jesuit missionary Francis Xavier (1506–52) traveled to India and Japan. He was followed by Matteo

Ricci's (1552–1610) mission to China to bring a Christian faith attuned to acculturation. As Protestants emphasized faith alone, Jesuits stressed good works (and encouraged downplaying the doctrines of predestination, faith, and grace explicitly[6]). As Protestants rejected the idea of Petrine supremacy based on a rereading of Matthew 16, Jesuits elevated the importance of papal obedience by adopting a fourth monastic vow. For the Jesuits, life was understood through the eyes of the church, even if the church's vision differed from one's own. (Famously, if the church says a white object is black, then it must be black no matter how I see it!)[7] Both groups, meanwhile, magnified the importance and necessity of Christian education through schools, catechism, and the use of printing.

But the Jesuits were not the only reforming voices making their mark on the future of the Roman Catholic Church. The observant movements within the monastic orders and the establishment of new religious orders proved transformative, though Rome met even these with scrutiny and restrictions.

The Jesuits were formed and led by **Ignatius of Loyola** (1491–1556), who overcame a soldier's injury and embraced a more devout life by 1522 to "help souls."[8] Pope Paul III confirmed the order in 1540, and they soon became known as "contemplatives in action."[9] Loyola's *Spiritual Exercises* was approved in 1548 as instruction for leaders in guiding others in a life of prayer and meditation through emphasis on human sin and God's mercy. The participant is led to heed Christ's call to follow and to meditate on the passion, death, and resurrection of Christ.

Barefoot and Reforming

Teresa (also called Saint Teresa of Jesus) was born in the city of Avila (1515–82) to an aristocratic family. During her time, the Spanish monarch was the most powerful in Europe. It was the Age of Exploration, and Spain's dominion included such a vast amount of land in either direction, east and west, that the sun actually never set on the empire's reach.[10] In 1536, she entered the Carmelite Monastery of the Incarnation at Avila. It was here that she encountered God in ways that transformed her into the Spanish mystic, Carmelite nun, Roman Catholic theologian, and critical reformer and founder of her monastic order we remember today.

The origin of the Carmelite Order is shrouded in mystery, though linked dubiously to the prophet Elijah and the Virgin Mary. Official acceptance of their rule by the patriarch Albert of Jerusalem in the early thirteenth century is the most credible dating.[11] At the start, they were hermits who emphasized poverty, piety, and contemplative prayer in isolation with no commitment to public ministry (that is, to the ministry of the friar), but they were soon assimilated into the mendicant ranks. It was not until 1452, with Pope Nicholas V's papal bull *Cum Nulla*, that the order began officially accepting women. By Teresa's time, accommodations for the wealthy and elite troubled Teresa's conscience, and she became critical of her laxity and sin. The Carmelite Order's emphasis on solitude in the context of community became key to her restoration movement.[12]

In June 1560, Teresa experienced the first of a series of visions of Christ that continued for the next couple of years and transformed her faith. She committed to unceasing prayer and care for the poor, which led her to establish a convent in Avila and eventually fourteen houses for nuns and friars in Spain. These encounters with Christ have been described as a kind of ecstasy in divine locution (or in hearing or experiencing God's voice with spiritual ears. They are recorded in her spiritual autobiography, *The Book of Her Life* (1565), which was suppressed by the Inquisition until its publication in 1588, eight years after her death. In 1567, a visit from the general of the Carmelites authorized Teresa's ministry of prayer and her founding of the Discalced Carmelites (discalced meaning "barefoot") for nuns and friars. Teresa's order defied many of the social customs of the time by rooting the criteria for entry in religious devotion rather than wealth and social status. At a time and place where "pure blood laws" (*limpieza de sangre*) constrained *conversos* (converted Jews), the Discalced Carmelites overlooked genealogy for piety.[13] This was extremely unusual and followed patterns of exception also practiced by the Jesuit Order. In 1577, Teresa wrote her most recognized work, *The Interior Castle of the Soul*, an instruction for contemplative prayer. Appreciation of her devotion and leadership elevated her into elite circles, which led her to meet King Philip II of Spain in the late 1570s, who protected her from charges of heterodoxy and ensured that all her writings were preserved at the library of the Escorial.[14] She even counseled in matters of war and peace, church and state tensions, and other crisis situations.[15]

In Castile, where Teresa was born, Renaissance humanism had made significant inroads in advancing access to the biblical text thanks to the work of Franciscan cardinal and chancellor of Castile Francisco Ximénes de Cisneros, who was also a known proponent of clerical reform. His greatest achievement, the Complutensian Polyglot Bible, was completed in 1517 and distributed in 1522; it was the first of its kind in print.

Teresa mentored **John of the Cross** (1542–91), who was also born in Avila and educated among the Jesuits. In 1563, he became a Carmelite monk and came to oversee the male reforming branch of the Carmelite Order established by Teresa. Opposition to reform led to his captivity and torture. After his escape, he wrote his famous *The Dark Night of the Soul* (ca. 1588–91): "Through the dark night pride becomes humility, greed becomes simplicity, wrath becomes contentment, luxury becomes peace, gluttony becomes moderation, envy becomes joy, and sloth becomes strength. No soul will ever grow deep in the spiritual life unless God works passively in that soul by means of the dark night." John of the Cross was canonized in 1726 by Pope Benedict XIII and later named doctor of the church in 1926 by Pope Pius XI.

Soon after, Spanish humanist and Reformer Juan de Valdés was the first to translate from the Greek portions of the New Testament and Psalms into Spanish paraphrase. Even so, before 1543, Spain was the only country during the Reformation without a printed translation of the vernacular Bible until Francisco de Enzinas's Spanish New Testament (based on Erasmus's Greek) was published. It was a momentous milestone, but Enzinas was rewarded with imprisonment.[16] A hidden network of prominent clergy with Protestant sympathies became connected to the Hieronymite Monastery of Saint Isidore outside Seville led by Cassiodoro de Reina (ca. 1520–94). Reina was condemned by the Inquisition and burned in effigy in 1562. That year, he escaped to Geneva and eventually in Basel published the first complete Spanish Bible based on the original languages, which became known as the Bear's Bible or *La Biblia del Oso* (1569).[17]

In these ways, the Spanish Inquisition was diligent in its efforts to homogenize religion as well as repress reform and mystical spirituality so that even Teresa's reform could not avoid its watchful eye.[18] The last decades of Teresa's life were consumed by traveling throughout Spain to extend the number of reformed and enclosed convents, when she was not grappling with censorship, slander, and misunderstandings by those in authority.[19] Today, Teresa is considered the paradigmatic saint of Counter-Reformation Catholicism, who also overcame the suspicions of the Inquisitions to eventually be canonized.

As the Americas were colonized by Spain, debates followed over how Christian doctrines of original sin and the image of God should be applied to indigenous peoples. Dominican friar **Bartolomé de las Casas** (1484–1566) is known for his campaign against slavery and colonial exploitation in the Americas in a debate (called the Valladolid debate) with theologian Juan Ginés de Sepúlveda. Spanish missionary zeal was tangled up in these dynamics, and the papacy favored Spain in the race to divide up the New World.[20]

Enclosing the Castle of Prayer

One of Teresa's great contributions to theology is her doctrine of prayer. Teresa embraced a stringent standard of enclosure for her order that promoted separation from the world through chastity and asceticism for female religious orders specifically. This was in keeping with the reform and renewal of the Roman Catholic Church after the Council of Trent (1545–63). Pope Paul III had called the council in 1545 with an eye toward responding to the Protestant Reformation, officially clarifying matters of debate over doctrine and practice, and introducing reform. The open communities of late medieval monasticism, which allowed a popular piety (think the Beguines and Tertiaries) to enter religious and secular worlds, was largely shut by the Council of Trent.[21] Teresa embraced that change, advanced it, and enforced it for the sake of reform and for the sake of elevating the most important element of the devout life: the interior life of prayer.[22]

Teresa's most significant work, *The Interior Castle of the Soul* (1577), teaches the soul how to progress toward union with God through prayer. To that end, Teresa employed imaginative theology to sustain the focus of the devout by comparing the soul to a diamond castle with many dwelling places (similar to Julian's citadel of the soul in revelations 16 of her *Showings*).[23] Prayer functions as the door to the castle, which enables the believer to move toward greater fellowship or union with Christ, starting with self-reflection.

Teresa's theology emphasized a deep awareness of human sin and the vast divide between humans as creatures and God as creator. She frequently described herself in diminutive manner, such as being no better than a worm (as she does in the epigraph to this chapter) or an ant. In her *Book of Foundations*, completed just a few months before her death, she wrote, "O greatness of God! How you manifest Your power in giving courage to an ant.

How true, my Lord, that it is not because of You that those who love You fail to do great works but because of our own cowardice and pusillanimity. . . . Who is more fond than You of giving, or of serving even at a cost to yourself, where there is someone open to receive?"[24] In the *Interior Castle*, a believer's humility should function like a bee making honey and, therefore, never cease to work.[25] By accepting the lowliness of humanity, Teresa conversely emphasized the goodness, mercy, and power of God, who is able to empower even the most insignificant of creatures to do his will.

In Teresa's teachings, the obstacles to a life of prayer are twofold: alienation from one's true self (not really knowing yourself as made in God's image), and caring more for the body than for the soul.[26] The unpracticed petitioner, meanwhile, addresses God as though he were a slave doing the human's bidding at the human's command, or practices either memorized prayer that does not come from the soul or mindless prayer that does not choose words carefully. In contrast, for Teresa, prayer functions in the life of the believer in line with Trent's teachings on justification and cooperative grace (God's gracious assistance that enables the work of believers to live into righteousness for the achievement of salvation). She writes, "True union can very well be reached, with God's help, if we make the effort to obtain it by keeping our wills fixed only on that which is God's will."[27] Yet this "way of perfection"—a work that she wrote for her nuns—was achievable only through the life of the monastery.[28]

Above all, the life of prayer focuses on the royal chamber of the castle at the center, where Christ the king resides. Rather than being burdened by earthly misery and fear, a tactic of

Satan's to trap souls, prayer seeks the center dwelling where union is offered with Christ. (In other works, she explicitly describes this as divine friendship.)[29] Teresa likens our bond to Christ as a marital union that brings deliverance and interior freedom. Drawing that connection, she echoes not only biblical explanations but also the medieval mysticism that had been articulated prominently by the reforming Cistercian, Bernard of Clairvaux. (Psst! Even Luther talked about union with Christ this way.) To be united to Christ, who is the bridegroom of the soul, requires taking up the cross of suffering on his behalf: "Embrace the cross your Spouse has carried and understand that this must be your task. Let the one who can do so suffer more for Him, and she will be rewarded that much more."[30] No doubt Teresa's book compels interest across traditions because it emphasizes the goal of the Christian life that is shared by all Christians: to be united with God eternally.

Matteo Ricci (1552–1610) was an Italian Jesuit priest who worked as a missionary in China. He is remembered for his cultural sensitivity, wearing the clothing of a Chinese scholar and growing a beard, and mastering Chinese in speech and writing. In 1601, Ricci became the first European allowed to live in Beijing during the Ming dynasty and converted the elite group of scholars and officials known as the "mandarins." Ricci's success ushered in a golden age of Christianity in China at the close of the Qing dynasty. Goodwill led to missionary Johann Adam Schall's becoming the first Jesuit to meet with a Chinese emperor.

For its safekeeping, the manuscript of *Interior Castle* was taken to Seville, the locus of reform, as it turned out, for both the Protestant and Catholic movements in Spain. There it found a home with the Discalced Carmelite nuns of Seville, where it resides to this day.

Shot through the Heart

Teresa's religious life involved fantastic, spiritual experiences, including trances, visions, and raptures leading her to union with Christ. Gian Lorenzo Bernini's sculpture *The Ecstasy of St. Teresa* (1647–52) captures a moment that she recounts of being pierced in the heart by an arrow. In chapter 20 of her autobiography, she describes in detail the different experiences of union and rapture (or levitation, "flight of the spirit," or transport).[31]

Although her experiences were not always received without question (and she even writes of her shame when involuntary ecstasies took over her in public), Teresa is an example of how mysticism provided a means of authority for religious women in the church that was both mystical and spiritual. Along her journey, Teresa read and was shaped by the life and visions of fourteenth-century mystic Catherine of Siena (1347–80). The next generation would be shaped by Teresa thanks to the translation of her work into multiple languages and her canonization in 1622 by Pope Gregory XV. Since 1970, her ministry gained prominence in the Roman Catholic Church when Pope Paul VI declared her to be a doctor of the church, making her the first woman in church history to be named as such. Her life of prayer and mystical experiences have informed Christian theology and practice within Rome's church and beyond. Her work is a helpful reminder of the diversity of theology that developed during the Reformation era, something that only expanded during the modern period.

Discussion Questions

1. One of Teresa of Avila's most significant contributions involves a theology and practice of prayer in the Christian life. What is the purpose of prayer, and how should we practice it?
2. Can you think of a time when you felt the presence of God? What did you learn from that experience?
3. Chastity and singleness have been important marks of Christian testimony throughout the church's history. How can they be values for the church today?

Further Reading

Teresa of Avila, *Teresa of Avila: The Interior Castle*, Classics of Western Spirituality (Paulist, 1980).

Robert L. Gallagher and Edward L. Smither, eds., *Sixteenth-Century Mission: Explorations in Protestant and Roman Catholic Theology and Practice* (Lexham, 2021).

George E. Ganss, ed., *Ignatius of Loyola: The Spiritual Exercises and Selected Works*, Classics of Western Spirituality (Paulist, 1991).

PART 4

MODERN
THEOLOGIANS

CHAPTER 13

THE WESLEY BROTHERS

PRAYER

O most holy God, for the passion of your Son, I beseech you to accept your poor prodigal, prostrating himself before your door now. I have fallen from you by my iniquity, and I am by nature a son of death and a child of hell by my sinful actions. But by your infinite grace you have promised mercy to me in Christ if I will but turn to you with all my heart. Therefore, upon the call of your gospel, I am now come, and throwing down my weapons, I submit myself to your mercy.

—John Wesley[1]

Here Come the Pastor's Kids

During the Age of Enlightenment, John Wesley (1703–91) and his younger brother, Charles (1707–88), became the instigators of spiritual renewal within the Church of England. Their ministry led to the establishment of Methodism, one of the most important global Protestant traditions today. The Wesley brothers grew up as pastor's kids in Epworth, England. Their father, Samuel Wesley (1662–1735), was a rector in the Church of England,

and their mother, Susanna Wesley (1669–1742), was a pastor's daughter before becoming a pastor's wife. In the brothers' formative years and into adulthood, their mother was a steady influence as spiritual mentor and educator and is often referred to as "the mother of Methodism."

Having been raised in a Puritan home, Susanna was equipped to offer lessons to her children in theology as well as biblical and classical languages (Greek and Latin). She held Sunday evening prayer and devotionals for the family when her husband was away. Gatherings ballooned to around two hundred in attendance before Samuel wrote her with concern.[2] Susanna's reply alluded to the parable of the talents and her commitment to being a good steward of her gifts for the sake of Christ. That stewardship is seen especially through the extended letters that she wrote to John and Charles over matters of Christian faith and practice.

Susanna's letters to her children are filled with rich theological and biblical teachings, including a commentary she wrote on the Apostles' Creed.[3] In it she explores questions of human anthropology, the impact of the fall, and God's redemptive design. Enlightenment-era concerns for human happiness and reason are woven into her theological questions and insights.[4] It was she who emphasized the Holy Spirit as spurring believers to Christian perfection and the necessity of directing one's "time and powers in working out their salvation, and making their own calling and election sure."[5] She was deeply grieved by the doctrine of predestination as an affront to God's justice and goodness and spoke negatively about "rigid Calvinists."[6] In these ways and more, Susanna's fingerprints are evident in the formation and output of the Wesley brothers' ministry and theology.

Oh, Holy Club

In the 1720s, the Wesley brothers began their studies at Christ Church College at the University of Oxford, where they earned graduate and postgraduate degrees as well as received ordination as priests in the Church of England. In 1729, Charles established a student group that pursued the pious life with a heavy emphasis on sanctification and which came to be called the "Holy Club." John was made fellow at Lincoln College that year and took over the leadership of the club. George Whitefield (1714–70), who later became a prominent Calvinist preacher in England and North America, also participated in the club. The group met early every morning for worship and practiced regular prayer times throughout the day. They were attentive to ministering to the poor, orphaned, and imprisoned, concerns that carried over into their formal ministries. Fasting and communion were also common practices. Instead of admiration, the club was met with ridicule by peers at Oxford over their methodical treatment of holiness, and so the name "Methodists" was born.

The Countess of Huntingdon, **Selina Hastings** (1707–91), embraced Methodism in 1739 and appointed George Whitefield as her personal chaplain.[7] In her drawing room, an eighteenth-century "sermonic society" flourished.[8] In addition to her financial support of Moravian missions, theological institutions, and orphanages, the countess built and endowed upwards of sixty chapels to promote opportunities for Methodist preaching.[9] The network came to be known as "Lady Huntingdon's Connexion," and Calvinistic Methodism was born.[10]

And Can It Be That I Should Gain?

The year 1735 proved to be an important milestone in the lives of the Wesley brothers as they set sail on the *Simmonds* for the new British colony of Georgia in North America. John recounted in his journal their early morning prayer, Bible study, preaching, and study of the church fathers. During that fruitful voyage, Charles wrote hymns that are well known today.

Upon landing in Georgia, the brothers began a ministry to Native Americans in Savannah.[11] Unfortunately, John's decision to enter into a romantic relationship with the niece of a judge in the colony put his ministry in jeopardy when the relationship ended in breakup rather than marriage. After the niece married another man, John refused to serve her communion, and she ended up suing him for defamation of character. A few months later, he was back in England, troubled and defeated. His was not the happy return of a successful ministry. But in that low point, a group of Moravians transformed Wesley's life.

The Moravians were a prominent part of the Wesley brothers' tapestry of faith and life. A group of them led by August Gottlieb Spangenberg were present on the brothers' journey to Georgia, and John admired their collective calm in the face of turbulent waters and stormy weather. They were descendants of Czech protoreformer Jan Hus and his followers, the Hussites, or Bohemian Brethren. The remnant that survived the Thirty Years' War (1618–48) were displaced by Catholic rulers until they found refuge under the patronage of Nikolaus Ludwig Graf von Zinzendorf (1700–1760). Zinzendorf inherited an estate in Saxony near Bohemia, and in 1722, he allowed the Moravians to establish a village there, which they named Herrnhut. They were among the first Protestants to prioritize global missions in the West Indies, Greenland, South Africa, and the Caribbean. Peter Böhler (1712–75) established the first Moravian church in Britain (called the Fetter Lane Society) and challenged the Wesley brothers to seek the assurance of their salvation.

On May 24, 1738, John begrudgingly attended a society meeting at Aldersgate Street, London. And yet, during a reading of Martin Luther's preface to Romans, a transformation of his heart took place that he described as his first experience of assurance of his salvation. In a famous passage he writes, "About a quarter before nine, while he was describing the change which God works in the heart through faith in Christ, I felt my heart strangely warmed. I felt I did trust in Christ, Christ alone for salvation; And an assurance was given me, that he had taken away *my* sins, even *mine*, and saved *me* from the law of sin and death."[12] As it was so often for the Wesley brothers, Charles too had just days before experienced a similar assurance of his salvation and renewal of faith after reading Luther's commentary on Galatians. To mark the one-year anniversary of that experience, he wrote one of his famous hymns, "O for a Thousand Tongues to Sing."

After a trip to Herrnhut and Halle to connect with the Pietists and Moravians there, John was invited to join George Whitefield's open-air preaching ministry in Bristol. By preaching outside, John provocatively challenged the classism of church attendance by bringing church to the poor. On April 2, 1739, in a field in Bristol known as "the Glasshouse," John preached his first open-air sermon at four o'clock in the afternoon to about three thousand people. Proclaiming Jesus' words from Luke 4, John and Charles began their itinerant ministry. Around this time, John also learned of the ministry of Puritan preacher and theologian Jonathan Edwards (1703–58) and the revivals that were taking place. A great awakening was afoot.[13]

Over the course of his ministry, John rode more than two hundred thousand miles on horseback and preached forty thousand sermons. His organizational leadership led to the formation of groups (societies, bands, classes) that met regularly and under spiritual direction. Women had a prominent role in these settings. In 1787, John authorized the first woman to preach at a Methodist conference, Sarah Mallet (1764–1846).[14] His appeal to a so-called extraordinary call opened the door for female leadership and their pastoral contributions in Methodism despite contemporary social pressures to maintain female propriety and opposition by male preachers.[15] In 1743, John published rules to guide the movement, though it was not until his death that Methodism separated from the Church of England in 1795.

Jonathan Edwards (1703–58) was a Calvinist pastor and theologian in Northampton, Massachusetts, when spiritual revival broke out. George Whitefield's arrival and preaching then extended and enlivened the First Great Awakening (c. 1730–55) throughout the American colonies. Edwards is often remembered for his sermon "Sinners in the Hands of an Angry God" (1741), but he was also a supporter of the doctrine of predestination and taught on affections and beauty in relation to faith. He eventually became president of what later became Princeton University, but he died of smallpox shortly after assuming the role.

Soldiers of Christ, Arise

Any consideration of the Wesley brothers' ministry and theology requires recognition of their place in the Enlightenment, which was characterized by confidence in human reason and scientific advancement, as well as concern for political liberty, human happiness, morality, and religious toleration. Theological and philosophical debates intersected with concern for miracles (see David Hume on miracles), the Trinity, and the problem of evil (or Gottfried Leibniz's "theodicy"). Can we know God simply by observing the natural laws of the world and using our reason, or do we require divine revelation? That was the question.

Although the Enlightenment is most often equated with a radical rejection of religion, not every Enlightenment figure was a materialist, atheist, or rationalist like Dutch Jewish philosopher Benedict Spinoza (1632–77). The religious Enlightenment[16] treated faith and reason as complementary (though God's reason always transcends human reason), while special revelation (Scripture) was deemed necessary. Similarly, Wesley claimed the need for Scripture, but not to the detriment of exploring God's creation with an eye for scientific understanding.[17] Faith and reason served as companions rather than enemies, and his letters and writings are filled with observations of natural science and mechanistic philosophy.[18] His ministry included establishing free medical centers and promoting the cutting-edge science of electrotherapy.[19] As his theology developed, it came to be described as rooted in Scripture and instructed by tradition, reason, and experience (known as the "Wesleyan Quadrilateral").[20]

Wesley's theology was also shaped by Dutch theologian Jacobus Arminius (1560–1609), who had studied under Reformer

Theodore Beza at Geneva's Academy. Beza's teachings on the doctrine of predestination, particularly on the idea of "supral-apsarianism" and limited atonement (that prior to the fall, God eternally elects only some people) became a sticking point with his student Arminius. At the Synod of Dort (1618), these matters were debated, and five-point Calvinism was born. Arminius emphasized the importance of freely accepting or rejecting the gospel, thanks to the gift of prevenient grace. This synergistic view of salvation distinguished Wesley from Calvinist contemporaries like Edwards and Whitefield.

In 1773, Wesley's *Predestination Calmly Considered* affirmed that God's grace restores free will to fallen humanity. Election, then, is rooted in God's foreknowledge of humanity's exercise of free will, rather than based on God's will alone. Wesley stressed rebirth in Christ and the potential for accomplishing Christian perfection in the heart through "entire sanctification" according to God's love and power. Though he denied the Lutheran doctrine of forensic justification (the idea that God regards us "as if" we are righteous, even though we are still sinful), Wesley rooted the assurance of salvation in Christ's righteousness and sacrifice on the cross. For Wesley, justification is the forgiveness of sins, and followers actually become righteous by the work of the Holy Spirit.

Holy, Holy, Holy

Wesley's *A Plain Account of Christian Perfection* (1777) grapples with Scripture's teachings on Christian perfection.[21] Although Wesley believed that entire sanctification is possible, he also nuanced the concept in important ways. For one, he clarified that he was not equating Christian perfection with God's absolute perfection. There is a difference between humans saved by Christ and Christ himself. Moreover, Christian perfection does not entail perfect health, knowledge, or a life free of temptation. And because Wesley denied the perseverance of the saints, that also meant that Christian perfection can be lost.

For Wesley, Christian perfection is the state of a believer governed by "perfect love in all things" and therefore living into holiness. Wesley offered several approaches for this. He described the importance of adopting the mind of Christ in both an inward and outward way (Eph. 4:23).[22] He also stressed the need for a circumcised heart (Rom. 2:29), since the true sacrifice that God desires is our hearts, which should "be continually offered up to God through Christ, in flames of holy love."[23] In addition, a mark of Christian perfection is the reception of a "double blessing" or "second blessing." The first gift is the forgiveness of sins from Christ, and the second is receiving the Holy Spirit.[24] Finally, Christian perfection entails being without outward and inward sin.[25] Entire sanctification requires fulfilling all of God's commands (Rom. 13:10). Thus, Wesley writes, "A Methodist is one who loves the Lord his God with all his heart, with all his soul, with all his mind, and with all his strength."[26] At a time when the Enlightenment was interested in religion's value as a moral compass necessary for human civilization, this teaching fit the cultural moment beautifully.

The outworking of Wesley's faith was evident in the way his preaching sought to reach the poor and prisoners, as well as in the social welfare policies that he maintained. He campaigned against slavery, and he advocated for temperance and the education of children. His *Thoughts upon Slavery* (1774) condemned the treatment of enslaved Africans, affirmed their full humanity, and rallied readers to help abolish slavery. Wesley's combination of evangelism *and* social activism contributed to the successful abolition of slavery in the coming century by way of the Second Great Awakening (1790–1830) and through the social gospel movement's attention to social issues.[27] This confluence of interests in evangelism and social transformation, informed by Pietism, forms the historic roots of evangelicalism.[28] Indeed, there is a through line from Presbyterian minister and revivalist Charles Finney (1792–1875) to later evangelists such as Dwight L. Moody, Billy Sunday, and Billy Graham, leading all the way to the establishment of the Lausanne Congress on World Evangelization in 1974.

Wesley's approach to theology, ministry, and piety also opened the door for the Holiness traditions led by American revivalist Phoebe Palmer (1807–74) and her teachings on "personal Pentecost" or "Spirit baptism," as well as the practice of the "holiness altar invitation."[29] Her revival ministry and popular writings are attributed with influencing the emergence of the Church of the Nazarene, the Salvation Army, the Keswick movement of Britain, and the Pentecostal and charismatic movements in the modern era.

William Wilberforce (1759–1833) was an English politician turned evangelical. He was the premier advocate in parliament for the abolition of slavery. In 1807, An Act for the Abolition of the Slave Trade was passed because of Wilberforce's efforts, but slavery was not abolished in England until the year of his death. Over the course of his campaign, he collaborated with former slave trader **John Newton** (who wrote the hymn "Amazing Grace" in 1773) and influential writer and abolitionist **Hannah More** (1745–1833).[30]

Come, Thou Long Expected Jesus

With the Wesley brothers at the helm, Methodism spread to Ireland, Scotland, Wales, and then across the Atlantic to North America before expanding worldwide through Protestant missions. Charles' composition of more than ten thousand hymns for congregational singing, many of which crossed the aisle of Protestant traditions, profoundly contributed to that expansion. By the end of the nineteenth century, Methodism numbered more than thirty million adherents on six different continents.[31]

In North America, Methodism as a movement began to develop in the 1760s through the efforts of Francis Asbury (1745–1816), an English Methodist missionary to America, called "the Father of American Methodism." The Methodist movement was formally organized as the Methodist Episcopal Church in 1784, and Thomas Coke (1747–1814) was its first bishop. Among African Americans, the formerly enslaved Richard Allen (1760–1831) and Absolom Jones (1746–1818) founded a separate congregation in 1787 in Philadelphia. By 1816, the African Methodist Episcopal (AME) Church was born, and Allen was installed as its first bishop. Nearly a hundred years later, the emphasis on the outworking of the Holy Spirit was powerfully seen in Los Angeles, California, with the Azusa Street Revival of April 9, 1906. African American preacher William J. Seymour (1870–1922) had begun a series of meetings that ended up drawing attendees from New York, London, Australia, South Africa, and many other places. Revival and the outpouring of the Holy Spirit in that moment and around the world launched Pentecostalism, which has more than 600 million adherents today, and counting.[32] A similar revival took place at Asbury

University in Wilmore, Kentucky, in 2023, drawing people from around the country and the globe. What started with a club at Oxford has become a worldwide movement rooted in the Holy Spirit. But Wesley was not alone in being profoundly shaped by the tradition of Pietism. So too was a nineteenth-century German theologian.

Korean **Yun Chi-ho** (1867–1945) was baptized while attending a school in Shanghai led by the United States Methodist Episcopal Church of the South. When the Southern Methodist missionaries arrived at his urging, he was likened to the Macedonian man of Acts 16:9. He attended the World Missionary Conference in Edinburgh (1910), where he bore witness to the thriving of Christianity in Korea. The Pyongyang Revival or Korean Pentecost of 1907 had contributed to the expansion of Protestantism in the region. **Kil Sun-ju** (1865–1935) was instrumental in leading revival and resisting Japanese colonization. He was one of the first ministers of the newly established Presbyterian Church of Korea.[33]

Discussion Questions

1. How does congregational singing shape Christian formation and worship? Reflect on the words of one of Charles Wesley's hymns.
2. Read Ephesians 1 and discuss its implications for the doctrine of predestination. What are some of the theological complexities that make this a difficult topic?

3. In the Sermon on the Mount, Jesus challenges us, saying, "Be perfect, therefore, as your heavenly Father is perfect" (Matt. 5:48). How do we reconcile this teaching with the reality of human sin in the Christian life?

Further Reading

Jeffrey W. Barbeau, *The Spirit of Methodism: From the Wesleys to a Global Communion* (IVP Academic, 2019).

Kyle C. Strobel, Adriaan C. Neele, and Kenneth P. Minkema, eds., *Jonathan Edwards: Spiritual Writings* (Paulist, 2019).

Randy L. Maddox and Jason E. Vickers, eds., *The Cambridge Companion to John Wesley* (Cambridge Univ. Press, 2009).

John Wesley, *John and Charles Wesley: Selected Writings and Hymns*, ed. Frank Whaling (Paulist, 1981).

CHAPTER 14

FRIEDRICH SCHLEIERMACHER

PRAYER

May God help us that we all may be true followers of Christ and not be ashamed of his holy life but follow the Lamb of God where he goes, so that he might lead us to the living water of life and wash away all tears from our eyes. Amen.

—Johann Arndt[1]

Theology on the Pendulum

The history of theology has often been marked by great pendulum swings. Periods of renewal that bring changes to the church are followed by eras seeking to clarify and codify those changes, which are in turn followed by periods of further reform. Particular doctrines are debated and refined in the midst of great controversy, then nearly forgotten, only to come roaring back under new circumstances. Appeals are made to one theological source over another, then the neglected source returns with greater urgency. This pattern can be seen in the life and thought of Friedrich Schleiermacher, a nineteenth-century German Reformed theologian, whose emphasis on experience in his theology reflected pendulum swings that predated him and was itself part of such a movement.

There would have been no Schleiermacher without Pietism, which emerged in the seventeenth century in response to the era of confessionalization. Following the tumult of the sixteenth-century Reformation, developing theological traditions in the Western branch of the church sought to clarify or institutionalize their doctrine and practices. This was often done by writing confessions, which formalized and summarized a tradition's beliefs. These statements were written within each major tradition: for the Anabaptists, the Schleitheim Confession (1527); for the Lutherans, the Augsburg Confession (1530); for Roman Catholics, the Council of Trent (1545–63); for Anglicans, the Thirty-Nine Articles (1571); and for Reformed Christians, there were several such confessions, including the Gallic (French) Confession (1559), the Scots Confession (1560), the Belgic Confession (1561), the Heidelberg Catechism (1563), the Second Helvetic (Swiss) Confession (1566), and the Westminster Confession (1646). While such statements helpfully clarified a tradition's beliefs and practices, they also tended to highlight contemporary theological disputes (for example, the Synod of Dort in 1618–19, a Reformed response to Arminian views) and even contributed to open conflict (such as the Thirty Years' War from 1618–48). In addition, concerns arose over the amount of attention dedicated toward ensuring right thinking. What about right practice? After all of these theological disputes and military battles, one might have asked, Where was Jesus?

In response, Pietism sought to bring an authentic Christian experience back to the faith. Its origin is traced to Johann Arndt (1555–1621), whose *Four Books on True Christianity* (1605) greatly influenced Philipp Jackob Spener (1635–1705). Spener, who is regarded as "the father of Pietism," was a pastor in Frankfurt when he published *Pia Desideria* (1675), which came to define the movement. In his effort to restore "true religion," Spener emphasized the inner life of the believer, piety through personal devotion, and the study of the Bible in conventicles or small groups. Though these gatherings were intended only to supplement life in the church rather than replace it, they came to be perceived as a threat to the established church, as well as socially subversive in the mingling of different social classes. For these Pietists, or "heart Christians," as they were known, personal piety, the experience of conversion by the Holy Spirit, and daily discipleship were far more important than debating and clarifying theological dogma.

Another important feature of Spener's work was his emphasis on the universal priesthood. Through works such as the *Spiritual Priesthood* (1677), he sought to restore Martin Luther's ideal of the "priesthood of all believers," which Spener thought had been left behind in the retreat to the ivory tower of Protestant scholasticism. His teaching thus empowered the active leadership and participation of women in pastoral roles, as seen in the life of Johanna Eleonora von Merlau (1644–1724). Spener was also instrumental in the founding of the University of Halle in 1694, which became the center of Pietist thinking. Like Peter's desire to build tents for Moses and Elijah when he witnessed Jesus' transfiguration (Matt. 17:4), there is always, it seems, the yearning to institutionalize and to make things last, even for a movement that began by pushing back on overly concrete expressions of faith.

Later expressions of Pietism are found in the work of August Hermann Francke (1663–1727), who taught at Halle—after being forced to leave his position at Leipzig—and was particularly known for his care of orphaned children, and Nicholas Ludwig von Zinzendorf (1700–60), who was Spener's godson. Educated at Halle, Zinzendorf was instrumental in revitalizing the Moravian Brethren, who later were formative in warming John Wesley's heart. Thus, although Pietism was first rooted within the Lutheran tradition, this "second Reformation" eventually became a transnational and transconfessional movement.

And it was the legacy of this theological tradition into which Friedrich Daniel Ernst Schleiermacher was born.

Catherine Booth (1829–90) was the cofounder of the Salvation Army, a church and charitable organization. Born as Catherine Mumford to Methodist parents, she was involved in the temperance movement before she met and married **William Booth** (1829–1912), a lay Methodist preacher. Encouraged by her reading of Scripture and the example of Phoebe Palmer (1807–74), a Methodist evangelist, Catherine became more involved in the ministry of the church. Along with her husband, she cofounded the Christian Mission in the east end of London in 1865, which sought out those most in need. It was later renamed the Salvation Army in 1878, and she is remembered as the "Mother of the Salvation Army."

Can't Stop the Feeling

As with any period, the theology of the nineteenth century was influenced by the social, political, economic, and historical factors of its time. The so-called long nineteenth century is said to have begun with the French Revolution (1789–99) and ended with World War I (1914–18). Between these bookends can be found events such as the conquests of Napoleon Bonaparte (1769–1821), the Industrial Revolution, the publication of Charles Darwin's *On the Origin of Species* (1859), and the American Civil War (1861–65). In many ways, the nineteenth century can be viewed as a reaction to the Enlightenment appeals to reason from the previous century. Seeing the limitations and the effects of human reason, nineteenth-century thinkers preferred instead to appeal to humanity's inner experience. This inward turn is reflected in Romanticism, which, broadly speaking, elevated emotion, individualism, intuition, and feeling. Artistically, these themes are found in the words of Goethe, Wordsworth, and Coleridge, the music of Beethoven, and the painting of Friedrich, Turner, and Delacroix. Theologically, they are most clearly represented in the theology of Friedrich Schleiermacher (1768–1834), the church's most significant theologian of the nineteenth century.

Often regarded as "the father of modern theology" and "the father of liberal Protestantism," Schleiermacher came from a long line of Reformed ministers. His father, Gottlieb, served as chaplain to the Prussian army and had encountered the Moravians. Schleiermacher himself attended a Moravian school and held a variety of positions—including as a private tutor, a pastor, and a hospital chaplain—before teaching theology at the University of Halle and then, from 1810 until his death in 1834, at the University of Berlin. Schleiermacher's writings reflect a wide range of interests, including hermeneutics, philosophy (he translated Plato's works), New Testament studies, ethics, psychology, and, of course, theology. Throughout his work, Schleiermacher engaged with classical Christian beliefs (including creeds and confessions across traditions), but he often reconfigured them or applied new terminology in light of the questions that had been raised about the credibility of the faith during the Enlightenment.

This method is clearly demonstrated in one of Schleiermacher's notable early works, *On Religion: Speeches to Its Cultured Despisers* (1799), which he wrote for some of his avant-garde friends in the German Romanticism movement. In it he defended religion, but he did so by redefining some of its basic concepts in such a way that would make it more appealing to the spirit of the age. For example, he defined religion as "essentially contemplative," such that theological doctrines "are all the result of that contemplation of feeling."[2] He thus cast a wide net for his definition of revelation: "Every intuition and every original feeling proceeds from revelation."[3] Similarly, he regarded *miracle* as a term that could be applied to everything: "Every event, even the most natural and usual, becomes a miracle, as soon as the religious view of it can be the dominant. To me all is miracle. . . . The more religious you are, the more miracle would you see everywhere."[4] Once again, the conversation had been set by the Enlightenment (see, for example, David Hume's rejection of miracles), but rather than rejecting the possibility of miracles, Schleiermacher flipped it on its head by regarding everything as in some sense a miracle.

Schleiermacher's magnum opus, however, was *Christian Faith* (*Glaubenslehre*, 1821–22), which encapsulated his theological emphasis on feeling. In it, we see the full flourishing of what has been described as Schleiermacher's "theology of consciousness."[5] Central to his thinking is the notion that religion is itself a feeling: "The piety that constitutes the basis of all ecclesial communities, regarded purely in and of itself, is neither a knowing nor a doing but a distinct formation of feeling."[6] According to Schleiermacher, religion is a "feeling of absolute dependence" on God, or what he calls "God-consciousness."[7] In its current state, humanity experiences both a relative freedom (or self-consciousness) and a feeling of absolute dependence (or God-consciousness), and these are "interwoven within and alongside each other."[8] For Schleiermacher, sin is that which inhibits the God-consciousness and creates instead a condition of "God-forgetfulness."[9]

Most important, Schleiermacher's response to humanity's condition is found in Christ, for "within Christianity everything is referred to the redemption accomplished through Jesus of Nazareth."[10] But what he means by Christ and salvation through Christ is not what the church has historically meant when employing those terms. Schleiermacher identifies four "natural heresies" with regard to the person and work of Christ: the docetic (which denies his full humanity), the Nazarean (which denies his full divinity), the Manichean, and the Pelagian.[11] At the same time, Schleiermacher specifically rejects the use of the term *natures* to describe the union of the human and the divine in the one person of Christ.[12] Instead, for Schleiermacher, Christ is ultimately the one who possesses a perfect God-consciousness. But what about salvation?

Schleiermacher describes salvation as the *experience* of redemption through Christ, who brings about a change in one's self-consciousness and enables the development of God-consciousness: "The nature of redemption consists in the fact that the previously weak and suppressed God-consciousness in human nature is raised and brought to the point of dominance through Christ's entrance into it and vital influence upon it."[13] Schleiermacher's theology of salvation is thus a significant departure from classical articulations of what it means to be saved by Christ, whether Calvinistic, Anselmian, Augustinian, or even Pauline: "Redemption does not depend upon the atoning death of Jesus of Nazareth but on the perfection of his God-consciousness."[14] For Schleiermacher, there is also a communal dimension to the experience of salvation: "We are conscious of all approximations to the condition of blessedness that are present in the Christian life as being grounded in a new, divinely wrought collective life."[15]

Another notable feature of *Christian Faith*—and one that has engendered much criticism—is Schleiermacher's location of the doctrine of the Trinity in the conclusion to the text.

Søren Kierkegaard (1813–55) was a Danish Lutheran philosopher and theologian who is considered to be the founder of modern existentialism. Born into an affluent family, Kierkegaard studied at the University of Copenhagen. Several of his works, including *Either/Or* (1843), *Fear and Trembling* (1843), and *The Sickness unto Death* (1849), were published under pseudonyms. In his *Attack upon "Christendom"* (1854–55), Kierkegaard was critical of what he perceived to be people's complacency toward their faith in the "Christian nation" of Denmark. Kierkegaard believed that lives could be categorized into three kinds: the aesthetic, which seeks only immediate gratification; the ethical, which is concerned with fulfilling obligations to others; and the religious, which is guided by a love that finds its source in God.

Many, including Karl Barth, would critique Schleiermacher for his relegation of the discussion of the Trinity to the end of his systematic theology and for limiting it to a mere twenty pages. For his part, Schleiermacher called it "the copestone of Christian doctrine" (a reference to a stone that is placed along the peak of a sloping roofline), suggesting that it was the culmination of his theological reflection.[16] But his decision also reflects a willingness to downplay certain aspects of traditional Christian orthodoxy. With its appeal to individual experience, its use of new terminology, and its departures from classic Christian articulations, Schleiermacher's theology is a decidedly modern expression of the faith.

(Post)Modernizing Theology

Schleiermacher's attention to human experience in his theology was reflective of increased concerns for human well-being and flourishing, not just spiritual but physical well-being. For example, the social gospel movement in late-nineteenth- and early-twentieth-century North America sought to address a number of issues, including poverty, race relations, alcoholism, the environment, education, and labor laws. With an optimism concerning humanity's capacities, this movement sought to bring about the kingdom of God on earth through social action, as seen in the ministry of Walter Rauschenbusch (1861–1918), a Baptist pastor and theologian. Undergirding this movement was a postmillennial theology, which held that the return of Christ would take place through the efforts of the church to combat social and structural sin.

Schleiermacher's influence can be seen directly in the work of Paul Tillich (1886–1965), a German Lutheran theologian, minister, and philosopher. Tillich, who was born the same year as Karl

Barth, studied at several universities, including the University of Berlin, the University of Tübingen, the University of Halle, and the University of Breslau before serving as a chaplain in the army during World War I. He began a teaching career after the war, but he was forced to flee from his native Germany with the rise of the Nazi party. He immigrated to the United States, where he taught at Union Theological Seminary in New York, Harvard Divinity School, and the University of Chicago. Theologically speaking, Tillich is particularly known for his "method of correlation," which begins "from below" with the human condition, from which existential questions of ultimate meaning arise. For Tillich, such questions could be answered only by the Christian faith: "In using the method of correlation, systematic theology proceeds in the following way: it makes an analysis of the human situation out of which the existential questions arise, and it demonstrates that the symbols used in the Christian message are the answers to these questions."[17] Tillich's existentialist methodology led him to affirm God as the "ground of being"[18] and Jesus Christ as the "New Being."[19] While the terminology was different, Tillich's methodology and the questions that arise from existential angst resonate with and demonstrate the influence of Schleiermacher's work.

Some, however, pushed back. German philosopher Ludwig Feuerbach (1804–72), for example, critiqued the appeal to experience: "Theology is anthropology. . . . [M]an's God is nothing other than the deified essence of man, so that the history of religion or, what amounts to the same thing, of God . . . is nothing other than the history of man."[20] While Feuerbach's response to the problem that he identified was a wholesale rejection of the faith, others sought to preserve the faith by swinging the pendulum back to more classical expressions.

Abraham Kuyper (1837–1920) was a Dutch neo-Calvinist pastor and theologian, whose wide-ranging interests and accomplishments included founding a denomination, starting a newspaper, founding the Free University, and serving as the prime minister of the Netherlands from 1901 to 1905. Among the features of his theology (and the Kuyperian tradition named after him) are the "cultural mandate," which calls humanity to make culture (based on a reading of Gen. 1:28); the affirmation of "common grace," which all people receive and according to which one might potentially find God's truth anywhere; and "sphere sovereignty," which affirms that while each sphere of life has its goals and responsibilities, Christ rules over them all: "There is not a square inch in the whole domain of our human existence over which Christ, who is Sovereign over all, does not cry, 'Mine!'" (from his speech opening the Free University in 1880).[21] Many of his views are articulated in his *Lectures on Calvinism*, based on the 1898 Stone Lectures that he delivered at Princeton Theological Seminary. His theological legacy is marred by his racist attitudes toward Black people, which contributed to the policy of apartheid in the Dutch colonial rule of South Africa.

H. Richard Niebuhr, for example, offered this devastating critique of what he perceived to be the naive optimism of liberal Protestantism: "A God without wrath brought men without sin into a kingdom without judgment through the ministration of a Christ without a cross."[22] Though not entirely reflective of or fair to Schleiermacher's theology, Niebuhr's summary criticism points to the concerns that many shared.

But even among his critics, Schleiermacher has continued to cast a long shadow. Karl Barth, perhaps his most noted critic, was trained in the liberal Protestant tradition under scholars who were shaped by Schleiermacher's theology, including Wilhelm Herrmann (1846–1922) and Adolf von Harnack (1851–1930). Barth later agreed with Feuerbach's assessment of nineteenth-century theology as essentially an expression of anthropology, but his response was not to reject the faith, as Feuerbach had done, but rather to turn more explicitly to God's self-revelation in Christ. For Barth, this ultimately meant a break with Schleiermacher's theology, but he could never quite leave him behind. At one point, in *The Theology of Schleiermacher,* Barth reflected, "As to a clarification of my relationship to Schleiermacher, what I have occasionally contemplated for here and now . . . and what I have already intimated here and there to good friends, would be the possibility of a theology of the third article, in other words a theology predominantly and decisively of the Holy Spirit."[23] Schleiermacher's ongoing influence can be seen well into postmodern articulations of the faith. Meanwhile, Barth's work, which rethought the Christian faith through the lens of Jesus Christ, brought yet another pendulum swing in the history of theology.

Discussion Questions

1. How is your faith informed by statements such as creeds and confessions? Do you find them helpfully clarifying or unhelpfully limiting?
2. What benefits do you see to Schleiermacher's approach to theology? What potential drawbacks?

3. Read Psalm 51. What is the place of human experience and emotion in the Christian life?

Further Reading

Johann Arndt, *True Christianity* (Paulist, 1979).

James D. Bratt, ed., *Abraham Kuyper: A Centennial Reader* (Eerdmans, 1998).

Søren Kierkegaard, *Fear and Trembling* (Penguin, 1986).

Jacqueline Mariña, ed., *The Cambridge Companion to Friedrich Schleiermacher* (Cambridge Univ. Press, 2005).

Friedrich Schleiermacher, *Christian Faith*, two vols., ed. Catherine L. Kelsey and Terrence N. Tice (Westminster John Knox, 2016).

CHAPTER 15

KARL BARTH

PRAYER

O Sovereign God! You have humbled yourself in order to exalt us. You became poor so that we might become rich. You came to us so that we can come to you. You took upon yourself our humanity in order to raise us up to eternal life. All this comes through your grace, free and unmerited; all this through your beloved Son, our Lord and Savior, Jesus Christ. . . . Be present now in our midst, we pray. Through your Holy Spirit open for us the way to come to you, that we may see with our own eyes your light which has come into the world, and then in the living of our lives become your witnesses.

—Karl Barth[1]

A Theology Born in Crisis

In May 1934, a group of theologians, pastors, and church representatives gathered in Barmen, Germany, to address an existential threat to both the church and the world: the rise of the Nazi party. The stakes could not have been higher. While the German Christian movement was coopting the church through its alignment with National Socialist ideology, others resisted by forming what became known as the Confessing Church movement. Among those gathered in Barmen was Karl Barth, a Reformed pastor and theologian, who was from Switzerland but who had spent much of his life and teaching career in Germany. Barth, who was a professor of theology at Bonn at the time, had drafted what became the Barmen Declaration. Rejecting the identification of the church with anything other than those who confess Christ as Lord, the statement reads, in part, "Jesus Christ, as he is testified to us in Holy Scripture, is the one Word of God, which we are to hear, which we are to trust and obey in life and in death."[2] This statement, while written in response to a specific threat, also serves as a kind of summary of Barth's theology, which has cast a large shadow over modern theology. The gathering at Barmen was not the first time he had been forced to take a stand for his beliefs in the midst of crisis. Rather, the declaration was the fruit of Barth's thinking through the implications of God's self-revelation in Jesus Christ.

As a theologian, Karl Barth (1886–1968) was initially a product of the liberal Protestant theology that traced its roots to Friedrich Schleiermacher. Born in Basel, Switzerland, and the son of a theology professor and pastor, Barth studied at the University of Bern and then at several German institutions in the liberal Protestant tradition, which broadly emphasized the role of experience in theology: the University of Berlin (under Adolf von Harnack), the University of Tübingen, and the University of Marburg (under Wilhelm Herrmann). Following ordination and a brief stint as an assistant pastor in Geneva, Barth undertook a pastorate in Safenwil, a rural town in northern Switzerland.[3] He might have remained in this relatively obscure position, but everything changed for him—and the world—with the outbreak of World War I in 1914. To his dismay, Barth discovered that nearly all of his German professors had signed a manifesto supporting the German war effort. If this is where the liberal Protestant tradition leads us, Barth asked, then how could he follow it? He decided that he couldn't. Reflecting later on his feelings at the time, he wrote, "An entire world of theological exegesis, ethics, dogmatics, and preaching, which up to that point I had accepted as basically credible, was thereby shaken to the foundations, and with it everything which flowed at that time from the pens of the German theologians."[4]

Where would he turn instead? Barth found a familiar yet surprising source by turning to Scripture, where he rediscovered what he called "the strange new world" of the Bible.[5] His reading of Paul's letter to the church in Rome led Barth to write a commentary, *Der Römerbrief* (*The Epistle to the Romans*), the first edition of which was published in 1919 and was said to have "landed like a bomb on the playground of the theologians."[6] Informed by Kierkegaard's notion of the "infinite qualitative distinction" between God and humanity, Barth described God not as something naturally available to humanity but rather as the wholly other and transcendent God who comes into the world in Jesus Christ.[7] This dialectic—between God and humanity, between eternity and time—came to characterize not only Barth's theology "from above" but also the theologies of those loosely affiliated through the so-called neo-orthodox movement. While some, such as Paul Tillich, continued in Schleiermacher's tradition, theologians such as Emil Brunner, Eduard Thurneysen, Reinhold Niebuhr, and Dietrich Bonhoeffer collectively responded to liberal Protestantism's emphasis on human experience by affirming God's self-revelation in Jesus Christ.

Brothers **Reinhold Niebuhr** (1892–1971) and **H. Richard Niebuhr** (1894–1962) were American theologians. Their parents were German immigrants, and their father was a Protestant pastor. Both brothers studied at Elmhurst College, Eden Theological Seminary, and Yale University. After serving as the pastor of a German-speaking church in Detroit, Reinhold taught at Union Theological Seminary in New York for more than thirty years. As seen in *The Nature and Destiny of Man* (1943), he is particularly known for advancing "Christian realism," which rejected what he viewed as the naivete of the social gospel movement's utopian goal of establishing the kingdom of God on earth in favor of a philosophy that acknowledged humanity's original sin and dependence on God. Richard, who taught for decades at Yale Divinity School, is best known for *Christ and Culture* (1951), which presents five paradigms for understanding the relationship between Jesus Christ and culture. Their older sister, **Hulda Clara Niebuhr** (1889–1959), also became a theologian and taught at McCormick Theological Seminary in Chicago.

Despite the fact that he did not have a doctorate in theology, Barth was offered a professorship in Reformed theology at the University of Göttingen in Germany, where he taught from 1921 to 1925. There Barth wrote his first attempt at a systematic theology, the *Göttingen Dogmatics*, and he met Charlotte von Kirshbaum, who became a theological colleague for decades (a relationship that caused friction in his marriage to Nelly Barth). Later, Barth taught at the University of Münster (1925–30) and the University of Bonn (1930–35), where he began working on his

Church Dogmatics. His anti-Nazi stance was made plain during this time, not only with the writing of the Barmen Declaration but also in light of his refusal to pledge loyalty to Hitler before his lectures. Forced to leave Germany, Barth returned to his native Basel. He spent the rest of his life in the city where he had been born: teaching, preaching, serving as a chaplain in the prison, and working on his magnum opus, the *Church Dogmatics*. Barth's intention was to write a five-volume theology (each of which has multiple volumes). The first half volume was published in 1932. Although he published several more volumes over the subsequent decades, Barth died in 1968 before he could fulfill his vision. To his mind, the *Church Dogmatics* was like many of the church's cathedrals or Mozart's *Requiem*: an unfinished work that even in its imperfections—and those of its author—pointed to the truth.[8]

God Only Knows

Following his dramatic turn from liberal Protestantism and to God's self-revelation in Scripture, Barth came to view every doctrine through the lens of Jesus Christ. His highly Christocentric theology can be seen throughout the *Church Dogmatics*, beginning with the first volume. For example, Barth developed a doctrine of the threefold form of the Word of God akin to the concentric circles that form after one throws a rock into a lake. When we think about the Word of God, Barth argued, the first thing that we should think of is Jesus Christ, who is the Word of God made flesh (John 1:14), the revealed Word: "He is the Word of God. From Him alone it may and will be experienced what the Word of God is."[9] The next circle is the Bible, which is the written Word, a secondary form of the Word that witnesses to God's primary revelation in Christ. Barth's doctrine of Scripture reveals both his high regard for Scripture and the actualism (an emphasis on God's agency) that permeates his theology: "The Bible is God's Word to the extent that God causes it to be His Word, to the extent that He speaks through it."[10] Finally, the third circle is the proclamation of the church, the proclaimed Word, which seeks to be a faithful articulation of what God has revealed in Christ and Scripture.[11]

In keeping with his emphasis on God's self-revelation, Barth was a staunch opponent of natural theology, which he defined as any attempt on the part of humanity to know God apart from God's self-revelation in Christ and Scripture. For Barth, such a view undermines the necessity and uniqueness of God's self-revelation because it makes knowledge of God a natural possibility for humans. This led to a debate with Emil Brunner (1889–1966), a friend of Barth's and a fellow neo-orthodox theologian. Brunner had argued for a "point of contact" between God and humanity within our nature because humans are made in the image of God. Barth's published response was blunt: *Nein!* (1934). In his view, there was no such point of contact within human nature; if any point of contact exists, it was established by God.[12]

Another striking feature of Barth's earliest volume of the *Church Dogmatics* is his treatment of the doctrine of the Trinity. The doctrine had fallen into relative obscurity in modern theology, as evidenced by Schleiermacher's decision to place it near the end of *The Christian Faith*. But Barth decided to put it front and center. Before going on to discuss what God has done—in the act of creation, in the redemption of sinful humanity through the life, death, and resurrection of Christ, in establishing the church by the Holy Spirit—Barth identified who God is. The God proclaimed and worshiped by Christians is the triune God—Father, Son, and Holy Spirit. The Trinity is not an optional doctrine but rather an essential feature of the Christian faith: "The God who reveals Himself according to Scripture is One in three distinctive modes of being subsisting in their mutual relations: Father, Son, and Holy Spirit."[13] For his emphasis on this doctrine, Barth is often credited with contributing to a resurgence of interest in Trinitarian theology, which flourished throughout the twentieth century.

But Barth's greatest theological contribution may have been his christological reframing of the doctrine of election in the second volume of the *Church Dogmatics*. Within the Reformed tradition, John Calvin's affirmation of the doctrine of election included a so-called double predestination by which God elects some to salvation and condemns others.[14] For Barth, the good news of election—which he called "the sum of the Gospel"[15]—is that it applies, first and foremost, to Jesus Christ. In the first instance, Barth argued that Christ is both the God who elects and the human who is elected. He is both the subject and the object of election: "Thus the simplest form of the dogma may be divided at once into the two assertions that Jesus Christ is the electing God, and that He is also elected man."[16] In addition, Barth applied both aspects of God's agency in election to Christ such that Jesus is both the elected and the rejected. In Christ alone do we see both what it means to be rejected, "the Bearer of all man's sin and guilt and their ensuing punishment,"[17] and what it means to be elected: "It is strictly and narrowly only in the humanity of the one Jesus Christ that we can see who and what an elect person is."[18] For Barth, then, predestination is still "double," but rather than referring to the salvation of some and the condemnation of others, both aspects refer to Christ. Barth still affirms that there are both communal and individual aspects to divine election, but primarily it should be understood in light of Christ.

Dietrich Bonhoeffer (1906–45) was a German Lutheran pastor and theologian. After studying at the University of Tübingen and the Humboldt University of Berlin, Bonhoeffer studied at Union Theological Seminary in New York, where he was influenced by Reinhold Niebuhr and shaped by his experience in the Black church of Harlem. Bonhoeffer returned to Germany to teach at the University of Berlin, but following Hitler's rise to power, he became an influential voice alongside Barth and others in the Confessing Church movement. During this time, he led an underground seminary at Finkenwalde, which is remembered in his work *Life Together*. After briefly fleeing to the United States in 1939, he returned to Germany. But he was arrested and imprisoned in Tegel Prison, and later implicated in a failed plot to assassinate Hitler. He was executed at Flossenbürg concentration camp on April 9, 1945, just weeks before liberation of the camp. Though Bonhoeffer's life was cut tragically short, he still managed to produce many influential works, including *Act and Being*, *Ethics*, *The Cost of Discipleship*, and *Letters and Papers from Prison*. As evidenced by a statue at Westminster Abbey in London, many regard him as a modern-day Christian martyr.

Barth's christological reading of God's act of creation argued that while creation is the first of the triune God's works, it is not disconnected from the rest of salvation history. While deism holds that creation does not require God's ongoing relationship with the world, Barth affirmed God's providential care of creation: the God who creates is also the God who redeems. The way Barth expressed this was by affirming that creation is "the external basis of the covenant" (it is the means by which Jesus fulfills the covenant between God and humanity), and the covenant is "the internal basis of creation" (it is the goal, aim, purpose, and *telos* of creation).[19] Not only did Barth affirm that Christ takes part in creation (John 1:10; Col. 1:16; Heb. 1:2) but also he argued that Jesus defines what it means to be human. According to his christological anthropology, the questions of what it means to be God and what it means to be human are both answered in Jesus Christ. It is not a coincidence that Barth's theology has been described as one of the most thoroughly Chalcedonian theologies in the history of the church.[20]

A particularly noteworthy feature of the fourth volume of Barth's *Church Dogmatics*—which has a complex structure addressing themes of Christology, sin, grace, the work of the Holy Spirit, and the doctrine of the church—is his consideration of the historicity of the resurrection. Of course, the claim of Jesus' disciples that he had actually risen has been challenged since the first Easter morning. But the doctrine of Christ's bodily resurrection was especially challenged in the modern era by philosophers, such as Scottish philosopher David Hume (1711–76), who rejected it entirely. Similarly, theologian Rudolf Bultmann (1884–1976) argued—as part of his "demythologization" project, which sought to strip away those parts of Scripture he thought were unacceptable to modern minds—that the resurrection was just a subjective event.

The only thing that rose on that Sunday morning, Bultmann contended, was the faith of the disciples, not Christ himself. Barth responded to Bultmann by arguing that the resurrection is not a purely subjective event, as evidenced by the empty tomb. At the same time, he noted, it is not like other historical events—like Jesus' crucifixion—because it is beyond historical investigation. He thus used the category of "saga" (as he had done with regard to the event of God's act of creation) to argue that while it was unlike other historical events, it did really happen: Jesus truly rose again.[21]

Dorothy L. Sayers (1893–1957) was an English Anglican novelist, playwright, and lay theologian. The daughter of the chaplain of Christ Church Cathedral in Oxford, Sayers studied modern languages and medieval literature at Somerville College, Oxford. Sayers is popularly known for her series of detective stories featuring Lord Peter Wimsey. Her more explicitly theological and philosophical reflections are found in a variety of works: plays such as *The Zeal of Thy House* (1937); essays such as "Are Women Human?" (1938); a BBC radio series, *The Man Born to be King* (1941); *The Mind of the Maker* (1941), which presents a reading of the doctrine of the Trinity inspired by her experience as a writer; and her translation of Dante's *Divine Comedy*. She was also friends with C. S. Lewis, J. R. R. Tolkien, and other members of the Inklings (though she was not officially part of their literary group). She never met Barth in person, but she corresponded with him briefly after Barth, who admitted learning English through her fiction, translated one of her works, *The Greatest Drama Ever Staged*, into German.[22]

Near the end of his *Church Dogmatics*, Barth—perhaps matured by the years—argued that God can reveal himself beyond Jesus Christ. In keeping with the broader Reformed tradition, which has regularly emphasized both God's general revelation as well as the necessity of God's special revelation in Christ and Scripture, Barth affirmed the existence of what he called "secular parables." While still maintaining the absolute priority of God's self-revelation in Christ, Barth argued that in light of God's freedom, there might be "other true words" spoken *extra muros ecclesia*, outside the walls of the church.[23] Yet these words are known to be true only in relation to the Word of God, Jesus Christ: they are "true words, genuine witnesses and attestations of the one true Word, real parables of the kingdom of heaven" insofar as they point to Christ, or rather, to the extent that Christ "declares Himself in them."[24] Elsewhere, Barth, who was known to have a deep passion for Mozart's music, reminded his readers that "the New Testament speaks not only of the kingdom of heaven but also of *parables* of the kingdom of heaven."[25]

The Last Word

After his retirement in 1962, Barth traveled to the United States and visited several places, including Princeton, where he briefly met Martin Luther King Jr., Harlem, and Chicago. During a discussion at the University of Chicago, a student boldly asked Barth to summarize his theology in a few words. He reportedly replied, "In the words of a song my mother taught me when I was a child: 'Jesus loves me, this I know, for the Bible tells me so.'"

Shortly before his death in 1968, Barth recorded a radio program. In between listening to recordings of Mozart's music,

Barth discussed his life and his theology. He offered the following as a closing word: "The last word which I have to say as a theologian . . . is not a term like 'grace,' but a name, 'Jesus Christ.' . . . What I have been concerned to do in my long life has been increasingly to emphasize this name and to say: There is no salvation in any other name than this."[26] Affirming that Jesus Christ is "the last word" enabled Barth to respond to the challenges of his day. More recent theologians have sought to express their faith in Christ in fresh ways and for their own contexts, giving new breath to the last word.

Discussion Questions

1. Are there aspects of Scripture that make it seem like a "strange new world" to you?
2. Can you think of an example when your understanding of the Christian faith was shaped by a crisis?
3. How important is the doctrine of the Trinity to your faith?

Further Reading

Karl Barth, *The Epistle to the Romans*, trans. Edwyn C. Hoskyns, 6th ed. (Oxford Univ. Press, 1968).

Eberhard Busch, *Karl Barth: His Life from Letters and Autobiographical Texts*, trans. John Bowden (Eerdmans, 1976).

George Hunsinger, *How to Read Karl Barth: The Shape of His Theology* (Oxford Univ. Press, 1991).

Christiane Tietz, *Karl Barth: A Life in Conflict* (Oxford Univ. Press, 2021).

John Webster, *Karl Barth*, 2nd ed. (Continuum, 2000).

CHAPTER 16

GUSTAVO GUTIÉRREZ

PRAYER

> *Lord, in your mercy, help us to "consider every neighbor without exception as another self, taking into account first their lives and having the means necessary to live with dignity, so as not to imitate the rich man who had no concern for the poor man Lazarus." Amen.*
> —Adapted from Vatican II's "Pastoral Constitution on the Church in the Modern World"[1]

In My Place

It is impossible in this final chapter to capture the scope of the complexity and diversification that took place in Christian theology during the twentieth century. That story, with its deserved fullness, is multidenominational, global, multiethnic, and beyond what can be fully represented here. To acknowledge that limitation is no admission of oversight but a reflection of the expansive nature of the topic. (The very problem is illuminating!) A multiplicity of voices from spaces far and wide have destabilized standard narratives as well as enriched the dimensions of theology in new, challenging, and important ways. These contributions have set out not necessarily to launch something new but to reinterpret and reimagine how we draw rightly from the biblical witness and the classical doctrines of theology. To till the soil of theology has led to paradigm shifts both disorienting and generative. Gustavo Gutiérrez's theology of liberation plays a crucial role in that harvest even as we recognize that there are many more contributions to highlight both before and after him.

With broad strokes, the aftermath of World War II and the grief and shame surrounding the Holocaust and the genocide of six million Jews has been regarded as triggering concern for the contextuality or space each person inhabits and how that informs the way they make sense of the world.

In response, postmodern theology became concerned with creating space for new demographics to contribute formally to the discipline, though it has been a slow and imperfect process. In the field, the category of "contextual theology" was adopted as an umbrella description for Black, feminist, womanist (Black female), and liberation theologies, as well as more recently Mujarista (Latina), Asian American[2], and Indigenous theologies.[3] All theologies are and always have been contextualized, shaped by the social, cultural, political, and intellectual realities in which theologians find themselves. This has not always been recognized, but contextual theology has brought the issue to the forefront. Each of these approaches with their histories and perspectives has made significant contributions to theological study in their own right, but one of the shared trends among them is this strong attention to context. They also share likeminded theological trends, which can be highlighted.

As with the beauty of polyphonic liturgical music (or organum), our ears may identify among the chorus of voices recurring themes and shared cadences. Contextual theology is noticeably

Christocentric; the person and work of Jesus Christ is the crux of it all. In him are found the truest solidarity, rest, and freedom for those on the margins, because Jesus is not only fully God but also a cosufferer among humans as fully human. Contextual theology shies away from the idea of a disembodied, gnostic suffering and salvation to embrace a powerfully embodied Christ. The redemption that we receive from Christ is bodily and visceral, born of blood, sweat, tears, and death. Christ's bodily suffering is an expression of his compassion and his solidarity with the poor, marginalized, and all who suffer. At the same time, Jesus is also fully God, which means that his body is also the place of shared victory on behalf of those who suffer. The bodily resurrection of Christ is the victory over oppression that not only promises wholeness in the next life but also demands justice in the life that we live now.

But divine solidarity is offered not only through the second person of the Trinity. A social model of the Trinity is favored. This model contends with any slanted views of an authoritarian, hierarchical Father God who is aloof and untouchable in his perfection. On the contrary, contextual theology emphasizes the relational dynamics of the three persons—Father, Son, and Holy Spirit—as that of mutuality and interconnection (akin to the perichoretic Trinity of Eastern Orthodoxy). The social Trinity is treated as exemplary, the ideal that our praxis should follow in our relationships with one another (though appropriating the dynamics of the Godhead for human relationships has also been controversial among theologians).

Finally, the desire for practical, everyday change is something that these theologies all share. Those changes relate to and include economics, police reform, voting rights, and women in ministry. If God's being and God's actions find no disconnect or inconsistency, then God's work is not merely the salvation of souls but the overturning of any human social order that does not align with his will. God is, after all, the God of justice. The question is, Do we work toward justice now or later? Liberation theology is quick to respond with "Now!"

A Tale of Two Vaticans

The history of liberation theology in the Roman Catholic Church is connected to the second of the two Vatican councils. The first was held in the nineteenth century (1869–70), and the second took place in the twentieth (1962–65). As it turns out, a span of nearly one hundred years between them made all the difference.

Vatican I set out to preserve and reassert the authority of the papacy in the face of the dangers of modernism. During the papacy of Pius IX, papal infallibility was claimed with two caveats: it pertained only to declarations made from the "seat of Peter," or *ex cathedra*, and only on matters of theology and ethics. As it turns out, this privilege has been sparingly used. Nevertheless, at a time when the pope's authority was in question, Vatican I doubled down on Petrine supremacy in a seemingly defensive and insular manner, even alienating many of the bishops voting. An imbalance of power between the papacy and the bishops was established not long before the world wars.

The Second Vatican Council could not have been more different from the first. The turmoil of World War II was replaced by the Cold War and the fear of communist atheism. The civil rights movement, the women's rights movement, and the ecumenical movement were in full force. During this time, it is said that Pope John XXIII experienced the leading of the Holy Spirit to "open the windows and let in the fresh air." John XXIII was nearing eighty years old and had been regarded as a caretaker pope rather than an innovator. He was only ninety days into the job when he announced the council, to the surprise of many. It's no coincidence that he was influenced by *La Nouvelle Théologie* or *La Ressourcement*, a movement in the Roman Catholic Church that sought to return to Scripture, the church fathers, and Thomas Aquinas.

The goal of the council was to bring renewal to the life of the church through the updating of teaching, discipline, and organization as well as the pursuit of Christian unity. What transpired, starting with the opening session on October 11, 1962, was remarkable. The Second Vatican Council was the largest ecumenical council in all of church history, with more than 2,600 bishops attending and some of the most significant Roman Catholic theologians contributing. Joseph Ratzinger (who became Pope Benedict XVI in 2005) and Swiss theologian Hans Urs von Balthasar (1905–88) attended, along with German Jesuit theologian Karl Rahner (1904–84), who served as papal advisor. Ecumenical overtures began with John XXIII, who invited more than one hundred Protestant and Orthodox observers (though it was two years before a woman was invited). The declarations of the sessions directly describe Eastern Christians as "separated brethren" (Protestants are implied in this according to the Decree on Ecumenism)[4] and sacramental regulations, once divisive with the East, were relaxed.[5] Christians were urged to pray for the unity of the church and hope for the restoration of full communion between East and West.

Lay devotion and participation were encouraged in a variety of ways. As a sign that Catholicism was opening its doors to the world, common languages were tentatively invited into the liturgy, even into the celebration of the Mass,[6] a practice once hoped for during the Protestant Reformation. Multilingual services were affirmed as a benefit to migrants[7] and a value added to pastoral ministry.[8] This attentiveness to local custom and inculturation reflected a new attitude and expectation. Also, the communion cup was extended to the laity at the discretion of the bishop (on certain occasions) for the first time officially since prohibitions by the Council of Constance (1415) and the Council of Trent (1545–63).[9] Lay and clerical study of the Bible, personal devotion, and participation in Mass were encouraged. Charity was shown even to people of other faiths, an impetus rooted in shared human experiences as well as fundamental human rights.[10] After the staggering number of deaths during World War II and the Holocaust, Vatican II was decidedly prolife and attentive to the poor. (See Pope Paul VI's papal encyclical *Humanae Vitae* rejecting artificial contraception.) From start to finish, Vatican II positioned itself for the good of the other and in dialogue with the world, compelled by God's love for the world through his Son, Jesus Christ.[11]

Although Pope John XXIII died before the council finished, his successor, Pope Paul VI continued in his footsteps and became the first Roman bishop to travel to the Holy Land. There, on January 5, 1964, he met with the ecumenical patriarch and bishop of Constantinople, Athenagoras I, a face-to-face that had not happened between leaders in those positions since 1439, five centuries before. The goal was to heal one thousand years of division: the Great Schism of 1054 between the East and the West, followed by the ransacking of Constantinople by Western Christians during the Fourth Crusade (1200–1204), the failure of the Council of Florence to mend divisions, and the fall of Constantinople by the Ottoman Empire (1453). In two, half-hour meetings, forgiveness and restored goodwill at the highest levels was modeled. That visit became emblematic of an era eager and hopeful for Christian ecumenism. The Vatican was moderating its old adage that "there is no salvation outside the Catholic Church" (*extra ecclesiam non salus est*).

In the end, Vatican II introduced a new definition of the church that included both clergy and laity as the "people of God" rather than being strictly tied to the supremacy of Peter's successor.[12] Collegiality also became a watchword between bishops and pope. In these ways, during the twentieth century, the Tridentine Catholicism of the Reformation was receding. Coming to the fore instead was liberation theology.

Dorothy Day (1897–1980) was an American convert to Roman Catholicism who practiced radical social activism. She became committed to addressing social issues that affected the poor after watching long lines of people waiting for food during the Great Depression. She became involved in the Catholic Worker movements and cofounded the *Catholic Worker* newspaper. She is attributed with saying, "If you have two coats, you have stolen one from the poor," based on John the Baptist's teachings (Luke 3:11) and Jesus' words in the Sermon on the Mount (Matt. 5:40).

Father Gutiérrez, I Presume

Gustavo Gutiérrez was born in Lima, Peru (1928), and currently holds a professorship at the University of Notre Dame. He earned his doctorate at *L'Institut Catholique* in Lyons, where he studied under French Jesuit Henri de Lubac. In 1959, he was ordained as a Dominican priest, and in 1971, his most famous work, *A Theology of Liberation*, was published in Spanish (then in English in 1973). While grappling with the history of violence and oppression that came with Spanish colonization, often in the name of evangelism, Gutiérrez adopted the example of the Spanish Dominican priest and bishop Bartholomé de las Casas (1484–1566), who advocated on behalf of the indigenous people in the era of Spanish colonialism and in opposition to their enslavement.[13]

Gutiérrez's pioneering work proved to be a major contribution to the development of Roman Catholic social teaching in the modern era. He was profoundly shaped by the conversations on human rights and social justice at Vatican II, as well as papal social teachings such as Pope Paul VI's 1967 encyclical, *Populorum Progressio*. Paul VI's piece struck a chord among the Latin American bishops by voicing shared concerns and bringing into sharp relief economic inequalities and the disadvantages faced by underdeveloped countries in the system of free trade. A group of Latin American bishops who attended Vatican II responded with "A Letter to the Peoples of the Third World." Within a year, Pope Paul VI became the first pope to visit Latin America, and the Conference of Latin American Bishops at Medellín in Columbia took place in July 1968.

The bishops called the church to side with the poor. The

conference used the term "solidarity," also used in Paul VI's *Populorum*, to rally a shared perspective and commitment to action in support of the impoverished. Subsequent open letters by Latin American clergy spoke with urgency about the necessity of an immediate response to the "heartrending reality of Latin America" and the despair experienced by those facing modern-day slavery.[14] Gutiérrez attended the conference and built on these teachings with Scripture and theology.

The message of liberation theology is that the triune God offers good news for the poor and oppressed through the person and work of Jesus Christ. It is a theological tradition that starts "from below" with the poorest of the poor. Total liberation is twofold, according to Gutiérrez: liberation from social and economic systems that oppress (material poverty that institution-alizes violence, destroys one's humanity, and leads to death),[15] and liberation from sin (spiritual poverty).[16] The primary concept of liberation theology—that God has a "preferential option for the poor"—was identified with John XXIII before Vatican II[17] and given expression at Medellín in 1968, ratified at Puebla in 1979, and confirmed in John Paul II's encyclical *Sollicitudo Rei Socialis*.[18] Gutiérrez explains that God's preferential treatment for the poor is not because the poor are somehow morally superior but because God works in such a way that the last are first.[19] This may appear baffling, he recognizes, but of course, God's ways are not human ways (Isa. 55:8). He clarifies that "preference" does not mean "exclusive," since God's saving love reaches beyond the poor as well.[20]

Numerous biblical texts and rich theological insight inform Gutiérrez's teachings. By taking on flesh, did not Christ side with the poor by becoming poor (Phil. 2:5–8)?[21] This kenotic

Christology, or the self-emptying Christ, is foundational to a liberation Christology. Similarly, Gutiérrez cites 2 Corinthians 8:9: "For you know the generous act of our Lord Jesus Christ, that though he was rich, yet for your sakes he became poor, so that by his poverty you might become rich."

Christ's ministry further reveals his mission to restore the full humanity of the poor and the outcast. Gutiérrez's reading of the Beatitudes[22] of Luke reveals a Christ focused on the physical and material sufferings of the poor.[23] To oppress the poor is an offense to God, he explains, and incompatible with God's kingdom of love and justice that Christ inaugurated with his coming.[24] To that end, Jesus confronted groups in power, from Jewish leaders to Roman leaders, and he "accompanied this criticism with a head-on opposition to the rich and powerful and a radical option for the poor."[25] His ministry is marked by preaching good news to the poor and proclaiming freedom for the prisoners as well as release for the oppressed (Luke 4:18–19), which proves that Christ's kingdom and social injustice are at odds.[26] Rooted in this biblical perspective, Jesus is seen as a liberator whose power is on full display in both his death and resurrection. Christ's willingness to go to the cross illustrates his solidarity with the oppressed. The cross is the expression of God's love for humanity and unity with our suffering. By his resurrection, God triumphs over the forces of oppression so that resurrection is not just about eternal life but about transformation of this life.

Liberation theology also developed in light of the doctrine of the Trinity. In 1988, Brazilian theologian and Franciscan Leonardo Boff asked provocatively, Is the Trinity good news for the poor and oppressed?[27] Absolutely! Boff taught that God's perfect, egalitarian fellowship as Father, Son, and Holy Spirit (called the immanent Trinity) provides a social model for human relationships since humanity is created in the image of the triune God. Our relationships should reflect the love that flows among the persons of the Godhead, which entails a struggle against social injustice on earth. As Gutiérrez taught years before, "To be saved is to reach the fullness of love; it is to enter into the circle of charity which unites the three Persons of the Trinity; it is to love as God loves."[28]

The struggle for a just society is central to salvation history, insists Gutiérrez.[29] By Christ's liberating action of death and resurrection, we have received liberation from sin and its consequences.[30] Gutiérrez envisions the church as living into her calling on earth as a "poor church" serving all, but particularly the lowly.[31] The church engages in critique of its past, particularly colonization, to resolve issues of injustice today. In this way, liberation theology is not satisfied with theory but is intent on praxis through political action and seeking social change that undoes the structural sins of society. God's triune love is liberating, and our communion as Christians with one another (primarily through the Eucharist) should be committed to solidarity and justice against exploitation and alienation.[32]

In 1988, for the fifteenth anniversary of the English translation of Gutiérrez's A Theology of Liberation, he wrote a new preface. In it he reflected on the maturation of liberation theology, clarified the meaning of terms, and recognized some of the blind spots of the movement. Most important, he noted the near total absence at Medellín of any consideration of the position of women in Latin America and the hidden challenges that they faced in the culture.[33] Ten years later, the Third General Conference of Latin American Bishops, which met at Puebla,

Mexico, in 1979, had grown in awareness of how women were "doubly oppressed and marginalized."[34] In response, Mujerista theology began to develop through the work of Cuban-American theologian Ada María Isasi-Díaz (1943–2012). This work has only just begun.

The reception of liberation theology has been complex. Realizing hope through social revolution has proven unsettling to many.[35] The assassination of Archbishop of El Salvador Oscar Romero (1917–80) while he was administering the Mass was an act of terror intended to frighten the church from entering the fray of reform in favor of the poor and suffering.[36] Meanwhile, the practice of "base communities" came under scrutiny by the Vatican for creating a church from the bottom up without the presence of local priests, sacraments, or the bishop. Concern also grew over Marxist economic theories attached to liberation theology to the point that the Vatican began to censor teachings and people involved. (See the Vatican's Instructions in 1984 and 1986.) Pope John Paul II and later Pope Benedict XVI navigated the tension between maintaining the Vatican's authority in the majority world and the desire to preference the needs of the poor. Argentinian Pope Francis, who is the first pope from the Southern Hemisphere, was deeply shaped by liberation theology.

A version of liberation theology was also advanced among Protestants in Latin America. René Padilla (1932–2021) was an Ecuadorian evangelical theologian and missiologist who proposed the idea of *mision integral*—the priority of evangelism and social activism. His work shaped the Latin American Theological Fellowship as well as the Lausanne Conference (1974), a global evangelical conference started by John Stott and Billy Graham.

Liberation beyond Latin America

One of the legacies of Gutiérrez's work has been to inspire liberation theology among others in other corners of the world. Feminist theology as a formal discipline also advanced in the 1960s the same year that Latin American bishops were meeting at Medellín in Columbia. Feminist theology expanded into a spectrum of views ranging from Mary Daly's radical or post-Christian feminism to Letty Russell's biblical feminism, which affirmed that the Bible teaches the full equality of women particularly through Christ's treatment of women, despite the Bible's patriarchal cultural context. The chance to formally evaluate, construct, and critique theology from a woman's perspective was dependent on key social and political changes. Through the work of Elisabeth Schüssler Fiorenza, Catherine Lacugna, Sarah Coakley, Janet Soskice, and many more, feminist theology has reflected on a range of theological issues, including the use of metaphor when talking about God, the gender of God, and implications surrounding Christology.

Meanwhile, Black theology was also formalizing after emancipation (consider the legacy of Sojourner Truth, a former slave turned abolitionist and advocate for women) and in response to the backlash that resulted. During a time of segregated churches, brutal lynchings, and Jim Crow laws, the National Association for the Advancement of Colored People formed in 1909. One of the founders of the NAACP, W. E. B. Du Bois (1868–1963), wrote "The Gospel according to Mary Brown," which retells the incarnation of Jesus by setting the story in the early twentieth-century American South. Rapid changes began in the 1950s with the desegregation of schools (1954), followed by Rosa Parks's

Montgomery bus boycott (1955), which inspired Baptist pastor and theologian Martin Luther King Jr. (who became the first president of the Southern Christian Leadership Conference in 1957) and launched the civil rights movement. King's nonviolent resistance, or "good trouble," led to his reception of the Nobel Peace Prize in 1964, but he was later assassinated in 1968. His impact aided the inauguration of "Black theology" as defined by the National Committee of Black Churchmen with Black liberation as the central theme.[37] From its formal inception and as expressed in the work of James Cone and others, Black theology advanced the idea that Jesus must be understood as Black as an indication of his identification with Black suffering.

The legacy of W. E. B. Du Bois is evident in **Albert Cleage**'s *Black Messiah* (1968) and the work of **James Cone** (1939–2018), including *A Black Theology of Liberation* (1970) and *God of the Oppressed* (1975). In Black theology, the cross is the focal point of God's suffering and liberating power. Jesus' solidarity with the oppressed is stressed: "God of Jesus is the Liberator of the oppressed from oppression."[38] Womanist theology began with two students of Cone's, **Jacquelyn Grant** and **Kelly Delaine Brown Douglas**, and seeks to highlight how Black women have "suffered the triple bondage of imprisonment" at the intersection of sexism, racism, and classism.[39]

This desire to identify closely with Jesus, as reflected in liberation theology and the many traditions of contextualized theologies, has always been part of the Christian narrative.

After all, Jesus Christ is Emmanuel, God with us. To confess the incarnation of the Son of God is to affirm the radical idea that God came near in an embodied way out of his love so that we might be saved. Thanks be to God!

Discussion Questions

1. How does Scripture encourage Christians to work toward human rights and social justice in the here and now?
2. How can the church better love our neighbor through political and economic systems?
3. Where does evangelism fit into the equation of the church's mission to love others? What can Scripture teach us about the dual nature of that work?

Further Reading

Robert McAfee Brown, *Gustavo Gutiérrez: An Introduction to Liberation Theology* (Wipf and Stock, 2013).

James Cone, *God of the Oppressed* (Orbis, 1997).

Gene L. Green, Stephen T. Pardue, and K. K. Yeo, eds., *Majority World Theology: Christian Doctrine in Global Context* (IVP Academic, 2020).

Gustavo Gutiérrez, A *Theology of Liberation: History, Politics, and Salvation* (Orbis, 1988).

Letty M. Russell, *Human Liberation in a Feminist Perspective: A Theology* (Westminster John Knox, 1974).

CONCLUSION
When Water Is as Thick as Blood

The wonder of the gospel message is that redemption through Jesus Christ is for all people, in all times, even as it reaches particular people in particular times, from the richest to the most vulnerable. Christianity is a global faith moving toward that blessed vision of "a great multitude that no one could count, from every nation, from all tribes and peoples and languages, standing before the throne and before the Lamb" (Rev. 7:9).

But there are other sides of this story that cannot be fully captured here. Of course, each one of us has experienced the disappointments, hurts, and failures that can come from being part of a family, even a Christian one. The church is no exception. Just as each of us is on a journey of sanctification, so too is the church, which requires repentance, confession, and the power of the Holy Spirit to follow Christ more faithfully again and again with each generation. The best still awaits us.

In the meantime, to know the theologians of the body of Christ means recognizing God's faithfulness in sustaining the church throughout its history and through the work of theologians and ministers over the centuries and around the globe. There are exemplars and successes to be celebrated that have brought glory to Jesus' name. Even in migration, war, and martyrdom, there has been extraordinary obedience and defiance of evil. But we must also grapple with the reality that, though the church has been called to carry the truth of Jesus Christ into the world, it also can fall grievously short of that calling this side of heaven. At points, parts of the church have struggled with civic allegiance and social custom, have fallen prey to avarice and power mongering, and have sometimes lost sight of God's Word. It has not consistently affirmed the full humanity and good creation of others, even among those who have embraced the good news of Jesus Christ and received God's adoption and Holy Spirit. And in those moments, when accountability has followed, Scripture has been brought to bear as a reminder that we are a family formed by God's gracious, mighty, and loving will.

Acts 17 recounts Paul's missionary journey to Athens. As he looked around, he was distressed to see not only the extent of the people's religiosity but its outworking: idolatry. He stood upon the Acropolis and addressed the Athenians as those who are counted among God's children:

> The God who made the world and everything in it, he who is Lord of heaven and earth, does not live in shrines made by human hands, nor is he served by human hands, as though he needed anything, since he himself gives to all mortals life and breath and all things. *From one ancestor he made all peoples to inhabit the whole earth*, and he allotted the times of their existence and the boundaries of the places where they would live, so that they would search for God and perhaps fumble about for him and find him—though indeed he is not far from each one of us. For "In him we live and move and have our being."
>
> —Acts 17:24–28, emphasis added

Paul teaches here that we are one family; indeed, we are "one blood." In the modern era of the church, this passage has been tremendously important in the fight for the abolition of slavery[1] and in the move toward greater ecumenism among Christians.[2] To embrace this passage is to recognize that out of a shared beginning, a new family is born of Christ's blood and baptismal water that we might be one with God and with one another: "For in Christ Jesus you are all children of God through faith. As many of you as were baptized into Christ have clothed yourselves with Christ. There is no longer Jew or Greek; there is no longer slave or free; there is no longer male and female, for all of you are one in Christ Jesus. And if you belong to Christ, then you are Abraham's offspring, heirs according to the promise" (Gal. 3:26–29).

This family is not possible by human means. It is only by the will of the triune God, revealed in the life, death, and resurrection of Jesus Christ and the outpouring of the Holy Spirit, that we are one. May we as the church find a way together to "run with perseverance the race that is set before us, looking to Jesus, the pioneer and perfecter of faith" (Heb. 12:1–2). And all God's children said, "Amen!"

NOTES

Chapter 1: Irenaeus of Lyons

1. Irenaeus, "For Growth in Grace," in *Prayers of the Early Church*, ed. J. Manning Potts (Nashville: Upper Room, 1980), 29.
2. Tertullian, *Apology* 40, in *Ante-Nicene Fathers*, vol. 3 (Peabody, MA: Hendrickson, 2004), 47.
3. "The Martyrdom of Polycarp, Bishop of Smyrna," in Henry Bettenson and Chris Maunder, eds., *Documents of the Christian Church*, 4th ed. (Oxford: Oxford Univ. Press, 2011), 9–13.
4. Tertullian, *Apology* 50, 55.
5. "St. Irenaeus," in *The Oxford Dictionary of the Christian Church*, ed. F. L. Cross (Oxford: Oxford Univ. Press, 2005), 851–52.
6. "The Gospel of Thomas," in *Readings in the History of Christian Theology*, vol. 1, ed. William C. Placher (Louisville: Westminster John Knox, 1988), 12.
7. Irenaeus, *Against Heresies*, 3.2.2, in *Ante-Nicene Fathers*, vol. 1 (Peabody, MA: Hendrickson, 2004), 415.
8. Irenaeus, *Against Heresies*, 3.18.3, 446.
9. Irenaeus, *Against Heresies*, 3.3.1, 415.
10. Irenaeus, *Against Heresies*, 3.19.1, 448–49.
11. Denis Minns, *Irenaeus: An Introduction* (New York: T&T Clark, 2010), ix.
12. Irenaeus, *Against Heresies*, 4.20.1, 487–88.
13. Irenaeus, *Against Heresies*, 4.20.2, 488.
14. Irenaeus, *Against Heresies*, 3.3.1, 415.

Chapter 2: Athanasius of Alexandria

1. J. M. Rodwell, trans., *Aethiopic Liturgies and Prayers* (Edinburgh: Williams and Norgate, 1864), 99.
2. Eusebius, *Life of Constantine*, trans. Averil Cameron and Stuart G. Hall (Oxford: Clarendon, 1999), 1.27–32, pp. 79–82.
3. "The Edict of Milan," in *Documents of the Christian Church*, 4th ed., ed. Henry Bettenson and Chris Maunder (Oxford: Oxford Univ. Press, 2011), 17.
4. Arius, "The Letter of Arius to Eusebius of Nicomedia," in *Christology*

of the Later Fathers, ed. Edward R. Hardy (Philadelphia: Westminster, 1954), 330.

5. Athanasius, *On the Incarnation* (Yonkers, NY: St. Vladimir's Seminary Press, 2011), 50.

6. "The Creed of Nicaea," in *Documents of the Christian Church*, 26, emphasis added.

7. Athanasius, *On the Incarnation*, 56–57.

8. Apollinaris of Laodicea, "On the Union in Christ of the Body with the Godhead," in *Readings in the History of Christian Theology*, vol. 1, ed. William C. Placher (Louisville: Westminster John Knox, 1988), 64.

9. Gregory of Nazianzus, "To Cledonius against Apollinaris (Epistle 101)," in *Christology of the Later Fathers*, 218.

10. Nestorius, "First Sermon against the *Theotokos*," in *The Christological Controversy*, ed. Richard A. Norris Jr. (Philadelphia: Fortress, 1980), 124–25.

11. Theodore of Mopsuestia, "Fragments of the Doctrinal Works," in *Christological Controversy*, 115.

12. "Cyril of Alexandria on the Incarnation," in *The Christian Theology Reader*, 5th ed., ed. Alister E. McGrath (West Sussex, UK: Wiley Blackwell, 2017), 238.

13. Leo the Great, "The Tome of Leo," in *Christology of the Later Fathers*, 364.

14. "The Definition of Chalcedon," in *Documents of the Christian Church*, 54.

15. "St. Athanasius," in *The Oxford Dictionary of the Christian Church*, ed. F. L. Cross (Oxford: Oxford Univ. Press, 2005), 121.

Chapter 3: The Cappadocian Four

1. Thomas Oden and Cindy Crosby, eds., *Ancient Christian Devotional* (Downers Grove, IL: InterVarsity Press, 2007), 67.

2. "St. Basil, 'the Great,'" in *The Oxford Dictionary of the Christian Church*, ed. F. L. Cross (Oxford: Oxford Univ. Press, 2005), 167–68.

3. "St. Gregory of Nyssa," *Oxford Dictionary*, 715–16.

4. "St. Macrina," in *Oxford Dictionary*, 1025.

5. Macrina, "On the Soul and the Resurrection" (380), in *In Her Words: Women's Writings in the History of Christian Thought*, ed. Amy Oden (Nashville: Abingdon, 1994), 48.

6. "St. Gregory of Nazianzus," in *Oxford Dictionary*, 715.

7. Tertullian, *Against Praxeas* 11, in *Ante-Nicene Fathers*, vol. 3 (Peabody, MA: Hendrickson, 2004), 605, emphasis in original.

8. Basil the Great, *On the Holy Spirit* (Yonkers, NY: St. Vladimir's Seminary Press, 2011), 53.

9. Basil, *On the Holy Spirit*, 55.

10. Macrina, "On the Soul," 49.

11. "The 'Nicene' Creed," in *Documents of the Christian Church*, 4th ed., ed. Henry Bettenson and Chris Maunder, (Oxford: Oxford Univ. Press, 2011), 27–28.

12. Basil, "Letter 236: To the Same Amphilochius," in *Nicene and Post-Nicene Fathers, Second Series*, ed. Philip Schaff and Henry Wace, vol. 8 (Grand Rapids: Eerdmans, 1955), 278.

13. Gregory of Nazianzus, *On God and Christ: The Five Theological Orations and Two Letters to Cledonius* 30.19 (Crestwood, NY: St. Vladimir's Seminary Press, 2002), 109.

14. Basil, *On the Holy Spirit*, 80.

15. Gregory of Nyssa, "On 'Not Three Gods,'" in *Nicene and Post-Nicene Fathers, Second Series*, ed. Philip Schaff and Henry Wace, vol. 5 (New York: Christian Literature Company, 1893), 332.

16. Gregory of Nyssa, "On 'Not Three Gods,'" 334.

17. J. N. D. Kelly, *The Athanasian Creed* (London: Adam and Charles Black, 1964), 18.

18. Gregory of Nazianzus, *On God and Christ* 31.8, 122.

Chapter 4: Augustine of Hippo

1. Thomas Oden and Cindy Crosby, eds., *Ancient Christian Devotional* (Downers Grove, IL: InterVarsity Press, 2007), 21.

2. "St. Augustine of Hippo," in *The Oxford Dictionary of the Christian Church*, ed. F. L. Cross (Oxford: Oxford Univ. Press, 2005), 106–8.

3. Augustine, *Confessions*, trans. Sarah Ruden (New York: Modern Library, 2017), II.9, p. 42.

4. Augustine, *Confessions*, II.2, p. 35.

5. Augustine, *Confessions*, V.10, pp. 114–15.

6. Augustine, *Confessions*, V.24, p. 132.

7. Augustine, *Confessions*, VIII.29, pp. 235–36.

8. Augustine, *Confessions*, VIII.29, p. 236–37.

9. Clement of Rome, "The First Epistle of Clement to the Corinthians," in *Ante-Nicene Fathers*, vol. 1 (Peabody, MA: Hendrickson, 2004), 1:32, p. 13.

10. Pelagius, "Letter to Demetrias," in *Theological Anthropology*, ed. J. Patout Burns (Philadelphia: Fortress, 1981), 44.

11. Pelagius, "Letter to Demetrias," 52.

12. Augustine, "On the Grace of Christ," in *Theological Anthropology*, 84.

13. Augustine, "On the Grace of Christ," 99.

14. Augustine, "On the Grace of Christ," 82.

15. Augustine, *The City of God*, XXII.30 (London: Penguin, 2003), 1089.

16. "Cyprian on the Unity of the Church," in *Documents of the Christian Church*, 4th ed., ed. Henry Bettenson and Chris Maunder (Oxford: Oxford Univ. Press, 2011), 77.

17. In Latin, this notion is expressed by the phrase *ex opere operantis*, meaning "from the work of the one doing the work."

18. Augustine, "On Baptism, against the Donatists," IV.12, in *Nicene and Post-Nicene Fathers*, vol. 4, ed. Philip Schaff (Buffalo: Christian Literature Company, 1887), 455. In Latin, *ex opere operato*, meaning "from the work worked" or "from the work performed."

19. Tertullian, *Against Praxeas*, chap. 8 in *Ante-Nicene Fathers*, vol. 1 (Peabody, MA: Hendrickson, 2004), 603.

20. Augustine, *The Trinity*, IX.2, ed. John E. Rotelle, trans. Edmund Hill (Brooklyn, NY: New City Press, 1997), 272.

21. Augustine, *Trinity*, X.18, p. 298.

22. Augustine, *Trinity*, IX.2, p. 272.

23. "Augustine of Hippo on the Relationship between Good and Evil," in *The Christian Theology Reader*, 5th ed., ed. Alister E. McGrath (West Sussex, UK: Wiley Blackwell, 2017), 172.

24. Augustine, *City of God*, XIV.28, p. 593.

25. Augustine, *City of God*, XV.1, p. 596.

Chapter 5: John of Damascus

1. John of Damascus, *Writings*, trans. Frederic H. Chase Jr. (Washington, D.C.: Catholic Univ. of America Press, 1958), x.

2. "Charlemagne," in *The Oxford Dictionary of the Christian Church*, ed. F. L. Cross (Oxford: Oxford Univ. Press, 2005), 324–25.

3. Sidney H. Griffith, *The Church in the Shadow of the Mosque: Christians and Muslims in the World of Islam* (Princeton, NJ: Princeton Univ. Press, 2008).

4. Dale T. Irvin and Scott W. Sunquist, *History of the World Christian Movement*, vol. 1 (Maryknoll, NY: Orbis, 2007), 377.

5. "Epitome of the Definition of the Iconoclastic Conciliabulum Held in Constantinople, A.D. 754," in *Nicene and Post-Nicene Church Fathers, Second Series*, ed. Philip Schaff and Henry Wace, vol. 4 (New York: Charles Scribner's Sons, 1916), 554.

6. Jason Mandryk, *Operation World: The Definitive Prayer Guide to Every Nation*, 7th ed. (Downers Grove, IL: InterVarsity Press, 2010), 802.

7. Irvin and Sunquist, *History of the World Christian Movement*, vol. 1, 57.

8. "St. John of Damascus," in *Oxford Dictionary*, 896–97.

9. John of Damascus, *Three Treatises on the Divine Images*, trans. Andrew Louth (Crestwood, NY: St. Vladimir's Seminary Press, 2003), 21–22.

10. John of Damascus, *Three Treatises*, 23.

11. John of Damascus, *Three Treatises*, 29.

12. John of Damascus, *Three Treatises*, 29.

13. "The Decree of the Holy, Great, Ecumenical Synod, the Second of Nicea," in *Nicene and Post-Nicene Church Fathers, Second Series*, ed. Philip Schaff and Henry Wace, vol. 14 (New York: Charles Scribner's Sons, 1916), 550.

14. "From the Fourth General Council of Constantinople," in *Theological Aesthetics: A Reader*, ed. Gesa Elsbeth Thiessen (Grand Rapids: Eerdmans, 2004), 65.

15. John of Damascus, *Writings*, 4.

16. Athanasius, *On the Incarnation* (Yonkers, NY: St. Vladimir's Seminary Press, 2011), 107.

17. John of Damascus, *Three Treatises*, 105.

18. Maximus the Confessor, *On the Cosmic Mystery of Jesus Christ*, trans. Paul M. Blowers and Robert Louis Wilken (Crestwood, NY: St. Vladimir's Seminary Press, 2003), 174.

Chapter 6: Anselm of Canterbury

1. Anselm of Canterbury, *Proslogion*, in *The Major Works*, ed. Brian Davies and G. R. Evans (Oxford: Oxford Univ. Press, 1998), 84–87.

2. "St. Anselm," in *The Oxford Dictionary of the Christian Church*, ed. F. L. Cross (Oxford: Oxford Univ. Press, 2005), 73.

3. "The 'Nicene' Creed," in Henry Bettenson and Chris Maunder, eds., *Documents of the Christian Church*, 4th ed. (Oxford: Oxford Univ. Press, 2011), 27–28.

4. "St. Anselm," in *Oxford Dictionary*, 74.

5. Mark A. Noll, David Komline, and Han-Luen Kantzer Komline, *Turning Points: Decisive Moments in the History of Christianity*, 4th ed. (Grand Rapids: Baker Academic, 2022), 110–11, 125.

6. "St. Anselm," in *Oxford Dictionary*, 73–74.

7. Anselm, *Proslogion*, 87.

8. Anselm, *Proslogion*, 87–88.

9. "S. Anselm on the Atonement," in *Documents of the Christian Church*, 147.

10. Peter Abelard, "Exposition of the Epistle to the Romans," in *A Scholastic Miscellany: Anselm to Ockham*, ed. Eugene R. Fairweather (Philadelphia: Westminster, 1956), 283.

11. John Calvin, *Institutes of the Christian Religion* (Philadelphia: Westminster, 1960), 2.16.7.

Chapter 7: Julian of Norwich

1. Julian of Norwich, *Showings*, trans. Edmund Colledge and James Walsh (New York: Paulist, 1978), 1:5, p. 184 (Long Text is LT—n.b. citation for revelation number, chapter, and page number).
2. Laura Swan, *The Forgotten Desert Mothers: Sayings, Lives, and Stories of Early Christian Women* (New York: Paulist, 2013).
3. Caroline Walker Bynum, "Religious Women in the Later Middle Ages," in *Christian Spirituality: High Middle Ages and Reformation*, vol. 2, *World Spirituality*, ed. Jill Raitt (London: SCM Press, 1988), 128.
4. Julian of Norwich, *Showings*, 2:127–128 (Short Text is ST—n.b. citation tracks chapter, then page numbers); 1:3, pp. 179–81 (LT).
5. Veronica Mary Rolf, *An Explorer's Guide to Julian of Norwich* (Downers Grove, IL: IVP Academic, 2018).
6. Nicholas Watson and Jacqueline Jenkins, eds., *The Writings of Julian of Norwich* (University Park, PA: Pennsylvania State Univ. Press, 2006), 1–10.
7. Watson and Jenkins, "Introduction," in *Writings of Julian of Norwich*, 5.
8. Elizabeth Robertson, "Julian of Norwich's 'Modernist' Style and the Creation of Audience," in *A Companion to Julian of Norwich*, ed. Liz Herbert McAvoy (Woodbridge, UK: D. S. Brewer, 2008), 140.
9. Bernard McGinn, *The Foundations of Mysticism*, The Presence of God, vol. 1 (New York: Crossroad, 1991), xvi–xvii.
10. Bynum, "Religious Women," 137.
11. Bynum, "Religious Women," 131–32.
12. Julian of Norwich, *Showings*, 1:125 (ST).
13. E.g., Julian of Norwich, *Showings*, 4:131, 6:134, 9:139–40, 13:147, 19:157, 20:161 (ST).
14. Julian, *Showings*, 1:2, p. 177 (LT).
15. Julian, *Showings*, 4:130 (ST); 1:5, p. 183 (LT).
16. Julian, *Showings*, 13:149 (ST).
17. Julian, *Showings*, 15:152 (ST).
18. John Aberth, *The Black Death: The Great Mortality of 1348–50; A Brief History with Documents*, Bedford Series in History and Culture (Boston: Bedford/St. Martin's, 2005).
19. Julian, *Showings*, 1:4, p. 181 (LT).
20. Julian, *Showings*, 8.16–17, pp. 206–9 (LT).
21. Julian, *Showings*, 4:130 (ST); 1:5, pp. 183–84 (LT).
22. Julian, *Showings*, 17:154 (ST); 13:39, pp. 244–45 (LT).

23. Julian, *Showings*, 17:155 (ST).
24. Caroline Walker Bynum, *Jesus as Mother: Studies in the Spirituality of the High Middle Ages* (Oakland, CA: Univ. of California Press, 1984), 113.
25. Bynum, *Jesus as Mother*, 111–18.
26. Julian, *Showings*, 1:4, p. 181 (LT).
27. Julian, *Showings*, 14:51, pp. 274–75 (LT).
28. Julian, *Showings*, 14:52, p. 279 (LT).
29. Julian, *Showings*, 14:58, p. 293 (LT).
30. Julian, *Showings*, 13:28, pp. 226–27 (LT).
31. Julian, *Showings*, 16:68, p. 315 (LT).
32. Lynn Staley, trans. and ed., *The Book of Margery Kempe* (New York: Norton, 2001), 18:31–34.
33. Staley, *Book of Margery Kempe*, 33.
34. Staley, *Book of Margery Kempe*, 32.
35. Bynam, "Religious Women," 129, 136.
36. See Kirsi Stjerna's *Women and the Reformation* (Hoboken, NJ: Blackwell, 2009) for chapters on Prüss and Shütz Zell.

Chapter 8: Thomas Aquinas

1. Thomas Aquinas, "For Ordering a Life Wisely," in *The Aquinas Prayer Book: The Prayers and Hymns of St. Thomas Aquinas*, ed. Robert Anderson and Johannes Moser (Manchester, NH: Sophia Institute Press, 2000), 5–13.
2. Jean-Pierre Torrell, "Life and Works," in *The Oxford Handbook of Aquinas*, ed. Brian Davies (Oxford: Oxford Univ. Press, 2012), 15–32.
3. For dating, see Torrell, "Life and Works," 21.
4. Torrell, "Life and Works," 17.
5. James Doig, "Aquinas and Aristotle," *Oxford Handbook*, 34.
6. Brian Davies and Eleonore Stump, "Introduction," *Oxford Handbook*, 4.
7. Doig, "Aquinas and Aristotle," 33–44.
8. Aquinas, ST I.2.3, in *Aquinas on Nature and Grace: Selections from the Summa Theologica*, ed. A. M. Fairweather (Louisville: Westminster John Knox, 1954).
9. Aquinas, ST I.3.7, *Aquinas on Nature and Grace*.
10. Aquinas, ST 22ae.2.8, *Aquinas on Nature and Grace*.
11. Richard Kieckhefer, "Major Current in Late Medieval Devotion," in *Christian Spirituality*, ed. Jill Raith (London: SCM Press, 1996), 97–98.
12. Aquinas, ST 3.75.2–6; 3.77.1–2, *Aquinas on Nature and Grace*.
13. Torrell, "Life and Works," 20.
14. Aquinas, ST 12ae.109.2–4, *Aquinas on Nature and Grace*.
15. Aquinas, ST 12ae.109.6, *Aquinas on Nature and Grace*.

16. Aquinas, ST 12ae.109.3, *Aquinas on Nature and Grace.*

17. Aquinas, ST 12ae, 112.2–3, *Aquinas on Nature and Grace.*

18. Aquinas, ST 12ae.109.3; 12ae.111.2, *Aquinas on Nature and Grace.*

19. Aquinas, ST 12ae.111.2–3, *Aquinas on Nature and Grace.*

20. Aquinas, ST 12ae.109.2, *Aquinas on Nature and Grace.*

21. Aquinas, ST 12ae.85.1–2, *Aquinas on Nature and Grace.*

22. Frederick Christian Bauerschmidt, *Thomas Aquinas: Faith, Reason, and Following Christ*, Christian Theology in Context (Oxford: Oxford Univ. Press, 2013), 26.

23. See Christopher Upham, "The Influence of Aquinas," *Oxford Handbook*, 511–32.

Chapter 9: Martin Luther

1. Thomas McPherson, ed., *Prayers of the Reformers* (Brewster, MA: Paraclete, 2017), 40.

2. *Luthers Werke: Kritische Gesamtausgabe* [Schriften], 65 vols. (Weimar, 1883–): WA 38:143.25–28.

3. "Preface to the Complete Edition of Luther's Latin Writings," in *Martin Luther's Basic Theological Writings*, ed. Timothy F. Lull, 2nd ed. (Minneapolis: Fortress, 2005), 8–9.

4. Wilhelm Pauck, ed. and trans., *Luther: Lectures on Romans*, reissued (Louisville: Westminster John Knox, 2006), 18.

5. Luther, "Preface," 9.

6. Theses 5, 13: Luther, "The Ninety-Five Theses," *Martin Luther's Basic Theological Writings*, 41.

7. Theses 43, 45–46: Luther, "Ninety-Five Theses," 43.

8. Theses 32–33, 41–42, 53–55, 67–68, 94–95: Luther, "Ninety-Five Theses," 42–46.

9. Theses 35–36, 39: Luther, "Ninety-Five Theses," 43.

10. Based on indulgences preacher Johannes Tetzel's famous saying, which Luther recalls in Thesis 27: Luther, "Ninety-Five Theses," 42.

11. Luther, "A Sermon on Indulgences and Grace," in *The Annotated Luther*, vol. 1, ed. and trans. Timothy J. Wengert (Minneapolis: Fortress, 2015), 57–65.

12. Martin Luther, "The Leipzig Debate," in *Luther's Works*, American edition, ed. Jaroslav Pelikan and Helmut T. Lehmann, 55 vols. (St. Louis: Concordia, 1955–86), 31:313–25.

13. Luther, "The Babylonian Captivity of the Church," *Martin Luther's Basic Theological Writings*, 216.

14. Luther, "Babylonian Captivity," 225.

15. Luther, "Babylonian Captivity," 224.

16. Luther, "Babylonian Captivity," 393.

17. Luther, "Babylonian Captivity," 394–95.

18. Luther, "Two Kinds of Righteousness," *Martin Luther's Basic Theological Writings*, 135.

19. Luther, "The Freedom of a Christian," *Martin Luther's Basic Theological Writings*, 408.

20. Kirsi Stjerna, "Argula von Grumbach," in *Women and the Reformation* (Malden, MA: Blackwell, 2009), chap. 6.

21. *Luthers Werke*, WA 7: 876.4–877.6.

22. Luther, "Freedom of a Christian," 394.

23. Andrew Pettegree, *Brand Luther* (New York: Penguin, 2015).

24. Bruce Gordon, *God's Armed Prophet: Zwingli* (New Haven, CT: Yale Univ. Press, 2021).

25. Amy Nelson Burnett, *Debating the Sacraments: Print and Authority in the Early Reformation* (Oxford: Oxford Univ. Press, 2019).

Chapter 10: John Calvin

1. Thomas McPherson, ed., *Prayers of the Reformers* (Brewster, MA: Paraclete, 2017), 86.

2. Erin Blakemore, "A Playmobil Figure of Martin Luther Has Become the Fastest-Selling of All Time," *Smithsonian Magazine*, June 11, 2015, www.smithsonianmag.com/smart-news/fastest-selling-playmobil-figure-all-time-coming-america-and-its-not-what-you-might-think-180955560/.

3. John Calvin, *Ioannis Calvini Opera Quae Supersunt Omnia*, ed. Wilhelm Baum, Eduard Cunitz, and Eduard Reuss, 59 vols. (Brunsvigae: C. A. Schwetschke, 1863–1900), 31:21ff.

4. Jennifer Powell McNutt, "In Her Own Words and Actions: Marguerite of Navarre (1492–1549) as a Theologian and Patron of Evangelicals," in *Women Reformers: Protestant Voices in Early Modern Europe*, ed. Kirsi Stjerna (Minneapolis: Fortress, 2022), 153–62.

5. John Calvin, *Institutes of the Christian Religion*, ed. John McNeill, trans. Ford Lewis Battles, vols. 1–2 (Philadelphia: Westminster, 1960): I.1.1.

6. This discussion also begins book 2: Calvin, *Institutes*, II.1.1–2.

7. Calvin, *Institutes*, I.4.4.

8. Calvin, *Institutes*, I.3.1.

9. Calvin, *Institutes*, I.6.1.

10. Calvin, *Institutes*, I.5.5; I.5.8; I.6.2.

11. Calvin, *Institutes*, I.13.1; III.21.4.

12. Calvin, *Institutes*, II.2.10–12, 26; II.3.5–6; II.4–5.

13. Calvin, *Institutes*, II.1.8–9.
14. Calvin, *Institutes*, II.2.14–16.
15. Calvin, *Institutes*, II.11.10; II.12.
16. Calvin, *Institutes*, III.19.15.
17. Calvin, *Institutes*, II.15.
18. Calvin, *Institutes*, III.1.1–3.
19. Calvin, *Institutes*, I.7.4–5; III.1.4.
20. Calvin, *Institutes*, III.2.34; III.6.1.
21. Calvin, *Institutes*, III.11.1.
22. Calvin, *Institutes*, III.11.16.
23. Calvin, *Institutes*, III.2.24; III.2.35.
24. Calvin, *Institutes*, III.11.1.
25. Calvin, *Institutes*, II.7.4–5; III.3.9–14.
26. Calvin, *Institutes*, III.20.
27. Calvin, *Institutes*, I.2.1; *Ioannis Calvini Opera Quae Supersunt Omnia* 2:34.
28. Calvin, *Institutes*, III.21.
29. Calvin, *Institutes*, II.12.5; III.22.1–2; III.24.
30. Calvin, *Institutes*, I.4.1; I.5.1; I.6.14–15.
31. Calvin, *Institutes*, III.21.6.
32. Calvin, *Institutes*, III.24.7.
33. Calvin, *Institutes*, III.25.
34. Calvin, *Institutes*, III.21.5.
35. Jennifer Powell McNutt, "Calvin Legends: Hagiography and Demonology," in *John Calvin in Context*, ed. R. Ward Holder (Cambridge: Cambridge Univ. Press, 2020), 383–92; Machiel A. van den Berg, *Friends of Calvin*, trans. Reinder Bruinsma (Grand Rapids: Eerdmans, 2009); Gary W. Jenkins, *Calvin's Tormentors: Understanding the Conflicts That Shaped the Reformer* (Grand Rapids: Baker Academic, 2018).
36. Calvin, *Institutes*, IV.17.31.
37. Calvin, *Institutes*, IV.14.9; IV.17.2.
38. Calvin, *Institutes*, IV.17.1.
39. Calvin, *Institutes*, IV.17.33.
40. Donald K. McKim and Jim West, *Heinrich Bullinger: An Introduction to His Life and Theology*, Cascade Companions (Eugene, OR: Cascade, 2022).
41. Jennifer Powell McNutt, *Calvin Meets Voltaire: The Clergy of Geneva in the Age of Enlightenment, 1685–1798* (New York: Routledge, 2014).
42. Calvin, *Institutes*, III.7.1.
43. *Heidelberg Catechism*, Modern English Version, 450th Anniversary Edition (Reformed Church in the United States, 2013).

Chapter 11: Menno Simons

1. Menno Simons, "A Meditation on the Twenty-Fifth Psalm," in *Early Anabaptist Spirituality*, ed. Daniel Liechty (New York: Paulist, 1994), 251.

2. See Ulrich Stadler, "Cherished Instructions . . . ," in *Spiritual and Anabaptist Writers*, ed. George E. Williams and Angel M. Mergal, Library of Christian Classics (Philadelphia: Westminster, 1957), 272–84.

3. See Jan Luyken's etching of this story in the 1685 edition of *Martyrs Mirror*.

4. Ward Holder, *Crisis and Renewal: The Era of the Reformations* (Louisville: Westminster John Knox, 2009), 135.

5. George Williams mentions the first reference to "Mennisten" in 1545 by a decree of Countess Anna of Oldenburg, who was regent of East Frisia (George Williams, *The Radical Reformation* [Philadelphia: Westminster, 1962], 393).

6. Menno Simons, "My Conversion, Call, and Testimony," in *Christianity and Revolution*, ed. Lowell H. Zuck (Philadelphia: Temple Univ. Press, 1975), 117.

7. Simons, "My Conversion, Call, and Testimony," 118.

8. Ulrich Zwingli writes, "Our opponents destroy the unity of baptism and rebaptize themselves" (Ulrich Zwingli, "Of Baptism," in *Zwingli and Bullinger*, ed. G. W. Bromiley, Library of Christian Classics [Philadelphia: Westminster, 1953], 166–67, 169).

9. Menno Simons, "Christian Baptism," in *The Complete Writings of Menno Simons*, ed. J. C. Wenger (Scottdale, PA: Herald, 1956), 235; Hans Hut, "On the Mystery of Baptism," *Early Anabaptist Spirituality*, 67.

10. Zwingli explains that pouring water does not wash away sin actually (Zwingli, "Of Baptism," 153).

11. Zwingli, "Of Baptism," 138.

12. Zwingli, "Of Baptism," 140–41.

13. Thomas Müntzer, "The Prague Protest," in *The Radical Reformation*, ed. and trans. Michael G. Baylor, Cambridge Texts in the History of Political Thought (Cambridge: Cambridge Univ. Press, 2008), 10.

14. Thomas Müntzer, "Sermon to the Princes," *Radical Reformation*, 31.

15. See article 3 of "The Twelve Articles of the Upper Swabian Peasants," *Radical Reformation*, 234.

16. Michael Sattler, "The Schleitheim Articles," *Radical Reformation*, 172–80.

17. George E. Williams and Angel M. Mergal, eds., "Martyrdom of Michael Sattler," *Spiritual and Anabaptist Writers*, 141.

18. Menno Simons, "On the Ban," *Spiritual and Anabaptist Writers*, 264, 270.

19. Simons, "On the Ban," 264, 270.

20. Simons, "On the Ban," 267.

21. See article 1 of "The Twelve Articles of the Upper Swabian Peasants," *Radical Reformation*, 232–33.

22. Andreas Karlstadt, "Letter from the Community of Orlamunde to the People of Allstedt," *Radical Reformation*, 33–34.

23. Balthasar Hubmaier, "On the Sword," *Radical Reformation*, 184–86.

24. Menno Simons, "Foundation of Christian Doctrine," *Complete Writings of Menno Simons*, 107.

25. Menno Simons, "Blasphemy of John of Leiden," *Complete Writings of Menno Simons*, 45.

26. Simons, "Blasphemy of John of Leiden," 49.

27. This emphasis continues with Dirk Philips, "Concerning the New Birth and the New Creature: Brief Admonition and Teaching from the Holy Bible" (1556), *Early Anabaptist Spirituality*, 200–218.

28. Simons, "Foundation of Christian Doctrine," 106.

29. Simons, "My Conversion, Call, and Testimony," *Christianity and Revolution*, 119.

Chapter 12: Teresa of Avila

1. Teresa of Avila, *The Prayers of Teresa of Avila*, ed. Thomas Alvarez (New York: New City Press, 1990), 21.

2. "Vittoria Colonna," in *In Her Words: Women's Writings in the History of Christian Thought*, ed. Amy Oden (Nashville: Abingdon, 1994), 219–22.

3. Elisabeth Gleason, ed. and trans., *Reform Thought in Sixteenth-Century Italy* (Chico, CA: Scholars Press, 1981), 32–33.

4. See Anthony N. S. Lane, *The Regensburg Article 5 on Justification: Inconsistent Patchwork or Substance of True Doctrine?* Oxford Studies in Historical Theology (New York: Oxford Univ. Press, 2019).

5. The concept is developed by Scott H. Hendrix, *Recultivating the Vineyard: The Reformation Agendas of Christianization* (Louisville: Westminster John Knox, 2004).

6. See articles 15–17 in Ignatius of Loyola, "The Spiritual Exercises," in *Ignatius of Loyola: The Spiritual Exercises and Selected Works*, ed. George E. Ganss, Classics of Western Spirituality (New York: Paulist, 1991), 213.

7. Ignatius of Loyola, "Spiritual Exercises," article 13.

8. Robert Bireley, *The Refashioning of Catholicism, 1450–1700* (Washington, DC: Catholic Univ. of America Press, 1999), 29–37.

9. Bireley, *Refashioning of Catholicism*, 33.

10. Bireley, *Refashioning of Catholicism*, 82.

11. Keith J. Egan, "The Spirituality of the Carmelites," in *Christian Spirituality: High Middle Ages and Reformation*, ed. Jill Raitt (London: SCM Press, 1988), 51–53.

12. Egan, "Spirituality of the Carmelites," 54.

13. R. Po-Chia Hsia, *The World of Catholic Renewal, 1540–1770*, 2nd ed. (Cambridge: Cambridge Univ. Press, 2005), 49, 147.

14. Bireley, *Refashioning of Catholicism*, 82.

15. Amanda J. Kaminski, "Teresa of Avila and Mary Ward: Spirituality and Re-imagining Mission," in *Sixteenth-Century Mission: Explorations in Protestant and Roman Catholic Theology and Practice*, ed. Robert L. Gallagher and Edward L. Smither (Bellingham, WA: Lexham, 2021), 290.

16. Emidio Campi and Mariano Delgado, "Bibles in Italian and Spanish," in *The New Cambridge History of the Bible*, ed. Euan Cameron (Cambridge: Cambridge Univ. Press, 2016), 372.

17. Jennifer Powell McNutt, "The Bible for Refugees in Calvin's Geneva," in *Global Migration and Christian Faith: Implications for Identity and Mission*, ed. M. Daniel Carroll R. and Vincent E. Bacote (Eugene, OR: Wipf and Stock, 2021), 18–36.

18. Kaminski, "Teresa of Avila and Mary Ward," 288.

19. Hsia, *World of Catholic Renewal*, 33–35.

20. Derek Cooper, *Twenty Questions That Shaped World Christian History* (Minneapolis: Fortress, 2015), 233–46.

21. Cooper, *Twenty Questions*, 37.

22. Cooper, *Twenty Questions*, 34.

23. Julian of Norwich, *Showings*, trans. Edmund Colledge and James Walsh, Classics of Western Spirituality (New York: Paulist, 1978): 16:56, pp. 288–90 (LT).

24. Teresa, *Prayers of Teresa of Avila*, 62.

25. Teresa of Avila, *Interior Castle*, ed. Amy Oden (Nashville: Abingdon, 1994), 226.

26. Teresa, *Interior Castle*, 224–25.

27. Teresa, "Meditations on the Song of Songs," *The Collected Works of St. Teresa of Avila*, vol. 2, trans. Kieran Kavanaugh and Otilio Rodriguez (Washington, DC: ICS Publications, 1980), 349.

28. Bernard McGinn, *The Growth of Mysticism: Gregory the Great through the Twelfth Century*, Presence of God, vol. 2 (New York: Crossroad, 1999), 128.

29. Teresa, "Meditations on the Song of Songs," 229–31.

30. Hsia, *World of Catholic Renewal*, 147.

31. J. M. Cohen, trans., *The Life of Saint Teresa of Ávila by Herself* (New York: Penguin, 1957), 136–46.

Chapter 13: The Wesley Brothers

1. John Wesley, *John and Charles Wesley: Selected Writings and Hymns*, ed. Frank Whaling, Classics of Western Spirituality (New York: Paulist, 1981), 143.

2. Jeffrey W. Barbeau, *The Spirit of Methodism: From the Wesleys to a Global Communion* (Downers Grove, IL: IVP Academic, 2019), 5–6.

3. "Susanna Wesley," in *In Her Words: Women's Writings in the History of Christian Thought*, ed. Amy Oden (Nashville: Abingdon, 1994), 250–64.

4. Jennifer Powell McNutt, "Reformed Preaching in the Age of Enlightenment: A Comparison of Jonathan Erskine's 'Enlightened Evangelicalism' with Geneva's 'Reasonable Calvinism,'" *Intellectual History Review* 26, no. 3 (September 2016): 371–89.

5. "Susanna Wesley," *In Her Words*, 253.

6. "Susanna Wesley," *In Her Words*, 254.

7. See Alan Harding, *The Countess of Huntingdon's Connexion: A Sect in Action in Eighteenth-Century England*, Oxford Theology and Religion Monographs (Oxford: Oxford Univ. Press, 2003); Geordan Hammond and David Ceri Jones, eds., *George Whitefield: Life, Context, and Legacy* (Oxford: Oxford Univ. Press, 2016).

8. Keith A. Francis and William Gibson, "Preface," in *The Oxford Handbook of the British Sermon 1689–1901*, ed. Keith A. Francis and William Gibson (Oxford: Oxford Univ. Press, 2012), xiii.

9. Mollie C. Davis, "The Countess of Huntingdon and Whitefield's Bethesda," *Georgia Historical Quarterly* 56, no. 1 (Spring 1972): 72–82.

10. David Ceri Jones, Boyd Stanley Schlenther, and Eryn Mant White, *The Elect Methodists: Calvinistic Methodism in England and Wales, 1735–1811* (Cardiff: Univ. of Wales, 2012), xii.

11. John R. Tyson, "John and Charles Wesley," in *The Blackwell Companion to Paul*, ed. Stephen Westerholm (Chichester: Wiley-Blackwell, 2011), 407.

12. John Wesley, *The Essential Works of John Wesley*, ed. Alice Russie (Uhrichsville, OH: Barbour, 2011), 38.

13. See journal entry for October 9, 1738, referenced in *John and Charles Wesley: Selected Prayers, Hymns, Journal Notes, Sermons, Letters and Treatises*, ed. Frank Whaling, Classics of Western Spirituality (Mahwah, NJ: Paulist, 1981), 21; John Wesley, *The Works of John Wesley*, vol. 19, *Journal and Diaries II (1738–1743)*, ed. W. Reginald Ward and Richard P. Heitzenrater (Nashville: Abingdon, 1990), 46.

14. David East, "Lightly Esteemed by Men: The Last Years of Sarah Mallet, One of Mr. Wesley's Female Preachers," *Methodist History* 42, no. 1 (October 2003): 58–63.

15. David Hempton, *Methodism: Empire of the Spirit* (New Haven, CT: Yale Univ. Press, 2005), 5, 78.

16. David Sorkin, *The Religious Enlightenment: Protestants, Jews, and Catholics from London to Vienna*, Jews, Christians, and Muslims from the Ancient to the Modern World, vol. 42 (Princeton, NJ: Princeton Univ. Press, 2008). For the category of "reasonable Calvinism," see Jennifer Powell McNutt, *Calvin Meets Voltaire: The Clergy of Geneva in the Age of Enlightenment, 1685–1798* (New York: Routledge, 2014).

17. John W. Haas, "Eighteenth Century Evangelical Responses to Science: John Wesley's Enduring Legacy," *Science and Christian Belief* 6, no. 2: 83–100.

18. John Wesley, *A Survey of the Wisdom of God in Creation; or, A Compendium of Natural Philosophy* (1763); Deborah Madden, "Experience and the Common Interest of Mankind: The Enlightened Empiricism of John Wesley's Primitive Physick," *Journal for Eighteenth-Century Studies* 26, no. 1 (March 2003): 41–53.

19. See John Wesley's *Electricity Made Plain and Useful* (1760).

20. The term was first coined by historian Albert Outler. This approach closely reflects the interpretive process that Protestant Reformers of the sixteenth century employed.

21. John Wesley, "A Plain Account of Christian Perfection," in *John and Charles Wesley*, 299–377.

22. Wesley, "Plain Account," 300.

23. Wesley, "Plain Account," 301.

24. Wesley, "Plain Account," 366.

25. Wesley, "Plain Account," 309.

26. Wesley, "Plain Account," 303.

27. For more, see David Bebbington, *Evangelicalism in Modern Britain: A History from the 1730s to the 1980s* (New York: Routledge, 1989).

28. Timothy Larsen, "Defining and Locating Evangelicalism," in *The Cambridge Companion to Evangelical Theology*, ed. Timothy Larsen and Daniel J. Treier, Cambridge Companions to Religion (Cambridge: Cambridge Univ. Press, 2007), 1–14.

29. Charles Edward White, *The Beauty of Holiness: Phoebe Palmer as Theologian, Revivalist, Feminist, and Humanitarian* (Eugene, OR: Wipf and Stock, 2008).

30. Mary Anne Phemister, *Hannah More: The Artist as Reformer* (Sisters, OR: Deep River, 2014).

31. Hempton, *Methodism*, 10.

32. Todd Johnson and Gina Zurlo, *World Christian Encyclopedia*, 3rd ed. (Edinburgh: Edinburgh Univ. Press, 2020), 6.

33. Sebastian C. H. Kim and Kirsteen Kim, *A History of Korean Christianity* (Cambridge: Cambridge Univ. Press, 2015).

Chapter 14: Friedrich Schleiermacher

1. Johann Arndt, *True Christianity* (New York: Paulist, 1979), 202.
2. Friedrich Schleiermacher, "From *On Religion: Speeches to Its Cultured Despisers*," in *Readings in the History of Christian Theology*, vol. 2, ed. William C. Placher (Louisville: Westminster John Knox, 1988), 133.
3. Schleiermacher, "From *On Religion*," 134.
4. Schleiermacher, "From *On Religion*," 134.
5. Walter E. Wyman Jr., "Sin and Redemption," in *The Cambridge Companion to Friedrich Schleiermacher*, ed. Jacqueline Mariña (Cambridge: Cambridge Univ. Press, 2005), 133.
6. Friedrich Schleiermacher, *Christian Faith*, vol. 1, ed. Catherine L. Kelsey and Terrence N. Tice (Louisville: Westminster John Knox, 2016), 8.
7. Schleiermacher, *Christian Faith*, vol. 1, 24.
8. Schleiermacher, *Christian Faith*, vol. 1, 273.
9. Schleiermacher, *Christian Faith*, vol. 1, 82.
10. Schleiermacher, *Christian Faith*, vol. 1, 79.
11. Schleiermacher, *Christian Faith*, vol. 1, 144.
12. Friedrich Schleiermacher, *Christian Faith*, vol. 2, ed. Catherine L. Kelsey and Terrence N. Tice (Louisville: Westminster John Knox, 2016), 581–90.
13. Schleiermacher, *Christian Faith*, vol. 2, 683.
14. Wyman, "Sin and Redemption," 130.
15. Schleiermacher, *Christian Faith*, vol. 2, 544.
16. Schleiermacher, *Christian Faith*, vol. 2, 1021.
17. Paul Tillich, *Systematic Theology*, vol. 1 (Chicago: Univ. of Chicago Press, 1951), 62.
18. Tillich, *Systematic Theology*, vol. 1, 156.
19. Tillich, *Systematic Theology*, vol. 1, 38.
20. Ludwig Feuerbach, "From *Lectures on the Essence of Religion*," in *Readings in the History of Christian Theology*, vol. 2, ed. William C. Placher (Louisville: Westminster John Knox, 1988), 139.
21. Abraham Kuyper, "Sphere Sovereignty," in *Abraham Kuyper: A Centennial Reader*, ed. James D. Bratt (Grand Rapids: Eerdmans, 1998), 488.
22. H. Richard Niebuhr, *The Kingdom of God in America* (Chicago: Willett, Clark and Co., 1937), 193.
23. Karl Barth, "Concluding Unscientific Postscript on Schleiermacher," in *The Theology of Schleiermacher* (Edinburgh: T&T Clark, 1982), 277–78.

Chapter 15: Karl Barth

1. Karl Barth, *Prayer* (Louisville: Westminster John Knox, 2002), 89.
2. "The Barmen Declaration, 1934," in Henry Bettenson and Chris Maunder, eds., *Documents of the Christian Church*, 4th ed. (Oxford: Oxford Univ. Press, 2011), 358.
3. For an excellent biography of Barth, see Eberhard Busch, *Karl Barth: His Life from Letters and Autobiographical Texts*, trans. John Bowden (Grand Rapids: Eerdmans, 1976).
4. Karl Barth, "Concluding Unscientific Postscript on Schleiermacher," in *The Theology of Schleiermacher* (Edinburgh: T&T Clark, 1982), 264.
5. Karl Barth, "The Strange New World within the Bible," in *The Word of God and the Word of Man*, trans. Douglas Horton (London: Hodder and Stoughton, 1928), 33.
6. Christiane Tietz, *Karl Barth: A Life in Conflict*, trans. Victoria J. Barnett (Oxford: Oxford Univ. Press, 2021), 90.
7. Karl Barth, *The Epistle to the Romans*, trans. Edwyn C. Hoskyns, 6th ed. (London: Oxford Univ. Press, 1968), 10.
8. Karl Barth, *Church Dogmatics*, ed. G. W. Bromiley and T. F. Torrance (London: T&T Clark, 2004), IV.4, vii.
9. Barth, *Church Dogmatics*, I.1, 137.
10. Barth, *Church Dogmatics*, I.1, 109.
11. Barth, *Church Dogmatics*, I.1, 47.
12. Karl Barth, "No! Answer to Emil Brunner," in *Natural Theology: Comprising "Nature and Grace" by Professor Dr. Emil Brunner and the Reply "No!" by Dr. Karl Barth* (London: Geoffrey Bles, 1946).
13. Barth, *Church Dogmatics*, I.1, 348.
14. John Calvin, *Institutes of the Christian Religion*, ed. John McNeill, trans. Ford Lewis Battles (Philadelphia: Westminster, 1960), III.21.5.
15. Barth, *Church Dogmatics*, II.2, 10.
16. Barth, *Church Dogmatics*, II.2, 103.
17. Barth, *Church Dogmatics*, II.2, 346.
18. Barth, *Church Dogmatics*, II.2, 351.
19. Barth, *Church Dogmatics*, III.1, vii.
20. George Hunsinger, *How to Read Karl Barth: The Shape of His Theology* (Oxford: Oxford Univ. Press, 1991), 85.
21. Barth, *Church Dogmatics*, IV.1, 336.
22. David W. McNutt, "A Surprising Correspondence: How an Exchange of Letters between Karl Barth and Dorothy L. Sayers Models Gracious Theological Discourse," in *VII: Journal of the Marion E. Wade Center* 38 (2021): 5–22.

23. Barth, *Church Dogmatics*, IV.3, 114.
24. Barth, *Church Dogmatics*, IV.3.1, 122–23.
25. Karl Barth, *Wolfgang Amadeus Mozart*, trans. Clarence K. Pott (Grand Rapids: Eerdmans, 1986), 57.
26. Busch, *Karl Barth*, 496.

Chapter 16: Gustavo Gutiérrez

1. Austin Flannery, ed., *Vatican Council II: The Conciliar and Post-Conciliar Documents*, vol. 1, new rev. ed. (Collegeville, MN: Costello, 1996): "Pastoral Constitution on the Church in the Modern World," in *Gaudium et Spes* (December 7, 1965), 27:928.
2. Jonathan Y. Tan, *Introducing Asian American Theologies* (New York: Orbis, 2008).
3. The fruit of that labor is evident in the popular *First Nations Version: An Indigenous Translation of the New Testament*, trans. Terry M. Wildman (Downers Grove, IL: InterVarsity Press, 2021).
4. *Vatican Council II*, vol. 1: "Declaration . . . Celebration of the Eucharist," in *Dans ces Dernier Temps* (January 7, 1970), 4:503.
5. *Vatican Council II*, vol. 1: "Decree on the Catholic Eastern Churches," in *Orientalium Ecclesiarum* (November 21, 1964), 24–30:449–51.
6. *Vatican Council II*, vol. 1: "The Constitution on the Sacred Liturgy," in *Sacrosanctum Concilium* (December 4, 1963), I.III.C.35:13.
7. *Vatican Council II*, vol. 1: "Instruction on the Proper Implementation of the Constitution on the Sacred Liturgy," in *Inter Oecumenici* (September 26, 1964), 41:53; "Instruction on the Worship of the Eucharistic Mystery," in *Eucharisticum Mysterium* (May 25, 1967), 19:115.
8. *Vatican Council II*, vol. 1: "Instruction on Music in the Liturgy," in *Musicam Sacram* (March 5, 1967), II.41; IV.47–51.
9. *Vatican Council II*, vol. 1: "Constitution on the Sacred Liturgy," I.II.55:19. Further instructions given in *Sacramentali Communione* (June 29, 1970).
10. *Vatican Council II*, vol. 1: "Pastoral Constitution on the Church in the Modern World," in *Gaudium et Spes* (December 7, 1965), 903–47.
11. Fathers of the Council, "Message to Humanity" (October 20, 1962), in Walter Abbott, ed., *The Documents of Vatican II* (New York: Herder and Herder, 1966), 3–7.
12. See Vatican Council II's *Lumen Gentium* (November 21, 1964).
13. See his book *Las Casas: In Search of the Poor of Jesus Christ* (1992 in Spanish).
14. Latin American Priests, ". . . Latin American Realities" (November 1967), in Alfred Hennelly, ed., *Liberation Theology: A Documentary History* (New York: Orbis, 1990), 58–61.

15. Gustavo Gutiérrez, *A Theology of Liberation*, rev. ed. (New York: Orbis, 1988), xxi.

16. Gutiérrez, *Theology of Liberation*, xxxviii.

17. Gutiérrez, *Theology of Liberation*, 162.

18. Gutiérrez, *Theology of Liberation*, xxvi.

19. Gutiérrez, *Theology of Liberation*, 7.

20. Gutiérrez, *Theology of Liberation*, xxv–xxvi.

21. Gutiérrez, *Theology of Liberation*, 172.

22. Gutiérrez, *Theology of Liberation*, xxvii.

23. Gutiérrez, *Theology of Liberation*, 170–71.

24. Gutiérrez, *Theology of Liberation*, 168.

25. Gutiérrez, *Theology of Liberation*, 132.

26. Gutiérrez, *Theology of Liberation*, 97.

27. See Leonardo Boff, *Trinity and Society* (New York: Orbis, 1988).

28. Gutiérrez, *Theology of Liberation*, 113, 146.

29. Gutiérrez, *Theology of Liberation*, 97.

30. Gutiérrez, *Theology of Liberation*, 103.

31. Gutiérrez, *Theology of Liberation*, 70, 162, 164–65.

32. Gutiérrez, *Theology of Liberation*, 150.

33. Gutiérrez, *Theology of Liberation*, xxii.

34. Cited in Gutiérrez, *Theology of Liberation*, xx.

35. Gutiérrez, *Theology of Liberation*, 148.

36. Gutiérrez reflects on his martyrdom years later: Gutiérrez, *Theology of Liberation*, xliii.

37. Joseph Washington, *Black Religion: The Negro and Christianity in the United States* (Boston: Beacon, 1966).

38. James H. Cone, *God of the Oppressed*, new rev. ed. (New York: Orbis, 1997), 178.

39. Jacquelyn Grant, "Come to My Help, Lord, for I'm in Trouble: Womanist Jesus and the Mutual Struggle for Liberation," in *Reconstructing the Christ Symbol: Essays in Feminist Christology*, ed. Maryanne Stevens (New York: Paulist, 1993), 66.

Conclusion

1. Timothy Larsen, "The Book of Acts and the Origin of the Races in Evangelical Thought," *Victorian Review* 37, no. 2 (2011): 35–39, www.jstor.org/stable/23646655.

2. "Dogmatic Constitution on the Church," *Lumen Gentium*, in Walter Abbott, ed., *The Documents of Vatican II* (Herder and Herder, 1966), 2:35.

Know the Heretics

Justin S. Holcomb

There is a lot of talk about heresy these days. The frequency and volume of accusations suggest that some Christians have lost a sense of the gravity of the word. On the other hand, many believers have little to no familiarity with orthodox doctrine or the historic distortions of it. What's needed is a strong dose of humility and restraint, and also a clear and informed definition of orthodoxy and heresy. *Know the Heretics* provides an accessible travel guide to the most significant heresies throughout Christian history.

As a part of the KNOW series, this book is designed for personal study or classroom use, but also for small groups and Sunday schools wanting to more deeply understand the foundations of the faith. Each chapter covers a key statement of faith and includes a discussion of its historical context; a simple explanation of the unorthodox teaching, the orthodox response, and a key defender; reflections of contemporary relevance; and discussion questions.

Available in stores and online!

Know the Creeds and Councils

Justin S. Holcomb

In every generation, the Christian church must interpret and restate its bedrock beliefs, answering the challenges and concerns of the day. This accessible overview walks readers through centuries of creeds, councils, catechisms, and confessions not with a dry focus on dates and places but with an emphasis on the living tradition of Christian belief and why it matters for our lives today.

As a part of the KNOW series, *Know the Creeds and Councils* is designed for personal study or classroom use, but also for small groups and Sunday schools wanting to more deeply understand the foundations of the faith. Each chapter covers a key statement of faith and includes a discussion of its historical context, a simple explanation of the statement's content and key points, reflections on contemporary and ongoing relevance, and discussion questions.

Available in stores and online!

Know Why You Believe

K. Scott Oliphint, author
Justin S. Holcomb, editor

The Christian life depends on faith, and there are good reasons for that faith. In *Know Why You Believe*, professor and author K. Scott Oliphint answers the "why" questions both Christians and non-Christians often ask, laying out a simple and convincing case for the core teachings of Christianity:

Why Believe in the Bible?
Why Believe in Jesus?
Why Believe in Miracles?
Why Believe in Salvation?
Why Believe in God Despite the Evil in the World?

And more!

As part of the KNOW series, *Know Why You Believe* is designed for personal study or classroom use, and for small groups and Sunday schools wanting to better understand the traditional defenses of Christian beliefs.

Each chapter covers a foundational teaching and includes a rationale for that teaching, responses to common objections, reflection questions to prompt further consideration, and suggested reading for readers wanting to dig deeper.

Know How We Got Our Bible

Ryan Matthew Reeves, author
Charles E. Hill, author
Justin S. Holcomb, editor

The easy accessibility of the Bible in most of the world's major languages can obscure a dramatic and sometimes unexpected story. In *Know How We Got Our Bible*, scholars Ryan Reeves and Charles Hill trace the history of the Bible from its beginnings to the present day, highlighting key figures and demonstrating overall the reliability of Scripture.

Reeves and Hill begin with the writing of the Bible's books (including authorship and dating), move into the formation of the Old and New Testaments (including early transmission and the development of the canon), and conclude with several chapters on Bible translation from the Latin Vulgate to the ongoing work of translation around the world today.

Written simply and focused on the overarching story of how the Bible came to us today, *Know How We Got Our Bible* is an excellent introduction for formal students and lay learners alike. Each chapter includes reflection questions and recommended reading for further learning.

McNuttshell Ministries

Christian faith in a nutshell.

McNuttshell Ministries is a teaching, preaching, and writing ministry that serves both the church and the academy by sharing the Christian faith "in a nutshell."

At a time when the church and the academy are increasingly separated from each other, McNuttshell Ministries seeks to demonstrate both the importance of faith to academic pursuits and the relevance of critical thinking in the life of the church. At a time when both the church and the academy are facing challenges and pressures, McNuttshell Ministries seeks to encourage both through the thoughtful, rigorous, and joyful presentation of the gospel of Jesus Christ. At a time when the church's body is increasingly fractured, McNuttshell Ministries seeks to model a co-ministry of men and women laboring together for the faith.

McNuttshell Ministries was founded by husband-and-wife team David W. McNutt and Jennifer Powell McNutt, both of whom are ordained ministers in the Presbyterian Church and both of whom hold doctorates in theological studies. They draw on their expertise in theology, church history, the Bible, the Reformed tradition, and theology and the arts to retrieve the wisdom of the church for Christians today.

McNuttshell Ministries presents the truth, wonder, and richness of the Christian faith through:

- Speaking and teaching at Christian colleges, universities, and seminaries
- Preaching and teaching at churches across Christian traditions
- Writing and publishing resources for use in both the classroom and the church

For more information or for speaking inquiries, please visit
www.mcnuttshellministries.com.